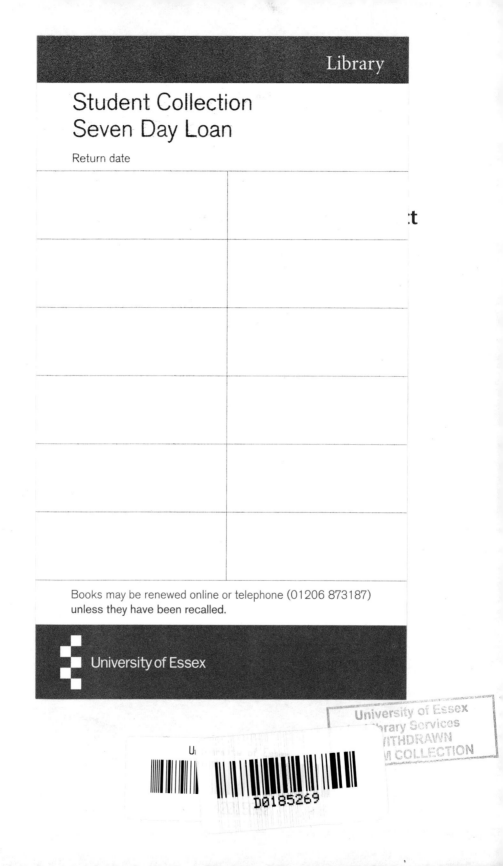

D0185269

CRITICAL PERFORMANCES
Presenting key texts by contemporary theater and performance artists with illuminating commentary by leading critics

Series Editors: Una Chaudhuri and Robert Vorlicky
Founding Editors: Lynda Hart and Paul Heritage

TITLES IN THE SERIES
from the University of Michigan Press:

The Reverend Billy Project: From Rehearsal Hall to Super Mall with the Church of Life After Shopping, by Savitri D and Bill Talen
    edited by Alisa Solomon
Say Word!: Voices from Hip Hop Theater, edited by Daniel Banks
Sex, Drag, and Male Roles: Investigating Gender as Performance,
    by Diane Torr and Stephen Bottoms
From Inner Worlds to Outer Space: The Multimedia Performances of Dan Kwong, edited by Robert Vorlicky

From Continuum Publishers:

Of All the Nerve: Deb Margolin Solo, edited by Lynda Hart
Hardcore from the Heart: The Pleasures, Profits, and Politics of Sex in Performance, by Annie Sprinkle, edited by Gabrielle Cody
Rachel's Brains and Other Storms: The Performance Scripts of Rachel Rosenthal, edited by Una Chaudhuri

The Reverend Billy Project

FROM REHEARSAL HALL TO SUPER MALL
WITH THE CHURCH OF LIFE AFTER SHOPPING

Savitri D and Bill Talen

Edited and with an Introduction by Alisa Solomon

THE UNIVERSITY OF MICHIGAN PRESS

ANN ARBOR

Copyright © 2011 by Bill Talen

Introduction Copyright © 2011 by Alisa Solomon

All rights reserved

Published in the United States of America by

The University of Michigan Press

Manufactured in the United States of America

♾ Printed on acid-free paper

2014 2013 2012 2011   4 3 2 1

A CIP catalog record for this book is available from the British Library.

Library of Congress Cataloging-in-Publication Data

D, Savitri.

   The Reverend Billy Project : from rehearsal hall to super mall
with the Church of Life After Shopping / Savitri D and Bill Talen ;
edited and with an introduction by Alisa Solomon.

      p.   cm.

   ISBN 978-0-472-07156-2 (cloth : alk. paper) — ISBN 978-0-472-
05156-4 (pbk. : alk. paper)

      1. Church of Life After Shopping (Theater troupe).   2. Street
theater—United States.   3. Experimental theater—United States.
4. Theater and society—United States.   5. Theater—Political aspects—
United States.   6. Consumer behavior—Moral and ethical aspects.
7. Consumption (Economics)—Moral and ethical aspects.   I. Talen,
William. II. Solomon, Alisa, 1956–   III. Title.

PN2297.C38.D22   2011

792.0973—dc22   2011007221

FOR THE SINGERS AND MUSICIANS OF THE LIFE AFTER
SHOPPING GOSPEL CHOIR—PAST, PRESENT, AND FUTURE.

Acknowledgments

For generously providing space and quiet, thanks to Beatrix Ost and Ludwig Kuttner, Melissa Savage, William and Elizabeth Monaghan, Harriet Barlow and the Blue Mountain Center, Charles and Patricia Gaines, Larry Harvey, Lightning Clearwater and Flash, Sal and Laura Leone.

For early encouragement and guidance, Una Chaudhuri, Bob Vorlicky, and Jill Lane.

Family thanks to Asha Greer and William Talen Sr., Joan von Briesen, all nine of our sisters and two brothers, and especially, Lena Nightstar.

For tireless documentation over the years, Fred Askew, Brennan Cavanaugh, Eric Brown, Tracey Luscz, John Quilty, Glenn Gabel, Rob VanAlkemade, and Morgan Spurlock.

Thanks to our NYC collaborators, Dee Dee Halleck, Mark Read, Frank Morales, Ben Shephard, Not An Alternative, and especially, Time's Up!

Special thanks to Michael O'Neil for seven years of media support.

And to the wonderful Marilyn Kleinberg Neimark for her fine-tooth reading, Jonathan Kalb for his incisive suggestions, and LeAnn Fields and Scott Ham and everyone at the University of Michigan Press for shepherding the project with enthusiasm and care, and as ever, to William Clark.

And, for faith and the work of the ages, to our editor, Alisa Solomon.

—BILL TALEN & SAVITRI D

Contents

Reverend Billy and the Life After Shopping Gospel Choir performing at the Highline Ballroom in New York City, 2007. (Photo by Eric H. Brown.)

1. A Dedication to Shouting

REVEREND BILLY

Why do I shout? Why do I preach? Because I think I hear something.

As you listen to me, I hear a shout in you. We're together in a silence that has the promise of a shout in it. We're working hard on it because there is a terrible emergency and we need to speak up. But there's a very bad echo in here. Here, in the world's largest economy.

How bizarre. That an economy has a way of speaking. But yes, products must open their mouths on the shelves. It's just good marketing. The packages scream perfectly and drown out our own original scream, interrupting us when we have a profound feeling rising in our bodies. Is it sex? Or a cry for peace? Or a shout to god? Whatever it is, whatever was about to be said, confronts an equal and opposite sales pitch. By the time we hand over our money at the cash register we believe that the product speaks for us.

And if we catch on to this silencing mimicry? If we suspect that the world's largest economy is forcing a duet on our oldest personal music? Do you keep preaching if you know that a corporation has got your tongue? This is no ordinary censorship. This shout-robbing is shushing the dead. That's what Consumerism does. It muffles the voices of the generations of old familiar lovers who founded us with their crying out at their moment of love. Those lovers who are slipping from us now, back into time—they gave us our sex and peace and a wide-open sky over everything. Our silence drives them away. Don't take that gamble, children. We remember the message of love only by expressing it.

When we let ourselves hear that good whooping through time,

then the marketing personnel have an impossible task. They must feel overwhelmed—are we some glorified nightmare? A cry for love howling up from the dead into the life of the living: Imagine that. We always have it somewhere inside us. We can always rear back and let it go. All we have to do to have the most powerful voice is hear each other from time to time. We're all preachers, and each of us has a way out of the all-consuming consumers' silence. As the thousandth advertisement of the day advances toward us, we can return to memories that are so much older and to acts of love that are so much newer.

As you listen to me, I hear a shout in you. Oh, let me preach. Let's stand up! Let's shout like we do when we are loving, like we do at a peace rally, like we shout in a church when the spirit tells us to give it up. Amen? We're safe from shopping now. How quickly our shouting becomes a kind of singing that gives the products nothing to say!

2. Introduction: A Theory of the Leisure Suit

ALISA SOLOMON

The *Wall Street Journal* liked Reverend Billy's economic proposals. With the financial system in collapse and the Dow Jones Industrial Average still scraping the low 8000s, David Weidner's column of April 16, 2009, took up the performer's call. "In place of a system where big banks and corporations enter neighborhoods only to profit from them," Weidner wrote, "Reverend Billy wants to empower small banks and credit unions that hold a stake in the communities they serve by offering incentives and making it harder for big finance to undercut local business." While the columnist admitted, "It's hard to imagine Timothy Geithner taking advice from an iconoclast dressed in a white suit, clerical collar and Elvis-inspired hair," he noted, too, that "[i]t's hard to argue against the system [Reverend Billy] envisions."

The *Wall Street Journal* promoting the principles of a radical, anti-consumerist, pro-union, tree-hugging, fake-preacher performance artist? What happened? Simple. It was the "Shopocalypse": Over-spending, de-regulation, and putting profit above people and planet were producing the catastrophe Reverend Billy had foretold for more than a decade as he railed away on sidewalks and in chain stores, theaters, and "contested spaces" in New York City and far beyond.

The actor and playwright Bill Talen created the persona of Reverend Billy in the late 1990s and began preaching against consumer frenzy—and against the spiritual malaise, worker exploitation, environmental degradation, and the monocultural malling of neighborhoods that support and flow from it. In a white jacket left over from a catering gig, a cardboard collar, and an emphatic bleached-blond pouf, he urged shoppers to "back away from the product" and cure themselves of "consumer narcosis" and "affluenza." He started solo on the streets of Manhattan's Times Square, staking out a patch of sidewalk amid sundry hellfire-and-brimstone street-corner evangelists. Then, attracting a flock of activist supporters, he moved inside the nearby Disney Store, and then into many of the more than 100 Starbucks coffee shops in New York, where interventions akin to Augusto Boal's "invisible theater" culminated in his leaping upon the countertops and attempting to "exorcise" the cash registers. Meanwhile, he began a weekly indoor show framed as a church service, featuring a rocking gospel choir, a finely tuned sermon, and the canonization of local lefty heroes, such as labor rights campaigners and community gardeners. Reverend Billy and the Church of Stop Shopping, as the project first named itself, became central figures in New York activism, and soon were bringing their new form of political theater to audiences and actions across the United States and the world.

Over nearly fifteen years, the project has sustained its core creed while adjusting nimbly to changing times. Reverend Billy took on something of a real pastoral role, for example, after September 11, 2001, when New Yorkers sought words of solace from him. (He has also obtained a state license to officiate at weddings.) The theatrics and politics have sharpened, too, thanks in no small measure to the addition in 2001 of a brilliant director, Savitri D. (She and Billy are also married to each other and the parents of a daughter.) Savitri joined the project at a critical moment. Reverend Billy had begun to garner international attention. An excellent story about the work, written by Jonathan Kalb, appeared in the *New York Times* in February, 2000, and ignited the first firestorm of interest from the mainstream. As Kalb later noted, it's a sign of Billy's integrity that he did not seize the occasion, as many artists might have, to build his "career." At that juncture, for instance, he could have taken the character in a more purely parodic direction and likely scored some commercial success, even a TV deal. Instead, he and Savitri have been walking a tightrope over America's celebrity culture, drawing the spotlight in order to deflect it: they steer the focus to the issues of their activism. It wouldn't do, after all, for Reverend Billy himself to become a commodity. Their website doesn't even sell T-shirts.

When, a decade into this work, the economy imploded, the project declared a recessionary name-change—it became Reverend Billy and the Church of Life After Shopping. According to their gospel, a plunging "consumer confidence index" may be a hopeful sign that sinners are seeing the light. On the surface, the new moniker celebrated that at least for a time, Americans no longer needed to be encouraged to "lift your hand from the product" as the Reverend's performances often implored. More deeply, the change reflected an inclination not only to keep a utopian ideal in front of the activism, but also to draw a distinction between the Church's cheery rejection of consumerism and the more general decline in spending wrought by the public's scant funds, but not matched by a drop in their desire.

For the most part at first, in the indoor shows at least, Reverend Billy—like most pulpit reverends—preached to the converted. Indeed, part of the genius of the televangelist character and church-service format of Reverend Billy's formal performances is that they disarm this condescending old phrase, which intends to mock political theater as somehow unsuccessful if it doesn't immediately turn opponents into devotees. (No one would discredit a priest, for example, for addressing Catholics, an imam for speaking to Muslims—or, for that matter, a movement leader rousing the rank and file; it's in the street and chain-store interventions that Billy functions more as a missionary.) Literally preaching in the theater, Reverend Billy trumps the snide accusation, and shifts attention from the presumed failure to persuade to the content of the already shared convictions—and to the active way an audience engages them by clapping along and chiming in with heartfelt "Hallelujahs" and "Amens." Still, in the early years, those audiences were mostly activists, hipsters, denizens of the counterculture, folks seething about their neighborhoods turning into generic strips of high-rises and chain stores, people with a social conscience that appreciated an occasional, entertaining nudge.

Then, suddenly, it seemed—faster than you could say "credit default swap"—Reverend Billy's reach broadened as his email box filled with invitations from such new and surprising hosts as the Yale Divinity School, CNN Money, Fox News, and even Glenn Beck. While of course the project has maintained a frequently updated website, Facebook page, Twitter feed, and regular email bulletin (which goes out to some thirty thousand subscribers), old-fashioned, if heightened, word-of-mouth seems to function as Reverend Billy's most potent form of advertising (evidenced by more than a thousand homemade movies of Reverend Billy posted on YouTube by the old-time faithful and new fans alike). This grassroots publicity, too, started to reach into new corners as the economy crashed. The troupe would show up for a gig in a gymnasium in, say, Columbus, Ohio, and find five hundred people waiting—predictably enough, janitors' strike committees and radical bicyclists, but now, also suburban housewives coping with slashed grocery budgets.

The troupe's 2007 movie, *What Would Jesus Buy* (produced by Morgan Spurlock and directed by Rob VanAlkemade), also struck deep chords in less-than-lefty places. The documentary tracked Reverend Billy and the choir as they crossed the country on a pre-Christmas tour singing against the "Shopocalypse" in Wal-Mart parking lots, on the escalators of the Mall of America, and at Disneyland on Christmas Day. "Many Christian churches could learn a few things from this secular outfit," wrote Brett McCracken, reviewing the movie for *Christianity Today*, agreeing that consumerism had cheapened the holiday.

The Green Party asked Reverend Billy to run as its candidate in New York City's mayoral election of November, 2009. In a campaign in which the incumbent Michael Bloomberg (having orchestrated the overturning of standing term limits) spent some $102 million—about $174 per vote—on his reelection, Reverend Billy didn't exactly pose a serious challenge, but the campaign was no joke. He used the platform to promote the vibrancy of the city's individual neighborhoods as bulwarks against the rampaging gentrification that Bloomberg has encouraged and—rather than the after-life paradise promised by many religions—as a heavenly vision of what life beyond corporate consumer culture could look like. Amid record low voter turnout—Bloomberg was elected with fewer votes than any New York mayor had ever received—some nine thousand New Yorkers marked their ballots for Reverend Billy (more tallies than any Green Party candidate for the office had ever garnered.)

None of this is to say that Reverend Billy has come anywhere close to achieving mass popularity—which is obvious enough in a country where even a wan public health option was burned at the stake. Indeed, the only highly visible movement the economic collapse and bank bailout have produced is the right-wing populist backlash of the Tea Party. Still, Reverend Billy has tapped into a strong counter-current that flows beneath the mainstream and he has helped it to gush up from time to time. You can hear it burbling—steadily and quickening—if you put your ear to the ground.

This book offers one means of doing so. Focusing on some signal Reverend Billy projects that took place between 2004 and 2009, it presents a backstage view of their planning, performance, and post-show assessment. Though some chapters contain performance texts—Reverend Billy's sermons—primarily the format is narrative: Billy and Savitri tell the stories of their exploits on three continents, and they consider how well the efforts worked (or didn't) and what it all meant.

Sometimes we view the action from inside Billy's head while he is performing—for example, dying up there in front of some three thousand stony-faced Germans at a Berlin comedy festival (Chapter 10). Or while he is in jail after a performance/action—for example, for three scary days in the Twin Towers Correctional Facility of Los Angeles, doing time for "harassing" a Starbucks cash register (Chapter 3). Sometimes we observe from Savitri's directorial perspective, following as her sharp dramaturgical eye shapes an effective protest spectacle against the privatization of Coney Island (Chapter 5), or as she breaks down the three-act structure of the American justice system (Chapter 3), or as she blocks out a scamper under a fence and up a scaffold to hang a banner on restricted property (Chapter 8). We follow the strategic planning of campaigns and on-the-fly adjustments to unexpected snags or opportunities, the thinking-through and carrying-out of some high-risk actions, the gleaning of insights from victories as well as from flops. We witness an expansive, justice-seeking worldview at work throughout—for example, as Billy and Savitri turn some conversations with exploited Ethiopian coffee farmers they meet at the World Social Forum in Nairobi into an effective local campaign back in New York; mull over the meaning of diversity in organizing during a meeting at an activist camp in Iceland; find a theatrical metaphor for the wanton pulping of Canadian Rockies forests to make pages of Victoria's Secret catalogues; preserve the First Amendment by publicly proclaiming it. We are privy to their internal debates over what can make activism meaningful: Is a lawsuit worth it? Does getting arrested accomplish anything? Are staged, contained protests "merely" theater? To tag along as they plan, enact, and, later, evaluate their projects is to take a rare and revelatory ride into a diverse, international world of local resistances and alternative cultures, and to see how two rigorous and radical imaginations engage and advance dreams of a more equitable world.

In sum, the reflective, narrative, analytical, and homiletic story-essays and sermons gathered here reveal a unique and surprisingly effective radical/spiritual/performance practice that is at once highly choreographed and improvisatory, non-ideological, and politically shrewd. (An interview with Billy and Savitri, addressing acting and preaching techniques, the evolution of the Reverend Billy character and the Church of Life After Shopping faith, among other things, closes out the volume.)

By design, it is not easy to classify this work. Is it best understood as theater? Religion? Activism? Maintaining what Billy and Savitri call "radical instability" that "resists the label" serves their project. And it means that one can't fully examine their achievement through a purely theatrical, religious, or activist lens. One needs trifocals—indeed, progressive lenses.

In the initial years, Reverend Billy could be understood as one early and particularly strong strand in a growing trend toward humor, parody, and pageantry (and occasionally, recklessness) in the activism of the late 1990s. Not that movements hadn't employed such antics before— Abbie Hoffman and fellow Yippies threw dollar bills from the visitors' gallery down onto the trading floor of the New York Stock Exchange in 1967; beginning in 1980 on America's west coast, the Ladies Against Women undermined anti-feminists by comically impersonating them. ("Mommies, mommies, don't be Commies," went one of their protest chants. "Stay at home and fold pajamas.") But the street-party atmosphere of late-1990s anti-capitalist actions felt fresh for several reasons. Primarily, the anti-hierarchical structure of the alter-globalization movement—there was no central leadership setting forth official slogans and agendas—opened up its mass marches to a giddy, anything-goes expressiveness. Hence the famous turtle-and-Teamster alliance at the Seattle 1998 protests against the World Trade Organization: environmentalists dressed as cute green reptiles linking arms with burly union men. A year later, the "Carnival against Capitalism," called by London's Reclaim the Streets in response to the G8 Summit, sparked spirited actions in more than forty cities around the globe. In 2000, the Republican and Democratic presidential nominating conventions in the United States brought out still more histrionic hi-jinks. The Bil-

Reverend Billy is arrested in front of New York's Disney Store after a cash register exorcism on Buy Nothing Day, 2004. (Photo by Fred Askew.)

lionaires for Bush, for example, cavorted in tuxes and evening gowns under such slogans as "Because Economic Inequality Is Not Growing Fast Enough." Whether deserved or not, activism of prior decades had acquired a reputation for being grim, sanctimonious, and supplicating—passionate, perhaps, in its anger (as ACT UP certainly had been), but not charged with playfulness and humor. In a festive fusion of form and function, the alter-globalization protests (so-called because "anti-globalization" falsely describes a movement that seeks not isolationism, but an alternative to the kind of globalization that dominates) took a stand against privatization of space by occupying it; they opposed neo-liberal economic policy and its axiomatic profusion of cheap-things-to-buy with their rollicking display of a hell of a fun time that didn't depend on any purchases.

While the Reverend Billy project belongs to that diffuse, exuberant outpouring of resistance to unbridled multinational capitalism, some of the ways it differs have enabled it to continue to surge long after the larger movement, in general, has ebbed (not least because of stepped up police aggression, the institution of "protest pens," and even the preventive detention of demonstrators, such as experienced by the "puppetistas" in Philadelphia during the 2004 Republican convention). Those differences have to do with a seeming paradox: Reverend Billy's wedding of radical commitment to spiritual sincerity and comic form. Post-religious worship and post-ideological engagement meet and prosper on the make-believe ground of performance.

Many commentators have remarked on the satiric laughs wrung from Reverend Billy's persona: a holy-roller in the smarmy and zestful style of Jimmy Swaggart, the pioneer of televangelism who suffered a spectacular fall from grace over a sex scandal in the 1980s. (His 1988 vague but tearful confession—"I have sinned against you, my Lord . . ." was broadcast repeatedly by news channels and became an icon of the period.) But it's not the preacher mode itself that makes Reverend Billy funny. Indeed, the characterization is not a parody in the style of Ladies Against Women or Billionaires Against Bush, which exaggerate a view in order to ridicule it. Reverend Billy does not make fun of the televangelist role; he makes use of it. This was evident from the beginning— writing about Reverend Billy more than a decade ago, I was moved to quip, "the collar is fake but the calling is real"—but in recent years, he has embraced the sincerity, and thus the fruitful contradiction, more forthrightly. It is a contradiction between artifice and authenticity that resolves itself in commitment. In his anti-materialistic church, Reverend Billy offers what one might call dialectical spiritualism.

The joke, as it were, depends not on sarcasm or mockery, but on irony—an audience's recognition of an incongruity: that this well-known type of character, who usually fulminates (frequently hypocritically) against non-marital, non-procreative sex and rallies behind war, big business, and good-old-boy patriarchy, is, in this astonishing instance, turning the preacherly performance tropes to opposite purpose. (Reverend Billy's frank exultation of sex is an especially enjoyable aspect of this classic comic reversal. His sermons happily call forth images of lovers—the importance of couples in Union Square park, for instance, "side-by-side on a park bench going at it, lunch-hour necking . . . Kiss-a-lujah!" And while there's no hip-swiveling in the reverend's own performance, it's not just his hair that recalls Elvis: Reverend

Billy's tall, lean frame clad in a snug leisure suit, along with his pouty good looks, contribute to his televangelical charisma.) The choir plays an important role in this process, too. No mere accompaniment to a central, straight-white-guy soloist, the strikingly diverse group (some forty singers of various ages, genders, races, ethnicities, sexual orientations, physical abilities, class backgrounds, national origins, and religious affiliations) often holds center-stage, a multi-culti community speaking to the universality of the Stop-Shopping creed and lending Reverend Billy his authority (not to mention, busting out with good, stirring music).

This neo-Brechtian process of making a familiar preacher figure strange opens an ironic gap through which a twenty-first century audience can enter a political discourse it might otherwise shun. That is, the comic frame makes space for the radical substance of the performance; laughter wipes away the sneer that has become America's standard-issue response to forthright leftism. It is not easy to break through a mass-media habit of dismissing progressive ideals as the immature longings of the naive, wimpy or anti-American. People born after, say, 1970—those as old as forty today—came to consciousness after the "Reagan Revolution" forced a far-reaching political realignment, casting regulation as dangerous, taxes as an offense, and social spending as a waste. This generation has no personal memory of a United States in which a considerable social safety net, progressive taxes, and corporate regulation could not only be earnestly proposed, but were enacted law. Instead, theirs is a dominant culture that regards appeals to the commonweal and collective responsibility as an embarrassment, the throwback lunacy of kumbaya-singing suckers. Reverend Billy's religious trappings remove the inhibition of such prevailing attitudes by giving spectators a tongue-in-cheek role to play. Behind the invisible mask of faithful churchgoers, we can express enthusiasm for ideals we might be too self-conscious to affirm, much less proclaim, otherwise. We can even go so far as to be utopian—a much-maligned, yet necessary element of any meaningful activism. A lead Stop-Shopping Choir member, the late Derrick McGinty, used to croon an enchanting solo and campily catch the spirit, jumping in sideways spurts of delight, as if he were being pulled across a runway for liftoff. Audiences perform that sort of dance metaphorically at Reverend Billy shows: We hop along with half-simulated jubilation—and pretty soon, we can fly. Often, performances end with Reverend Billy leading the crowd outside for an action: planting seedlings in a vacant lot, massing in Union Square. In the early years, some of these ventures seemed impulsive or incompletely thought-through: they subjected participants to danger they might not have anticipated and certainly had not assented to risking. Once, for example, Reverend Billy guided the audience out of a theater into Manhattan's downtown streets to cheer on the defacers of giant billboards that had recently been erected in the residential area; the ads' gleaming-toothed, airbrushed models had been the villainous figures in the show's sermon about the "malling" of Soho and "the street formerly known as Prince" and now we were going to witness and encourage the splattering of those relentlessly perfect faces. Several men with giant paintball guns aimed globs of primary color at the offending billboards looming above us—and within moments, the spinning red glow of police-car lights illuminated the scene. In a crowd in the dark, those paintball guns could easily have been mistaken for real weapons and skittish cops could have threatened the crowd—possibly even fired—with live ammunition. I remember the high-adrenalin anxiety of the police officers' sudden, aggressive arrival. They threatened us with arrest for defacing property and ordered us to disperse. Apart from some snarky verbal exchanges, we escaped serious confrontation and went our separate ways. Only later did I realize how lucky we had been. In more recent years—thanks to the ballast Savitri has brought to the work, the maturing of the project, and the wariness with which the post-9/11 take-no-prisoners enforcement mode has chilled the activist atmosphere—the post-performance actions Reverend Billy leads have been more considered and conscientious, more focused on meaning than on daredevil antics.

Like the shows themselves, these actions have more ritual than revolutionary efficacy—but the two are related in Reverend Billy's church. As in traditional religions, ritual takes on power here through repetition and communal assent; the recurring, collective enactment of a deed confers its significance. By shouting "Amen," or singing along with the choir, or patting a flower into rocky urban ground, we call ourselves forth as civic participants, as vitally as a man crossing himself both expresses and creates his Catholicism, or a woman lighting Sabbath candles performatively produces her Jewishness. We may put quotation marks around our activities with Reverend Billy—that Brechtian irony that keeps sanctimony and sentimentality at bay—but we still believe the expression inside them; like Reverend Billy, we mean what we are saying. The Church of Life After Shopping services and the symbolic actions that follow are rehearsals for political participation, and at the same time, they are real, sometimes genuinely risky, events. Like Reverend Billy himself, they are at once both fake and true. Which is another way of saying, this is good theater.

In particular (like so much that is post-modern), it's a kind of pre-modern theater. Western theater, after all, began in ritual; fictional drama secularized it. By removing the invented storytelling and replacing it with songs, sermons, tales of real-life conflicts between good and evil, reference to a providential order (at least one that is implied), and the search for a righteous life, Reverend Billy harks back to a form in which audiences have a direct stake in the action. This link between theater and religion has long ghosted America's radical performance, not only in the holiness pursued by such groups as Bread and Puppet Theater and the Living Theatre in the 1960s and '70s, but also in the very institutions that cultivated New York's experimental theater in the early '60s: Theater Genesis at St. Mark's Church under rector Michael Allen; Judson Poets' Theatre under minister Al Carmines at the Judson Memorial Church; and the Theater at St. Clements, under its vicar Sidney Lanier, Billy's mentor in the creation and development of Reverend Billy. (This relationship is discussed in Chapter 12, the interview with Billy and Savitri.)

While his moral imperative couldn't be starker—"stop shopping!"—Reverend Billy demonstrates that much more than abstract, noble principles are at issue. And this is one more reason the project succeeds. Quite simply, it's fun. Reverend Billy connects the enjoyment we can have in the theater or in the streets with the need to free our colonized imaginations, to detach ourselves from the long-standing idea that shopping offers the most direct route to pleasure (and to patriotism). Part of the delight comes from one more set of old comic tropes: exaggeration (as if anyone actually could stop shopping—and indeed, Reverend Billy sings the praises of local mom-and-pop outfits as much as he does of gift economies) and obsession. Onstage, Reverend Billy can be as hilariously single-minded about the evils of shopping as Molière's Harpagon is about hoarding money or as Dr. Strangelove's General Ripper is about the imminence of Soviet attack. That we can laugh at him—and in turn, be uplifted by his grandiloquence—helps rescue the critique of consumerism from a tone of reproach. (One danger, as the work has shifted the balance more toward earnestness, is that the target of its opprobrium can slip from the exploiters and polluters to Reverend Billy's audiences. If we consumers are the sinners, then—to invoke Greg Tate's memorable phrase about the 1997 "Promise Keepers" march on Washington—are we meant to protest ourselves? Only comic irony prevents Reverend Billy from tumbling into self-righteous moralizing; his performance must always remind spectator-participants that he is wearing a disguise, transparent as it may be.)

By counseling us to stop shopping, Reverend Billy pulls on one end of a long-standing tug-of-war in assessments of American consumer habits. On one side, for at least a century—since Thorstein Veblen wrote *The Theory of the Leisure Class* in 1899—critics have warned against the folly and the moral decay of status-driven purchases and the promotion of spending over saving. On the other side, champions of mass consumption, such as Veblen's contemporary Simon Patten (head of the Wharton School of Business), cheered on what Patten called an "economics of abundance," arguing that in modern times, when technology could provide for everyone's basic needs, there was no reason to function in the old scarcity mode of scrimping and sacrifice. Though such provision of needs hardly materialized for everyone, Patten's view easily won the day, especially as shopping was elevated to a practice far grander and more satisfying than the mere chore of picking up basic necessities. It became entertainment and, eventually, a marker and conferrer of "lifestyle." Those who objected, from Veblen onward through Herbert Marcuse and Marxist critics in the New Left, couldn't help but sound like scolds, as they blamed consumers for being, at best, unwitting dupes of nefarious capitalism, and worse, eager collaborators. In contrast, Reverend Billy snatches pleasure from rampant consumerism—and indeed, recalls the loneliness and passivity one experiences when her life revolves around a series of advertising-manipulated purchases—and reclaims it for the live, communal satisfactions of theater and action. This church's pious practice is not one of abstinence and self-abnegation, but of agency.

As a form, theater suits the nature of this activism: first and foremost, it is corporeal—live, immediate, dependent on bodily presence. There's a literalness, then, to the dissident's willingness to put her/his body on the line, and Billy does so again and again, submitting to arrest and incarceration (in increasingly more planned and thoughtful ways as the years go by. Indeed, he and Savitri have come to regard the legal system—police on the streets, juries in courtrooms, opponents in lawsuits—as elements in the spectacles they construct. They consider when it's dramatically and politically effective to engage them on purpose, and how to turn legal intervention to their advantage—if they can—when it arrives unbidden.) Bodies become the very substance of performance-protest sometimes, when, for example, Savitri takes the extreme measure of going on hunger strike (Chapter 5) or Billy leads an audience through an improvisatory transformation into forest creatures (Chapter 7) or persuades a group of activists to lick the fixtures in a Starbucks in Spain (Chapter 4).

Theater serves their project in a more abstract way, too. While Reverend Billy and the choir participate in traditional protests that demand the rights of aggrieved people—whether locked-out factory workers, residents of gentrifying neighborhoods, gays and lesbians prohibited from marrying, Appalachians trying to save their landscape and water from coal-mining destruction, and so on—their politics are expansive, transformative. That is, about envisioning a different, more compassionate, world. As a place for seeing things anew, experiencing unfamiliar and fuller feelings, and flexing the imagination, theater is indispensable to such productive dreaming. Life After Shopping: What a reality-rearranging idea, which the theater allows us to try on.

Finally, the Reverend Billy project offers one more powerful critique by slyly mirroring the state of transnational corporate capitalism itself: both a religion that fosters blind faith in "market fundamentalism" and a kind of theater, whose increasingly unmoored financial instruments depend on a collective willing suspension of disbelief among investors and brokers. Derivatives like collateralized debt obligations, after all, are about as real as Tinker Bell. They exist and have value only because enough people clap their moneyed hands together. (I refer to the Tinker Bell, I hasten to add, beloved in J. M. Barrie's *Peter and Wendy,* not to the Disney branding icon.)

As this book goes to press—with the pace of publishing always lagging behind that of world events and agile performance artists—the economy continues to slump and the US still feels the repercussions of its biggest environmental calamity ever (the result of profiteering corner-cutting and lack of regulation). The Reverend Billy project has always included some good, pagan ardor for nature (it comes to the fore in the Victoria's Secret campaign, Chapter 7), and even before the BP oil spill, they got involved in the movement to end "mountaintop removal," an aggressive means of strip-mining for coal that is razing Appalachia. The process involves blasting into mountains with toxic explosives and scraping away a layer of earth hundreds of feet deep, in order to expose coal seams. Some three million pounds of explosives are detonated every day in the region; several ridgetops are destroyed each week. Tons of "removed" dirt, bearing chemicals from the explosives, are dumped in nearby valleys and riverbeds while the ridges are left deforested, the landscape devastated, the mountain cultures undone. Local residents and environmentalists have been fighting for years, through the courts, the legislatures, and with their bodies, seldom managing, in this era of de-regulation, to restrain "King Coal." Meanwhile, coal's price keeps rising on the global market.

In the spring of 2010, Reverend Billy and the Church of Life After Shopping began taking the battle to the banks that underwrite the coal companies. They received some mountain soil from activists in West Virginia's Coal River Valley and brought it ceremonially to Manhattan bank lobbies. First they went into some twenty branches of J.P. Morgan Chase, which financed eighty percent of mountaintop removal in Appalachia, and then, when J.P. Morgan Chase quickly pulled out, the troupe paraded into the midtown headquarters of the Swiss bank UBS, which rushed in as the new financiers. Singing and praying and handing out leaflets about poisoned water and local children with unusual cancers, Reverend Billy and the choir sculpted the dirt into little peaks, symbolically depositing the soil in the bank, thereby tying the abstractions of stocks and bonds and free-floating capital to the earthly damage moving some numbers on a computer screen can do.

This latest campaign extends the Church of Life After Shopping's long-standing resistance to rampant consumption—of energy as well as products—and its doting parent, unchecked free-marketeering. And it brings yet a new dimension to the Reverend Billy project's stirring blend of spectacle, spirit, and action. The ruination wrought by mountaintop removal is all too literal. It is also powerfully symbolic for activists who honor their radical history and try to project us into a just future: If we destroy our mountaintops, from where will we glimpse the promised land?

3. City of Angels: Banished, Convicted, and Free
Northridge, Reseda Boulevard Starbucks
REVEREND BILLY

It was to be an afternoon of "Retail Interventions." More or less routine. Enter the interior of a corporation that is behaving badly in the world, camouflage ourselves for a time in the faux bo-ho environment of the chain store, and then pull off an action that is brash but not utterly suicidal—just rising out of the garish retail enough to break it open and deposit new thoughts, research, and such gifts to the customers there: to offer a view of the world that is for a moment not Consumerism.

Fifteen students from the Northridge campus of California State University (this is north of Los Angeles in "the Valley") and a like number of Life After Shopping singers would rise to their sly disruptions. Our stage, on this April day in 2004, would be the unsuspecting Starbucks at 9420 Reseda Boulevard, the heart of a numbingly suburban wasteland, featuring thousands of automobiles hesitating this way and that, nudging each other, honking and stopping. And there it was, the Starbucks, with its sign, the Mermaid With No Nipples, tucked away in one of those little strip-malls with people inside standing in line, waiting at the condiments, nudging and pushing forward like the cars outside.

On a little grassy area on campus, the singers and eager students practiced the scripts for our slow-release plays: "Sponsored Love," "The Post-Doctoral Consultant of Bare-Faced Lies," and "Jail House Rocks." Passersby watched us, slack-jawed and frowning, or grinning and elbowing a friend—then they moved on. Savitri was stopping and starting the students over, modulating their volumes, encouraging them. They bit into their roles voraciously, as if ready to sink their canines into the ankles of the coffee giant. Watching it all from the side, I remember reflecting that the monoculture would be bristling with complications today! The rehearsal was very energized, but I had no idea . . .

We walked toward Reseda and the film crew making *Preacher With An Unknown God* (Rob VanAlkemade's 2005 documentary about our work) was walking with us, circling us, brandishing those shiny lenses. It was midday in the San Fernando Valley and the pavement slipped under the empty apartments and dusty hedges like a hot spatula. The students were walking here easily, second-generation immigrants, handsome and happy and not intimidated by Starbucks, clearly. They marched ahead and morphed into customers as they neared the coffee shop, with their role-playing making their eyes lively. This was a new kind of politics we were witnessing. I was looking at these people: working-class children of the American Dream detecting the con in that dream a couple of generations earlier than the planners at Starbucks would've guessed.

Savitri staggered their entry. They circled the corner of the closest building in twos and threes and the Starbucks started filling up. I watched with the camera crew in an area behind some small palm trees out near Reseda. I could see two of our thespians pursuing the lesbian love story in the corner, "Sponsored Love." I know the words because I wrote them. I read their lips:

"Oh honey, I love you so much, Lizzie, SO much."

"Yes, I love you too, brought to you by American Apparel hosiery."

"What? But . . . I love you . . . I just love you."

"Yes, I love you too, brought to you by Nike Peak Performance."

"What? But honey . . . I . . . you . . . your love for me is . . ."

"That's right, it's SPONSORED LOVE! Courtesy of your local Coca Cola Bottler . . ."

"NO! NO!'"

I could see them, their voices rising, pulling the focus of the audience of the coffee shop, people sneaking looks over the tops of their laptops. Meanwhile, "Jailhouse Rock" was clearly picking up steam. This is the one with the prisoner just freed that morning, now being brought to the Starbucks by his cousin, and the prisoner is having some trouble with the "outside world."

"Wait a minute, Solomon."

"What is it?"

"This coffee. This Christmas special here. This bag with the Santa sticker . . ."

"Calm down, Sammy. What's the problem? It's chocolate-covered coffee beans."

"I know these beans. I mean, I . . . I . . . packed this bag of beans. I put the chocolate-covered coffee in there and I sealed it. I did this in prison."

"Sammy, cool it. Breathe deep now."

"I'M NOT OUT OF PRISON AT ALL. I'M STILL THERE! I'M AT THE TWIN RIVERS CORRECTIONAL FACILITY IN MONROE, WASHING-TON AND I'M STUFFING CHRISTMAS CHOCOLATE COFFEE IN THESE BAGS HERE AND I'M DOING IT FOR FIFTY CENTS AN HOUR—OH OH OH!"

And I could see the hysterical ex-con and his cousin, played by our choir master James Solomon Benn, sort of staggering in circles around the coffee shop. By this time the Sapphic sisters had risen from their table in the corner. I can practically hear—

"I LOVE YOU, MADE POSSIBLE BY TOYOTA! TOYOTA! We've got what you're looking for!"

Savitri, the action manager, was standing at the door. She signaled, "Not quite yet." Inside, the store manager, a large woman, had come out of the back office, and now the third intervention was kicking in: five or six of the students following our diva Laura Newman; she is the Post-Doctoral Consultant of Bare-Ass Lies.

"Now here you see we have pictures of the old Chavez Ravine, from before the Dodgers, back when this town was a kind of paradise, with the deco buildings and orange groves. That is, of course, a time that is no longer possible, and we here at Starbucks are killing it as surely as anyone, but here we have the picture, and that helps us with our concept of the half-hour vacation, the stop at Starbucks for the $4 latte, an unreal buzz, a bit of mild amphetamine rush that makes our customers feel as if their lives are a temporary movie, living in another time, before Starbucks was here, before LA died under an avalanche of cheap strip malls like this one we're standing in. We are selling not just coffee, but the lie that people choose for a tawdry lunchtime escape, and so this photo, a damn lie but a nice high . . ."

"I LOVE YOU BROUGHT TO YOU BY POLO DECK-WEAR!"

"WORKIN' ON THE CHAIN GANG, CHAIN GANG—I'M PACKIN' YO CHOC-BEANS FOR YOUR STARBUCKS CHRISTMAS!!"

Then Savitri turned in the doorway: NOW!

I crept from behind the palm trees out near Reseda with the film crew. We crossed the parking lot, toward the glassy box of a café, the madcap contents of which went on like soundless shadow-boxing inside. I raised my long white megaphone and pushed through the door. Savitri whispered, "Go to the end and work your way back to the register. It looks good."

Crossing the pavement, I inhaled the whole way. I have a practice breath I take at the beginning, when I want my exhalation to fill a whole business with sound. I think of my entire body as a lung that fills, inhaling through my feet, my ass, and my ears. Then "THE COFFEE IS NOT FAIR TRADE AND WE MUST NOW SPIT OUT THE DEVIL'S JUICE" comes through the bodies of the cappuccino sippers more like a crying train whistle slicing through the side of a town. I don't want to screech at a secretary point-blank. I don't want a retired postal worker's eyeglasses to crack. Causing upset is not what we want.

The full-body breath tries for a mythic in-the-present sort of sound, hoping for a response more like "Oh, this is the Reverend Billy wind; it is the protest wind that comes off the desert like the Santa Anas, the breath of the Unknown God blowing dust and smoke straight west right through the billboard models and the low-hanging police helicopters of LA, nothing to do but change."

But I hadn't gotten to the phrase "Fair Trade" before I sensed the room had changed a lot before I got there. Something had happened here. The docent of lies, our diva Laura Newman, was sweepingly praising the way that Starbucks tries to be hip and beatnik, environmental and "green," labor-friendly and in love with smiling coffee peasants, in a lying smorgasbord of false good intentions, but something in the way that the students were responding was breaking open the air. "Wow!" "Wow!" "So many lies at once!" "How do they do that?" "I have to tell my business professor!"

The corporatized lesbian had gone Pavarotti—she was blasting her aghast lover with "I LOVE YOU BROUGHT TO YOU BY THE REPUBLICAN NATIONAL COMMITTEE!" What? Meanwhile, the first-day-free prisoner was fully realizing a return to prison in the middle of suburbia. He was on his knees gibbering, while James tried to console him, reminding him that he actually was free. The prisoner, a nice graduate student from Glendale named Ravi, was doing an assembly-line kind of automated dance, like a mime caught in a nightmare, stuffing Christmas candy beans in the bags, sneaking submissive looks at the warden, "Back in the can, workin' for the man, put this under your tree, before you go out to ski . . ." Several patrons abandoned their lattes and were consoling him. Laura was singing her marketing advice now. Why had the lesbians lifted chairs in the air?

I realized that if I wanted to be the big train making this town cry, these actioneers had already flooded the town with firecrackers, Bible-thumpers, and psychologists doing burlesque. This was a Method Acting scene class on somatic mushrooms plus Marx, or something. What had happened here? I was preaching like I do, but the retail hypnosis was already cultivated by superior performances. I was only the aging Elvis impersonator that I really am, merely an anti-consumerist with an Unknown God. The retail stage had already been thoroughly seized by the most virulent sort of show-stealer, the amateur revolutionary with absolutely no fear.

I was preaching about Reseda Boulevard's new moral fervor, the Fair Trade zoning that would require Starbucks to leave the San Fernando Valley! Then my entire field of vision was rounded with one large face—the manager, a stocky, fierce woman with glasses, who seemed to be trying to stuff her tie into my mouth. She was defending her computerized cash register. A man off to my left was shouting, "Will you shut the fuck up?" There seemed to be a complicated collapsing in the center of my plans for mythic presence. This guy looked like an ex-marine and, amazingly, he was lifting me into the air. Then Savitri was lifting him into the air. I turned and, the riptide of scene class pandemonium breaking over my back, I somehow stepped up onto the counter between the two registers. The sound in the room, every word that each person was at that moment exhaling, went up a note-and-a-half, with a shower of squealings over the top, for I was up on the altar; the Unknown God was confronting the God who paid the rent.

The ex-marine in mortal combat with my wife, the lesbian lovers now bloodcurdling the Fortune 500, the docent of lying now Leontyne Pricing the walls, and now five or six prisoners moving all the merchandise from place to place—"I'm locked UP, locked UP, locked UP!" I remember clearly having a moment of marking this, marking it for my own life, for what I would be made of and what I would remember—from my silent control tower up on the counter. I felt the beauty of human imagination overwhelming a major corporation. You wouldn't do business here now, not with that conversation that Starbucks thought it would continue day and night with the half-drifting public. This was a return to our native fierceness, which we could sustain if we wanted to. This moment in this coffee shop on this unlikely day: This was our proof.

In that expanding moment, all the hundreds of assumptions that we all say yes to together, that thick consensual wall of yes ok yes of course this is normal—this agreement that goes automatically forward and governs, that dominating thing that we might call Consumerism—it was turned inside out. I looked around the flimsy suburban aluminum and glass room, set among the automobiles of the blazing afternoon of Los Angeles, and each consumer was inside out. The advertising lurched, trying to catch them, but their senses were inverted. The roses opened. The dark Freudian interiors were filled with light. Childhood traumas and glories bloomed up into the eyes and erogenous zones. I saw a woman stand up, walk three steps, and have a deep thought, but then some prison beans made her laugh and look around.

I was back on terra firma. Savitri had the manager's cravat in her fist. Somehow that tie was the joystick of this flying circus. "Information!" cried Savi, and the students and singers who had all this time stayed in the passive cross-legged choreography of café customers, sitting there quietly as the mayhem rose, but holding their fire and trying not to shout—they all greeted the folks at the neighboring tables, some of whom still had iPods in their ears, some at laptops or on cells. Now they had the opportunity to confront, for instance, the question of how many doctors per 100,000 Guatemalans are working in the Western Highlands where Starbucks gets its beans in that country. The answer is: One doctor per 85,000 people. So after defeating the strategic culture of this chain-store café, now we gave everyone the facts.

The three overweight male cops stood in the doorway and you could see their faces sampling crimes in the scene they surveyed. You could see the wide-eyed analysis: negative, click, next, no, click, next, click. Peg the crime. They tried to fit dozens of square crime pegs into hundreds of round holes. Their reckoning swiftly descended to regular discon—disorderly conduct. Just to do something and get the crazy preacher and his followers into the parking lot, they began a march toward the cash register, led by Ms. Manager stomping with her strap-on pumps. Save the cash first. They understood this. As law enforcement advanced, the vortexes of retail-replacing drama hesitated toward a murmur. Savitri saw the cops and turned to me.

"Honey! You said you wouldn't pray over any more cash registers!" I took my cue and reached for the register, with the other arm in the air and the hand up like a little satellite dish. "Oh radical creator, Oh fabulous Unknown! Blow this money the other way, back from the billionaire to Guatemala, to Colombia, to . . ." I couldn't quite touch the cash registers because Sergeant Bilko was now saving the economy from the evil preacher, but mostly Savitri had the floor. "Why did you do this again? What is it with these cash registers!" It was working! The police stopped in their tracks. "YOU COME HOME THIS INSTANT! THEY MIGHT THINK YOU'RE STEALING SOMETHING!" The police were taken in completely. They looked at Savi and back at me. "BILLY YOU COME HOME!" The police, by stopping, gave us the option of leaving without their interrogation. They handed over authority to the crazy preacher's wife. The marriage obviously was the authority here, a governmental entity more important than the local precinct. I pleaded with Savitri that this was not a Fair Trade company and she pulled me from the marine and started toward the door, with our political troupe following our lead.

We left the cops there with the manager, echoes of their own wives' voices in their heads. So we made our getaway, feeling that some kind of unexpected crack in the retail wall had revealed a new promised land. We didn't have words for it, beyond "wow" and "what the hell was that!" But we talked throughout the afternoon about how deep Consumerism's spell is in an average Starbucks—the shape of the room and the light and acoustics of it, the particular set of customers with the sergeant. We had to accumulate so much energy with the three intervention-plays to shatter it. We backed up and broke open the marketing calculations, apparently, and the gravitational horizon completely changed. That day we kept explaining that we were having unlikely old memories. Our bodies felt different. Our dreams turned over.

As confused as the police may have been in that monocultural café turned magic cauldron, they regrouped and drove our tour bus to the Northridge city line. They were polite, though, and careful with us. We thanked them for letting us go, and asked them not to drink their coffee at Starbucks. One officer said that there was a new Fair Trade café, near the college. Change-a-lujah!

Almost four months later, in July, we received a curious fat envelope in the mail from the Los Angeles Federal Court. One astonishing document announced that William C. Talen, aka Reverend Billy, was now banished from all Starbucks establishments in California, and was enjoined from "annoying, disturbing, stalking or sexually harassing the computerized cash registers of the Starbucks Coffee Company." The envelope also contained documents charging said William Talen with trespassing and vandalism. We would have to go back to the San Fernando Valley in the fall to stand trial.

On Trial in the Valley

SAVITRI D

IN ORDER TO PROVE THIS CRIME EACH OF THE FOLLOWING ELEMENTS MUST BE PROVED: ONE, A PERSON INTENTIONALLY INTERFERED WITH A BUSINESS OPEN TO THE PUBLIC; TWO, A PERSON DID SO BY OBSTRUCTING OR INTIMIDATING THOSE ATTEMPTING TO CARRY ON THEIR BUSINESS OR THEIR CUSTOMERS; THREE, THAT PERSON REFUSED TO LEAVE AFTER BEING ASKED TO DO SO BY THE OWNER OR AGENT OF THE OWNER.

FOR THE PURPOSE OF 602.1 (A) OF THE PENAL CODE, THE MEANING OF THE WORD 'OBSTRUCT' IS BE OR COME IN THE WAY OF, HINDER FROM PASSING, ACTION OR OPERATION. 'IMPEDE' MEANS RETARD, SHUT OUT AND PLACE OBSTACLES IN THE WAY.

THE DEFENDANT IS CHARGED WITH A VIOLATION OF 602.1 (A) OF THE PENAL CODE, A MISDEMEANOR. IF IT IS DETERMINED THAT A PERSON FALLS IN ANY OF THE FOLLOWING CATEGORIES, SECTION 602.1 (A) DOES NOT APPLY: ONE, A PERSON IS ENGAGED IN LAWFUL LABOR UNION ACTIVITIES THAT ARE PERMITTED TO BE CARRIED OUT ON PROPERTY BY STATE OR FEDERAL LAW; OR BY THE CALIFORNIA CONSTITUTION OR THE UNITED STATES CONSTI-

TUTION. IF A PERSON FALLS IN EITHER CATEGORY, SECTION 602.1
(A) DOES NOT APPLY AND A GUILTY VERDICT MUST NOT BE RE-
TURNED. (California vs. Talen 2004)

Secretly I love Los Angeles. New Yorkers talk trash about it, even
though most of them have never even been there. People everywhere
just hate it as a matter of principle, the same way they hate the Yan-
kees, but I have clarifying visions when I am there. A kind of juvenile
revolutionary spirit courses through me while we sit in traffic jams
trolling for classic rock or soul music from the seventies. The catastrophe stimulates me. When we stop at the forty-seventh red light in a
row, surrounded on all sides by Applebee's and Mattress Warehouses
and sunlight so bright my whole face has to squint, I find myself excited, buzzy with response. I see each overpass and interchange as if
from the sky, like I'm driving and flying, gazing down at the Byzantine
complex of overgrowth and hubris, the cloverleafs and the subdivi-
sions, the cul-de-sacs and the swimming pools, canyons dammed by
wealth, wetlands clogged by pollution, ten-lane highways. Jesus, am I
even human? Is my skin still working? We pull into the courthouse. It
looks like a suburban middle school.

Billy's fate would be determined here, in a modest room with a deep
red carpet that sucked the sound out of everything. The tables and
desks were low and flat. The judge was somewhat elevated but appeared
to have no face—all robe and gavel. Prospective jurors sat shoulder to
shoulder in rows; their eyes, with nothing to look at, nothing to wander to, flickered like little screens. All hands were out of sight, the newspapers and books disappeared, and the straight-backed chairs de-
manded good posture. We were waiting for the proceedings to begin.
There was nothing else to do. Heavy drapes and curtains cloaked the
windowless walls. Mysterious doors revealed uniformed interlopers carrying stacks of paper from here to there.

Art Goldberg, our tall, slightly rumpled, but somehow saintly
lawyer, asked the prospective jurors how many of them had ever been
to Starbucks. Every single person raised a hand. Then he asked how
many went regularly, like once a week. Every single person raised a
hand. He asked how many of them went every day and an astounding
seven out of thirteen raised their hands. Art abandoned that line of attack. A few minutes later the man who would soon be elected foreman

of the jury laughingly admitted that "lately" his family had been calling him "Mr. Starbucks."

Art: And what is your occupation sir?

Mr. Starbucks: Well, I'm retired.

Art: And what was your occupation before you retired?

Mr. Starbucks: I worked for the government.

Art: In what capacity?

Mr. Starbucks: I worked for the Central Intelligence Agency.

Art: And you go to Starbucks every day?

Mr. Starbucks: Yes.

Art: What do you do when you are at Starbucks?

Mr. Starbucks: Surf the World Wide Web, maybe send some email, socialize, read, work on some writing. It's kind of like being at home, only without my family.

Art struck only two jurors, a red-faced car salesman whose unfocussed hostility gave Art what he later called "a bad feeling," and a frail elderly woman who said she could not imagine that a person being charged with a crime hadn't done "at least something to deserve it." The prosecutors dismissed a labor organizer and two others who said they had protested the war in Iraq.

We were staying at my Aunt Dabney's ranch way up on a ridge in Altadena. We slept in a little cabin perched on the side of the hill, woke up with the rooster and spent the early mornings wandering around the old property with our coffee cups.

As the trial went on the ranch seemed more and more fantastic, more remote, like another planet. One night a torrential rain came and a series of leaks sprang in the roof of the cabin. The water drained from the ceiling into the center of my chest. After a while the blankets soaked through and I couldn't ignore it any more. Billy was still asleep. The hair on my arms was standing up with static electricity and I started having cataclysmic visions—lightning strikes, mudslides, the cabin in shards at the bottom of the arroyo. "Billy wake up, wake up," I said. "We have to get out of here." The rain was getting heavier. I was possessed, irrational. The power was out. I put on my headlamp and packed everything, loaded the car. "Billy get up," I said. "Wake up." I handed him pants and shoes and hustled him out to the car. We started down the hill, water and mud oozing off the slopes. There was debris everywhere and we couldn't get through. I stopped the car and we rolled away a rock the size of a tire and a little farther, a tree that had fallen across the road. It was 3:00 a.m. by the time we found a motel, and I couldn't sleep. I lay there in the fake bed, in a fake hotel built for secretive lovers, ten miles from the ranch where my aunt and uncle had lived since the forties, raising animals and children and making art and building barns. The motel was awful. It was still raining. I watched back-to-back episodes of *Law and Order*—fake courtrooms, fake juries, fake judges, fake morality, fake commercials.

Back in court just a few hours later, with the Method actors and formulaic plotlines of *Law and Order* fresh on my mind, I saw how the drama comes from being accused, being judged, being tried. The stakes are high no matter the charge. The court itself is so meaningful, and our cooperation in the legal system is so primary to the covenant of our society. We all agree to some of these rules some of the time. It's not just the marshal's gun that makes us stand up when the judge walks in. Something makes us regard a jury's decision differently from how we might the decisions of our neighbor or brother or boss. We oblige ourselves to some aspect of the proceedings, and most of us take it seriously, even as we know the proceedings will almost always favor the acquisition and protection of property, even as we know the conditions of the courts are basically racist, basically punitive, basically flawed. We know all that, but we cooperate. It's the best we've got. The brokenness of the system started to play like a drama within the drama, like an internal monologue in the middle of a fight.

We stood in front of the jury to be judged—in this case for turning Starbucks into a courtroom and ourselves into prosecutors, judge, and jury. We invited customers to join the sentencing. We had done the same many times and will undoubtedly do it again. We see into the business practices of a corporation and denounce them, call them wrong, call them evil, call them immoral, greedy, excessive. We put Starbucks on trial because our government creates regulations and trade agreements that make certain corporate practices inevitable, because our government doesn't seem to have a way to put corporations on trial itself. Not really. We take the law into our own hands. A dangerous prospect, except when you consider the trappings of our enforcement: a self-proclaimed preacher, a choir, some improvisational comedy routines, press releases, YouTube videos.

So we were being prosecuted for a minuscule "crime," while Starbucks continued its misleading advertising (not a crime), its iron grip on the coffee market (not a crime), its overuse of resources (not a crime), its intimidation of small businesses (not a crime), its union busting (not quite a crime), its exploitation of coffee farmers (not a crime), and on it goes. I had to remind myself that Starbucks was not on trial here—we were in a courtroom in Northridge, California, and it was Billy who was on trial.

Inside a courtroom nestled among the dark wood, caught up in the ritualized proceedings, things became binary in a hurry. It was hard not to feel that the world was made up of two kinds of people: those who think you did it and those who think you didn't, or, in this case, those who think you did but that you had a good reason, and those who know you did and don't care what the reason was, because the video plainly shows you did. It's not my favorite way to look at the world, and especially in those dark days, on the eve of the 2004 presidential election, it was hard not to feel that the nation itself was similarly divided. I wondered if this was really a jury of our peers. Once in a while I tried to abandon my own assumptions, neutralize my position, and listen to the lawyers' arguments. Would I have found Billy guilty were I on that jury? Would I have been shocked by the video playing in slow motion, even the 243rd time? Would I have cared that in the other twenty minutes of video there were thirty other people of many races and ages participating, that there was lots of conviviality all around and absolutely no threat or danger to anyone and even some smiling, nodding workers behind the counter? Would it have mattered that the girl whose commercial transaction was disrupted was laughing?

Deep into the trial, under questioning from our other lawyer, Mark Wolfe, the manager of the Starbucks defined the concept of the Third Place, Starbucks' ultimate corporate aspiration: "We want to be the third place, not work or school and not home, but the third place, where people feel comfortable and safe and can go to just, you know, to *be*." Art, a lifelong free-speech activist, jumped in, asked her if "in the so-called third place, just, you know, 'being,' includes talking about issues of the day, what's on your mind, current events," to which she replied, "Well, I mean, as long as it isn't bothering anyone. I mean as long as everyone is being, you know, nice."

Art was never optimistic about our prospects; he didn't think we had a chance in hell in that valley. Northridge is a series of strip malls, shabby condos, and tucked-away neighborhoods where a significant percentage of the world's pornography is made. Countless bargain stores and quasi-Italian restaurants, long strings of traffic lights, mysterious office parks and gas stations, storage lots, and billboards line the main strip. There are fairly regular pockets of diversity—a taco truck, maybe an Iranian grocery—but in general Northridge is dominated by blankly mainstream commercial culture. The only real evidence of the immigrant presence there, or even the native Angeleno culture, are immigrants or Angelenos themselves, in live flesh, walking, driving, shopping: their faces, an occasional sari, a candy-red lowrider, a cowboy boot.

Lunchtimes we ate in a Chinese buffet across an eight-lane road. It was the best we could do. One day I noticed one of the jurors was also there. He didn't seem to register our presence in the least. Then I noticed a young woman was reading the menu to him, and that when he went to the buffet he held her arm and walked slowly. I realized he was, if not blind, then seriously visually impaired. I was relieved actually, as I had noticed him staring at me almost constantly in the courtroom, so much that it made me uncomfortable. One day I smiled at him, but got no response. Watching him at the restaurant, as he pressed his face almost flat against the cough-guard, I realized he probably couldn't even see me in the courtroom; it wasn't me he was looking at. But what about the surveillance tape? Didn't the whole trial rest on a piece of visual evidence? I asked Art what he thought and he shrugged, "That's the least of your worries." He was telling Billy how he and Mario Savio stood on top of a trapped police car in Sproul Plaza while thousands of students rallied around them, and how he knew the Berkeley Free Speech Movement was a real movement from the way people took information from him, how eager they were to read. I said we could barely get people to make eye contact with us. "They are hypnotized, mesmerized," Billy said. "Just like our jurors," Art said.

The District Attorney, Nancy Rodriguez, called some of the students to the stand, ones who were with us the day of the action. The DA asked them to describe our "training," how Billy and I led them into Starbucks in order to perform "subversive" theater. Billy and I, along with our host professor, Tony Perucci, seemed more and more sinister every minute, more dangerous, more radical. We were terrorist zealots instigating chaos, dangerous criminal activity; we were corruptors of wholesome youth. (And back at his university, Tony took some flack from his administrators for having invited us in the first place.) It was going well for the DA. For a second, even I forgot that we were basically just doing comedy bits in the Starbucks with some gospel music and a high-volume preacher—I forgot that we had a really good reason too, a purpose. Are we criminals? Are we? I had spent a fair share of time with less than savory characters in my lifetime, minor players in various dark economies, even some dangerous people. Was I missing something? Were we really so bad? "NO," I wanted to shout. "Starbucks is the criminal! They're the subversive ones! Their ads are full of lies! They keep kids from going to school!"

I wondered what the hell we could expect to gain from this experience. I meditated on the jurors' faces a lot. Their upper lips and eyebrows, the smooth planes of their foreheads. I marveled at the many textures of hair, the variety of postures. They didn't look at Billy much and it was easy to see that their sympathies lay with the Starbucks manager, Angelica Polito, and why wouldn't they? A single mother making a living, a kind of everywoman. She said Billy scared her, intimidated her, that she felt she had to protect her store and her workers. Art and Mark reminded the jury that this woman was not the owner of the Starbucks, that Starbucks is a multinational chain store with more than 14,000 locations, that she was the one who touched Billy, and that the workers in the video were actually smiling. Art asked her to refrain from calling it "my shop." None of that seemed to help at all. Billy just looked like an out-of-control aggressor.

The original charges against Billy included a restraining order that enjoined Billy to refrain from harassing, confronting, or sexually intimidating the Starbucks cash register. Again and again, we re-read the notice that had come by certified mail.

> The Honorable J. Harkavy hereby enjoins William Claire Talen, aka Reverend Billy, from coming within 250 yards of all the Starbucks in the State of California. The defendant shall not annoy, harass, strike, threaten, sexually assault, batter, stalk, destroy personal property of, or otherwise disturb the peace of the Starbucks cash register or the Starbucks Corporation.

"Starbucks cash register" was written with a thick black Magic Marker in a childlike hand.

Billy and the choir exorcise a cash register in Liverpool, England, 2009. (Photo by John Quilty.)

I live in a city where women get killed and seriously injured by sexual violence on a daily basis, in a country where a woman actually has to be hurt or have her life threatened before she can even file for a restraining order. To use the language of sexual violence for what was obviously a political act aimed at an object, not a person, to portray Starbucks as a victim, struck us as totally offensive and completely hilarious at the same time. We spent a few weeks making jokes about how Billy couldn't possibly land at LAX without coming within 250 yards of a Starbucks cash register. We imagined canoeing up the LA river to the courthouse to avoid violating the restraining order, or touring the state of California in a hot air balloon, hovering just 252 yards above the Starbucks. We mapped the area and were disappointed to discover that the courthouse itself lay just a few yards outside the 250-yard perimeter.

In the years since the trial, Billy has been pulled aside at customs every time we have reentered the country from a trip abroad. Billy is taken into a small room and asked if he is traveling with his alleged victim. Billy then explains that his alleged victim is the cash register of the corporation "Starbucks." Meanwhile I am pulled aside and asked if I am traveling with William Claire Talen "of your own volition" and asked to swear I am not being "coerced." I resist the urge to make jokes. I say, "No, I am not being coerced, officer. Yes I am here of my own volition." Then I wait for Billy by the luggage carousel and about an hour later he emerges and we go through customs.

The DA and the judge made it very difficult to talk about context, to discuss the meaning of what we were doing, the purpose. The judge made it abundantly clear to the jury that they were there to decide only one thing: whether or not Billy had interrupted the flow of commerce. So our lawyers could only try to expand the criminal moment to include the context, the motivation, the imperative of political protest. Everything revolved around those few seconds when money was exchanged across the counter. I wasn't surprised. Billy and I spent years perfecting the exorcism action for exactly that reason, so it would heighten and expand that very moment, the critical, ancient exchange of value from hand to hand.

In the court though, the whole thing was inverted. We were on the wrong side of a fun house mirror. The moment was not expanding to absorb the true history of the product—its labor history, its resource history, the distribution cycle, its future as waste, trash, landfill. Nor did it include the parsing of those dollars into massive profits for the corporation and meager earnings for the workers. No, here in the court the moment expanded to highlight our criminality, our shocking invasion of the simplest, most innocent, and legally protected actions, that exchange of value from hand to hand.

Finally Art was able to ask Billy to reconstruct exactly what happened, but only in order to illustrate precisely how long it took. So in the end Billy did get to stand in the courtroom, on the witness stand in front of the jury and deliver, to the best of his memory, a version of the exorcism he performed at the cash register that day. And so, after all those days the politics did ultimately make it into the courtroom, the words "impoverished," "hunger," "poverty," "globalization," "union busting," "neighborhood shop." But it was too late, like trying to pump

blood into a dead body. I watched the jury, their earnest, almost prayer-
ful listening, knowing how easily, how automatically, they could di-
vorce themselves from Billy's words, the meaning there. Indeed the
judge instructed them to ignore the meaning. They could declare Billy
guilty while insisting on their own innocence, perpetually startled that
anyone would ever even say anything bad about Starbucks.

During closing arguments the prosecuting attorney sanctified the
cash register. "Ladies and gentleman of the jury," she said, her eyes
turning heavenward. "He intentionally interfered with business, he did
interfere with business and this was beyond, beyond any right any of
us has to go in and have a skit, have a play, have any actions, because
there is a sacredness, there are places that people can't go grabbing registers and disturbing the flow of business. That's just *beyond*." The judge
read the charges again, reminded the jury of the rules, and they were
dismissed. Forty-five minutes later they returned with a guilty verdict
for Billy. Billy was sentenced to three days at the Twin Towers Correctional Facility in downtown Los Angeles.

On Election Day, I dropped Billy off to go do his time. The courthouse, a local voting site, was absolutely packed. I spent the day sending out press releases, catching up on work. That night I watched the
returns with Tony and his students. They made a party out of the disaster, drinking wine coolers and smoking on the patio. I sat frozen on
the couch as Bush and Cheney lifted their arms in victory, then dozed
off to the sound of students laughing, doors opening, empty bottles
falling, un-recycled, into the trash.

On Trial in the Jail

REVEREND BILLY

I felt some activist pride when I told the judge that I would go to jail.
No, your honor, I won't pay that fine—I will serve my time. It was a
way to defy the judge and jury who found me guilty of "impeding lawful business" when the choir and I drove the devils out of the Starbucks
cash register. Here we have a corporation that refuses Fair Trade moni-
tors for its coffee, and you're worried about that lady who had to wait
with her $5 bill while we prayed? Give me the cuffs.

Two days after my impulsive decision, we returned to the North-ridge courthouse so I could sign in, commit my wallet and shoelaces to the manila envelope, and embrace my curiously worried—but she's so strong that I have to say it's very dramatic when she finally does worry—beautiful wife. Then I walked under my own power toward the first of many windowless rooms. Somewhere in the approach to the door of the lockup is that subtle moment when the shadow of incarcer-ation pulls the citizen forward. There was a feeling in my legs and chest. I could not run anymore. I could not shout. I was not free. I was . . . con-tained. I knew it the moment that the sunny Californian civil servants were behind me about thirty or forty feet and I took this one turn in the concrete block wall hallway. Then I was standing there, not free, un-easily feeling that. A policeman said, "Come on guy," and caught the back of my elbow with his cupped hand. Freedom was completely gone by the time I stood in the holding-tank doorway. The eyes of the men on the bench along the wall all had the same look of dull pain.

This would be the beginning of three days and three nights of im-prisonment. When the judge said, "I sentence defendant Talen to three days . . ." it didn't feel like such a long time. Well, it felt like a far, far longer period of time now, as I took my seat on the bench. I geared down consciously. Having been arrested scores of times, I had become a practitioner of the "Zen of Jail-time," the lowering of all expectations, the dream state of well-performed incarcerations. Then a shout, "You, Mr. Space-Out, get on the fuckin' bus." Oh, our asses needed to get up from the bench at precisely the same moment. My meditation prepara-tions left my ass on the bench a couple seconds too long. Prisoners are like consumers who also move in lockstep, I was thinking as I went into my political head—it's the monoculture.

Walking across the pavement in the San Fernando Valley had a quality of unrealness. The light was soft and fluffy, the temperature eighty degrees, the buildings were lollipop colors and pastels. The bus was a bit raggedy, true, with metal mesh on the windows. The vinyl seats had stuffing poking through rips. Los Angeles, the land of dreams, features a rusty spring boinging through the upholstery.

The first hour of my jail-time we sat on the Ventura Freeway. I was thinking to myself, this is more like jail than jail, suspended here, in-carcerated between what we did and where we will end up. This was the perfect sense-deprivation tank-like context for me consciously to begin gearing down into my Jail Zen. So I started walking down my interior road, my alternative universe, while the candy-colored stucco of Los Angeles floated in the windows. As I slowly hypnotized myself, there was really nothing to interrupt me—only the occasional bark from the armed guy up by the driver with the fast-food stain on his belly.

There wasn't much talk among the prison population, just a nice patina of cussing and farts. Nothing you wouldn't expect—although coming up the valley by Universal Studios, I noticed an uneasiness in the bus for the first time. Something in the murmur of conversation hung just above the volume of the bus's old engine: a nasty unhappiness in the air. Men were staring straight ahead, folding their arms with their death's-head tattoos watching from the muscles. Of course, they were frowning and full of regret. OK. I overheard something, though, that would be my first full step down into hell. "My kid left a joint in the glove box and they took it from there. Cleaned out the house. Damn him to hell. Now I got me some heavy time." What?

I felt compelled to ask the guy sitting to my left, in the easy pastor voice, "What's your rap?" And he said quietly, "I'm fucked. Five, maybe eight. Who knows cuz of the vote?"

"Five years? Oh." When he said "You?" I swallowed down hard on my "three days," not wanting anyone to hear. And he gave me a laughing look like I was not going to jail at all. Then, out of the murmur a couple seats back, "I guess I'm three strikes and I'm out, could be ten years I'm lookin' at. Goddamn it, that damn vote . . ." Vote? I started hearing about the "three strikes referendum." Then a kid off to my right popped the back of the seat in front of him with his fist and let out a cry of strangled agony. The bus lurched over and stopped on the shoulder, while the goon with the gun in the wheel well got real nervous and gave an incomprehensible lecture full of threats. The kid was bleeding on his legs. An old man, a version of Willie Nelson, sat next to the kid and talked him down.

Now everybody broke the silence, ignoring the "Shut THE FUCK up" again and again from the guard. They talked about the three-strikes-you're-out law. Designed to put away "habitual offenders," in California it puts you away for up to twenty-five years on the third felony. This is mandatory sentencing—the judge cannot show mercy. A state-wide referendum to repeal three-strikes was defeated the Tuesday before our ride to the can. The dangerous feeling I detected in the bus

was the years and years of hard-time that anything more than a misdemeanor was getting some of these guys.

And there was a lot of ragging on Governor Arnold Schwarzenegger.
"The Austrian fucking oak, you fuckin' cunt"—this because Arnie came
out against the repeal of three-strikes just before the vote. The whole
ride felt different now and I imagined I had "three days" written all
over my face. There was no one on this bus with my easy, breezy life.
This was a gaggle of rage from inside a border, looking through the im-
penetrable steel mesh, looking out at the stardom of Los Angeles that
becomes such a demimonde of liberal bullshit, a famous person with
cosmetic compassion on every billboard.

We pulled in under a strange round building and we were marched
out and stood in a line against an orange-painted concrete wall while a
bull shouted at us like a sergeant in a movie about boot camp. As I best
recall it, this is how his spiel sounded: "You have arrived at the Twin
Towers Correctional Facility and you won't ever forget it." (What? Did
he say "Twin Towers"?) "This will be a lousy experience for each and
every one of you with no redeeming social value whatsoever, but this
building, the Twin Towers, wants to eat you and digest you in its bow-
els very slowly. Yes old Twin Towers wants to swallow you whole." (Is
this a well-advised line of talk for a New Yorker? The Twin Towers as
Godzilla?)

The cop was just getting going. "Let me tell you something about us
incarceration professionals. We're unhappy in our personal lives, you
see, and we get our kicks in unusual ways. For instance, we're already
losing your papers. You'll never see your girlfriend again or your loving
momma either. That was another life and it's too bad that this happened to you. It's like death. There's nothing to say. Your mommy
won't even get a telegram. And every badge here in the Twin Towers
knows you're innocent, most of you. It's the corrupt justice system of
Los Angeles County. You were framed. But each and every one of you is
a jackass for being here. Now another kind of evolution is taking over
and you didn't survive cuz you're not one of the fittest. You are little
meat units with sad cartoon faces. And you're in the no-one-could-
possibly-give-a-shit-anymore jungle of LA justice."

Our bitter orator took a few steps, suddenly so bored he was disas-
sociating from his surroundings. Then he inhaled sadly and we came
into focus again.

To my mind, he sounded like he was delivering a polished, eloquent monologue, whose performance he had "frozen," so that, like an actor in a long-running show, he could present it the same way every time he welcomed the next group of inmates. At least that's how I remember it: "Why am I talking to you right now? Why the hell am I talking to you slugs? Yeah, well, that's what I'd like to know. This must be like the moment in the James Bond movie where the ugly thug gives a speech before he blows up the orphanage. Yes, that must be me. I'm the character who gives a long speech to the cute actor who is in love with the cute actress and I have a long long speech while I deal with my pent up homosexual life, which is in turmoil within my soul. So while I'm revealing myself to be a terrible person, the cute actor is sawing away with a piece of broken glass on the knot of rope around his hands. It's a movie device that goes back generations. A leitmotif of melodrama that goes back to Restoration Comedy. And one more thing. I hate you. I hate each and every one of you little citizens because I hate myself. Now turn around, put your hands on the wall shoulder-width apart, stand out from the wall one yard and spread your legs."

Unbelievable. What *was* this guy's story? Leitmotifs and the history of Restoration Comedy? Was he a drama major who ended up here? My jaw was so dropped. I wanted to have a long talk with this cop about comic strategies, the relationship between certain vaudeville routines and authority over the audience. Fascinating. But as I turned around to face the spit-covered stinking wall, I thought, well, this was only a slightly more sophisticated version of the actor in all Los Angeles cops. They want to be on TV or in the movies. They have the *Hollywood Reporter* rolled up on the dashboards of their cruisers. This sadistic Police Academy comedy routine did have the quality of a movie scene to me. It really felt scripted. But wow, it was special. . . . Then a jolt of sound in my ear, a mouth up close: "HEY YOU, SPACE CADET FROM MARS!" I answered, "Yes?" "I didn't say SIDEWAYS. Put you're fuckin' nose ON THE FUCKIN' WALL."

I guess I was daydreaming again. I do that a lot. Savitri says I'm a dreamer. I had just been wondering if lots of folks doing everyday domestic actions throughout the Los Angeles basin think they are actors in a movie scene. It's such a company town—but does the industry distort everyone's personality all the time? There are surveillance cameras everywhere in this town, on the ledges, in the trees, up on the overpasses. Maybe the populace can't distinguish between surveillance and Hollywood stardom. James Cameron's eyes are everywhere, a seeing-eye landscape. Ten million people living every day like Jim Carrey in Celebration, Florida. I used to live in Los Angeles and I was trying to remember if this was the case. Maybe even as I shuffled in this line toward jail, maybe right in that moment there were thousands of people throughout this town doing Jack Nicholson scenes in their everyday life, while Nicholson himself lives up on Mulholland Drive looking down from his picture window on this vast town that is imitating him. "HEY HEY SPACE FUCK. Are you asking for solitary before you even check in?"

Another cop was red-faced inches away, spitting and upset. What the hell. Was I starting to become a problem prisoner? Already separating myself out as some kind of special case? My Jail Zen isn't working right. The thing I do, my little trick whenever I'm ushered into these places from a Starbucks cash register, is proactively to create a rich interior life, make my head a symposium of questions, images.

I get into these daydreams and then as I'm imagining things, I don't walk in line right or I smile to myself when everyone's in this macho pressure-cooker. It started occurring to me that I was very different from anyone here, and my approach was not a good thing at all. The monologuist who greeted us at the door and took us to the other side of the River Styx—he was right. There was an evolutionary law at work here. The patterns of compassion probably still existed, but they were hidden. All the signals had shifted, the way they do for a young vole on the forest floor who comes out into the sunshine for the first time and feels the talons of a sparrow hawk lifting it into the air before the television is turned off forever.

For one thing, I had never been in a jail like this. It was shiny, fluorescent light everywhere. It felt like the Wal-Mart of prisons. And so maybe this was like hell, a cross between a big box store and the Twin Towers. It was definitely not The Tombs, formerly the Bernard Kerrick Correctional Facility in Manhattan, where I've visited so many times. That place has a human scale. It has old-fashioned things like bars over the windows—a reassuring signal. (You can't find any bars in Twin Towers.) The Tombs' bars stay in the background like in black-and-white classics we go to see at the Film Forum. They are like very old friends who never say anything but you know what they mean. And in

The Tombs, the doors are shaped to fit bodies. The whole place could be from a Richard Price novel. It *is* from a Richard Price novel. I never thought I would miss The Tombs in the way you miss a summer camp that you loved as a child but . . . "HEY BOZO-MAN! YEAH, YOU! HALLUCINATOR WITH THE BLOND SURFER BOY HAIR!" I cleared my throat. "Yes, ma'am."

"WHAT DID YOU SAY? WHAT DID YOU CALL ME?" I was staring at a new kind of bull who arose from some godforsaken back aisle of this Wal-Mart of a prison. I was staring at her with a fascination that gave my whole game away. She was smiling back at me watching my agogness. She was wearing her sex life on the outside, and what was she? A dominatrix straight from the Halloween Parade, a deep, extreme bull drag, in a very tight uniform like in that Reno cop comedy, but with silver face-jewelry and a big fucking bullwhip. "What? I'm sorry. Not ma'am . . . OFFICER. I'M SORRY OFFICER." "That's better, white meat. Get in the cell." "Yes, officer."

Everything I was doing was wrong now. The news stories about knifings in this place were starting to repeat over and over in my mind. I was having that moment that all self-conscious ironists seek: Raw innocence. When death is real. Nothing that I thought made me smart was remotely applicable to the situation here, which was that I was hanging from the edge of some kind of cliff. I was drifting toward getting cut because I didn't know what to do.

Bullwhip woman walked away and guards were nowhere in sight, not even in the fluorescent middle distance; about forty of us in a small cell were having trouble breathing. After the afternoon of prison admissions, standing in this line and that line, I ended up with only one or two of the men I remembered from the bus. Now the sense that we got pushed into a cul-de-sac, a forgotten back alley in the labyrinth, with my last contact with the prison authorities and thus with the possibility of freedom—that glazed-eyed sensualist, the woman demon with the whip who sized me up for a submissive with professional dyed hair—now there was nothing but the humming silence of glaring lights. The vicious comedian with his "forgot your papers" joke really knew his varieties of spiritual pain. This was the point in the movie when the soundtrack rises to indicate the passage of many hours. Meanwhile, a distinguished looking man sitting next to me, well-dressed with an erect, quiet mien, who had been talking amiably in a mysterious but well-modulated accent about the traffic ticket that got him here, burst out crying and then fell forward on the floor and had a seizure like a dying animal.

We were so crowded that only some of us could respond. Our claustrophobia was so extreme that we had ratcheted down our responses collectively, an agreed-upon kind of collective jail yoga. Some of us were down on the floor, trying to sleep in the incubator-bright light, leaning heads on each others' legs. We became encased in an otherworldly kind of steam room. A fart became a very big deal and there was one big one at the beginning—but only one—because after our funny reacting to the gaseous gift, we weren't just funny. The culprit was identified and properly ostracized. There is honor among thieves. We all agreed to keep our gasses inside, self-enforcing this mandate with glances that were fairly serious. And now we had this seventy-year-old, nattily dressed grandfather, passed out at our feet, occasionally jerking, eyes rolled back. Who would dislodge from this tableau and go to the little window in the door and try to get a guard?

Certain people took a nursing role with the man who was down. Others spontaneously cast themselves in the role of town crier at the window. The trouble with this window was you could poke your facebones into the smudged thick glass and try to crane your eyes, but you wouldn't be able see down the hallway, which reached out of sight like some architecture out of Kafka. So our shouts of "We need a doctor here!" might or might not have been heard by someone. There might have been a guard nearby, but we wouldn't know and the guard or guards would know that we couldn't possibly be sure. We shushed everyone at one point and in complete stillness listened for signs of life. We heard distant echoes only, the hollow clanging of cell doors in the distance.

We loosened the man's shirt collar. One prisoner, who looked like a full-blooded Mayan, whispered in the man's ear in an unpanicky way. His language wasn't English, and I found myself relieved to hear the soothing sounds. I thought that this man from Central America would be the only source of a prognosis, as the prisoners began a new approach—shouting single sentences in unison, the result a cross between a raucous sports chant and the screaming of a violent domestic quarrel. I thought that sound might get through the Twin Towers because it sounded very different from the usual cries and murmurs. I became alarmed when the hardened men that you knew had coexisted with corpses in prison before, wore an expression of sudden softness in their faces, like a thug at a funeral. This man was dying here.

I wedged my way over to the window and made it clear that I would take a turn. I looked at the window for a moment. I thought of *No Exit*, the Sartre play. My idea was to treat the window like a person who would listen to me: "Did you notice this gentleman who came in here, did you see him come through the door? He's a grandfather, and he looks out of place here. Thought you might have noticed. His English is his fourth or fifth language, I would guess. He is like many civilized immigrants. He meets the challenge of being a new American, of countering all the riddles of our tough cities and our nationalism that is sometimes so cruel, with a belief that if he is deferential—helpful to a fault—with those of us who have been Americans longer than he has been, that things will work out in some system of decency that foreigners still think we have in this country." I stopped and wondered about what I was doing. The men were looking at me funny, but no one was stepping in with his own speech. I decided to re-address the little window.

"This man might possibly be dying on the floor here before us, because a teenage grandson took out his car and got a ticket and didn't tell anyone, and here is this gentleman, so classy and forgiving, but you could see this too, from the first time you saw him in processing, that he was startled. Perhaps he knew the whole time that his medication needs could not be adequately communicated to the representatives of the authorities here, but then comforted himself that he would get a phone call out to his lawyer son-in-law who would leverage, with rhetorical flair, a response through a politician he knows on the Los Angeles City Council. Our grandfather here, escaped from Stalinist Latvia or Estonia, I believe, now living with grandchildren around him out here in suburban Glendale, shared in his polite way, his story, with us, seemingly only to be generous, as he asked for our stories in return. He apparently felt that the generosity and allowance of civilized talk would somehow deliver him back to his necessary caretaking, despite that the clock was ticking on his heart condition."

Suddenly a big black face filled the window and stared downward at our gentleman on the ground where he lay. Maybe the guard was seated just around the corner by the door against the wall where we couldn't see. The door opened and the forty of us inhaled the slightly fresher air as one. The cop stepped into the room with his hand on his gun, but you could see he registered the temperature and airlessness of the room and it put a little frown on his face. He was in his fifties, with a potbelly and a weary face. He kept turning with his hand on his gun, instinctively knowing which of us was dangerous, and suddenly he dropped to his knees and put his ear to the man's chest. He shot up again with surprising ease, then backed out of the door and slammed it. We could hear him talking on his prison walkie-talkie.

All this was happening in a good way, not just for our stricken gentleman, but a good thing for all of us. Our room was being put in the system. Good, I suddenly sensed, for everyone but me. Eyes were on me now. There was a quiet in our little cell and we sat there together, stunned. Gradually everyone in the cell was sharing the same thought and one by one eased his focus over toward the tall, blond surfer dude. I wasn't a surfer dude at all. I was not who I pretended to be. I revealed my identity because some plan I was a part of was going badly. I didn't have a callus or a tattoo. I had a graduate degree. My clothing couldn't be traced to a store that anyone in the cell knew. The plan that I was a part of wasn't going down and I was forced to talk in that educated gibberish to the guard who probably worked for me. A guard who was at that door because of me. When I spoke that way, the microphones in the walls for this place would pick me up and someone would alert a desk. No, I was the only one here who knew that the guard was by the door. I was an educated cop and I blew my cover because I thought I was suffocating. Got in over my head and had to narc myself out.

The door flapped open and shoved aside six broadsided men who were instinctively packed in around the gate to their freedom. (There are always some guys who want to be closest to the door.) Then the stretcher carriers hustled in—hard-time good-behavior guys in orange jumpsuits. A nurse got down and she was fast: ear to the heart, fingers to the artery in the neck, opening the mouth, rubber mouthpiece and oxygen, up on the gurney and back out. Before the door closed, I saw Madame Whip and beside her stood a man who read out our names and each of us called out with tremendous relief (they found my papers!), got out the door and stood against the wall. After my name was called, I walked toward the door self-consciously, trying not to trip or bump anyone. I turned left and there was a small crowd of cops. Were they looking at me funny, too, or was I hallucinating again?

We filed into the general population over the next hour, received white bread with a slap of peanut butter on it and a miniature carton of skim milk. The new cells had long cafeteria-style tables, larger rooms with more connection with the outside world by good-behavior flunkies pushing carts, laundry, food, and cleaning supplies past the window on the door. I was feeling better now in this new place. I instinctively felt safe. Not being a prison person, I found that last episode in the holding tank disconnected from the rest of the world, the rest of my life, and the rest of the prison. One motherly cop with a clipboard and Bic pen sticking out over her ear came by my table to discuss our meds with us. I thought, now here's a touch of civility, and I instinctively added up the hours to my release. I asked her for news about the Eastern European elderly man who fainted in the holding tank back there. She looked at me, enjoying my naïveté.

I sat there for a while staring at the table. I tried to look around casually, not feeling comfortable with any conversation or eye contact. I was thinking, well, for all the excitement of this unusual day, I had almost the whole seventy hours still to do, and now might be the time to go back into my Jail Zen. And the bulls who screamed at me en route from the Valley—they were right: It is spacing out. I start with an image from way back in my life; in fact I don't know if it is a memory or a dream or what. I can't remember when I first had this image. I call it "my field" when I'm talking about it with Savitri. But when I go to that image on purpose and sit with it for awhile, it acts like a switch or a doorway opening into a series of little movies of my life. I say movies because when my Jail Zen is working, I am so entertained that it doesn't matter where I am. I don't know if my eyes are closed or not—it doesn't matter. I'm looking straight ahead at a ship on the Mississippi rising and covering the sky over a little green hill; I'm seeing a Catholic schoolgirl laughing in the grass under a willow tree. Now, these scenes hummed in my eyes and over-powered the gray paint and pain of prison.

"OFFICER! HEY OFFICER!" My reverie was broken. I turned to the men doing the shouting and realized they meant me. *I'm* the officer. "What are you doing communicating with someone like that? What agency do you work for, you fuck?" "Oh no, Jorge, do not be impolite. In inglés, anyway." As I listened to the cold laughter I started shaking. My heart raced in my chest and neck. I was holding my breath. The quiet, menacing comments around me continued with thick Mexican accents—eight or nine of them. They had pushed aside the people who had been sitting near me at the table and gang members stood at the door checking the hallway. About half of the group were the size of sumo wrestlers, with shaved heads and tattoos that I tried not to look at, but they were naked to the waist and their tattoos were panoramic, in Technicolor. They made a circle around me, like a mural with a flesh background: Mayan temples, Aztec princesses sleeping on their shoulders, and on their chests and backs, eagles with warriors inside them. I thought I'd better at least claim that I'm not a cop. "I'm not a cop."

A couple of them laughed a little bit except not the more serious one, the leader. No laughter from him—I felt his presence. It made the whole room's energy radiate from him. He sat there like a monument. Finally I told myself that I'd better look him in the eye and repeat myself. I turned and there he was. I nodded. "That's right. I'm not a policeman of any kind, not even a little. I was put here by a trial that I lost, I was convicted by a jury trial in Northridge." Silence. I felt that every word was a couple seconds in which I wasn't being killed. I kept talking and then with my eyes locked with this powerful man, I started gushing with no control of my voice's tone or my facial expressions. My head was spraying words to not die. They went something like:

"I know I should be afraid right now and I am afraid right now. All I can defend myself with is the truth and you'll believe me or you won't. I'm a political activist named Reverend Billy Talen and my wife's name is Savitri D and we're political activists together and we have a church of people who are from different backgrounds and different countries and we're from New York City and we all live in New York most of the year and we rehearse once a week and our activism is against this economy, the way this economy is all chain stores and super malls and Wall Street investors run them and they overrun communities and we try to defend neighborhoods and we especially don't like sweatshop companies like Wal-Mart and Disney or companies that aren't Fair Trade and don't pay their workers and Starbucks is a good example and that's how I got here in this mess—we came to a college in Northridge because a professor found $800 for us and we put it on our tour with the choir and this is about half-a-year ago so we took them to the Starbucks near the school and helped them research about the purchasing policies— what that company pays the families that bring the beans to market.

We especially concentrated on Ethiopia and Guatemala because we have friends there that we trust to get the best information, like in Guatemala there is an 85,000-to-one ratio of people to doctors in the Western Highlands region where Starbucks, this company, buys coffee beans and Starbucks has this principal stockholder named Schultz who is a billionaire and so we went into Starbucks, the one near the campus on Reseda Boulevard with about fifteen students after we showed them this research and I got into my Reverend Billy collar and my white suit—I'm a televangelist, a whooping and hollering preacher although lots of Christians wouldn't find me strictly a Christian, but the choir and I and the students put our hands on that cash register and tried to get some kind of holy spirit to blow that money away from the company's CEO and blow it back the other way down the supply chain the other way back to the coffee families who can't get nourishing meals for their kids and the children can't go to school even if there was a school because of course the . . . families . . . everyone even the grandparents . . . have to go out to the coffee groves to tend to the . . . because the profit margin is kept so low per pound . . . because of the Wall Street trading and driving down the price . . . so the whole family is out there all day long . . . dawn to dark . . ."

And then the field I imagine in my Jail Zen came and got me. It wasn't that I was daydreaming. No, rolling grasses swirled around me like water and I started shuddering. I was confused for a moment. I lowered my head into my hands and cried. I don't know how long I sobbed. It wasn't a quiet cry; it was a harsh coming-up of energy from somewhere. I lost the image of the field. I was coming back to my situation. I remember feeling extreme embarrassment, acting this way in the jail surrounded by tough guys. I tried to recollect what my strategy had been and then I recalled that I was trying to keep eye contact with the leader. I had given up looking at him long before this outburst, and suddenly panicked. I tried to see him, but he wasn't in the same spot. He had moved. I found him, a couple seats over toward the right. There he was, sort of peering in my direction, but he was seeing something else.

I finally tore my eyes from the leader and looked at the others. The same look was on their faces. In fact, in that moment most of us in this prison cell were dealing with images from outside. It was as if a fierce daydream had broken into our cell. I wiped my face on my sleeve and sat there like I was waiting for them to stop praying. I looked back at the big guy again and he was frowning at me. I knew for a fact that I should not say anything. One by one the men in the gang joined me in looking into his face for a signal. He began to smile and then the room erupted in laughter and Spanish exclamations.

"Well, yes, we know about those familias. We can tell you all their names." And then the leader said in a quiet voice that made the laughing quiet down, "You are not safe here, Starbuck. Do you know how not safe you are?" I said, "No, I don't know." And then they all looked at each other without speaking for a while. Then the leader said, "Starbuck is not safe. He's not a surfer. He's not a cop. He's a very unsafe activisto." Then he turned to me and said, "We will pray for you, preacher man. That you have a safe and comfortable time in our hotel." By the trading of glances that was going on I knew there were signals being sent and received. Then some kind of sign came from the sentries at the door and my strange trial was over. The Latino men stood up and mixed in once again with the prisoners, the other men scurrying away to give them back their old seats on the benches. I sat there expressionless.

From that moment to when I was let out, two or three of these guys were always near me. I vaguely felt the strategies of power shift in the air nearby, but knew that I could not read those currents. I gradually understood that I didn't have to know anything. When I woke up in the middle of the night on the metal cot, I looked over and one of them was there wide awake next to me. During my three days, a lockdown took place—sirens, flashing lights, and all doors electrically locked. At that moment I was surrounded and it was them again. When we would be in the hallways or in line for the medical check, getting blankets or food, they would call out, "You still surviving, Mr. Coffee Hero?"

When I finally walked to the door to the street that following Monday, I felt a crush of echoes in the fluorescent halls: "Good luck with those Devils, Starbuck! Blow some money back to my cousins down in Santiago. Watch out they don't bite your ass, Reverendo!" and then a trailing off of laughter as the door shut behind me.

And there, outside the door, was Savi. And across the street? A Starbucks.

4. New York and Barcelona: Ceremony in the Action

In February, 2007, Billy and Savitri attended the World Social Forum in Nairobi, Kenya, as a part of a delegation of American theater artists organized by Melanie Joseph of the Foundry Theatre. There, at the African Bio-Diversity Network tent on the WSF's grounds, they chatted with some Ethiopian coffee farmers and were stunned to learn that Starbucks had blocked Ethiopia's efforts to trademark its indigenous old coffee strains, Sidamo, Yirgacheffe, and Harrar. The farmers had hoped that such licensing—along the lines of French champagnes—would give them more dealing power at commodity markets and help them earn enough money to overcome the high rates of hunger and malnutrition in their communities. Meanwhile, Starbucks was selling Sidamo beans at $24 per pound; less than a dollar from each of those $24 sales made its way back to the coffee farmers.

As soon as they returned from Nairobi, Billy and Savitri joined various advocacy groups and American and Ethiopian coffee activists in demanding that Starbucks recognize the African nation's efforts to control its own commodities. Following a three-act structure, they devised three interventions: an "exorcism" of the cash register at Manhattan's Astor Place Starbucks (for which Billy was arrested and held overnight); a wedding ceremony at Astor Place with an exuberant, love-fueled protest/reception (recounted in this chapter); and, a week later, a parade led by Reverend Billy and the choir among the three Starbucks shops in the area. All the events were documented on video and quickly uploaded to YouTube, sparking an online battle with Starbucks, which posted various explanatory (and desperate sounding) responses. The actions helped generate considerable press about the dispute between Ethiopia and Starbucks.

The Sidamo Campaign was ultimately successful: Ethiopia was awarded trademarking rights the following November. The key activist in the US throughout the struggle—and a central guide for the Reverend Billy efforts—was Wondwossen Mezlekia, based in Seattle, whose website, Coffee Politics, http://poorfarmer.blogspot.com, explained the international legalities and history of the dispute.

The Precise Moment of "I DO!"

REVEREND BILLY

February 11, 2007, Astor Place, downtown NYC: About a hundred of us walked in our overcoats and scarves to the icy traffic island in the center of the intersection of five streets, Astor Place. We encircled the famous "Black Cube" sculpture, frozen on its point. The choir sang the gospel hit, "Remove Starbucks." Police cars followed us at a surveillance distance. When the lieutenant from the Ninth Precinct jumped from his cruiser, I blurted out the truth: "We have a wedding now, officer—let's talk when it's over."

"Oh!" he said, "Yes of course! A wedding!"

And it was a wedding, a real legal one, between Anna Oman and Matthew Ott. Their friends and loved ones cheered them on and wiped their eyes. But then something else happened. With the lieutenant standing with us in our wintry outdoor church, the big circular signs the singers were holding—covered with hearts and cupids for the wedding—were flipped over, and there was the Starbucks logo with a red slash through it.

The beautiful bride Anna, and her groom Matt, still beamed with bliss, but the wedding rhetoric was including more than the wedding itself now. I was preaching blissfully as a wedding officiant should—but spicing it up with righteous indignation, and the choir harmonized. "Look around us, these cars and trucks whizzing by, look around at these buildings, and at our citizen friends, and the clothing we wear, the food in our bellies, the vapor trails above us crossing the highways of blue sky. Where do the things we have, in this city, where do these

Reverend Billy, John Quilty, Monica Hunken, and Ben Dubin-Thaler protest Starbucks in New York's Halloween parade, 2005. (Photo by Fred Askew.)

things come from?" The lieutenant—we have him on tape—looked around at the cityscape, spaced out and fell for a short while into the rhythms of the wedding message. But then he suddenly frowned and did a double-take. He hustled over toward his cops keeping themselves warm in the police cars. He was right to notice the wedding veering off, but he was almost too late.

The wedding party had turned its gaze to the Mermaid With No Nipples across the street. My talk and our song became prosecutorial. "The children of the farmers who bring us the $2-a-pound champagne of coffees—Sidamo coffee from the volcanic soil of Ethiopia—the children in these families are dying of starvation. Starbucks has taken advantage of the collapsed world coffee market, paying rock bottom for these famous coffees. As in so much of the globalized economy, the perpetrators count on us not finding out. We have found out, Starbucks. We know all about it."

The officer was shouting through the open window of the cruiser. His boys in blue were caught flatfooted. What, the bride and groom shouting about coffee? They had to scamper out of the cruisers and they barely beat us to Starbucks' front door, about two hundred feet away. They couldn't picture going from the loving vows of commitment, Anna and Matthew with the rings, the embrace and the kiss, to "Fair Trade! Fair Trade! Fair-Trade-a-lujah!" The wedding guests by now had surrounded the Starbucks, facing the windows where the sipping sinners looked up from their Macs. The protesters placed their hands and their slashed-logo signs forward on the windows and we began our Exorcism . . .

Later that night, I went over the action point by point, waiting in line in my handcuffs in a dank underground hallway in the municipal correctional facility known as "The Tombs." The city jail has this name because it is down below the courtrooms way downtown on Centre Street. One is led in handcuffs down, down, down sets of stairs—and the descent generates a sense of doom in the prisoner. As I walked to the pens, I was lost in thought, reviewing the afternoon's action. In my point-by-point recalling, I detected a skip in the story of our Sidamo action. Something was missing in my mental account. Or, a space in the event existed that I couldn't remember, to be more precise. There was a bubble, a distortion in the middle of the afternoon.

The officer asked, "Where's your sheet?" I was yanked out of my reverie. I was standing in the cuffs between my two arresting officers, facing the medical desk. They would question me here about allergies and health history—I knew the drill. The medical official seated at the desk said, "Next!" and my rap-sheet with my Xeroxed Elvis impersonation was slapped in front of him. The medic's head snapped up, he looked at me bug-eyed, and burst out laughing. He shouted, "Sidamo! Reverend I was following the action on my computer. So they nailed you for trespassing? How weird! You didn't even go inside!" He said the charge should be "Unlawful Exorcism!" and he doubled over laughing at his desk and couldn't stop. Soon the officers and I were laughing, too.

The medic then got imperious. "Officers, I will take the reverend from this point forward. We'll put him in Special. And he laughed as he took me from the cops. I descended with him farther down into the Dante levels beneath Manhattan and was admitted into the special cells. There I sat on the bench and breathed through my mouth so I wouldn't smell the shit-hole toilet and then it happened again—I let the afternoon's action come through me and, again, sensed a gap. I was organizing it into little chapters, going from one dramatic moment to the next. And something in the center of it all was disappearing, or speeding up, or something. Then one of my cellmates poured milk on himself and started dancing the cool jerk. I came to realize that the special cells, this aristocratic vacation spot, were reserved for schizophrenics and drug-jonesers headed for the ward in Bellevue or some doctor deeper in the system.

I called Savitri and she said the Legal Aid people were informed and it looked good to get in front of a judge in the morning and get out. We reviewed the afternoon's action together. We slowed down the screening of it in our heads, like a detective running a surveillance tape back and forth, looking for something. The thing that made the lieutenant so angry was also troubling us. The wedding gave us all unexpected energy, and we sped up, we floated, out across the street to the Starbucks, with the sermonizing, the dancing, and the quick move to the ritual at the chain-store café. It was like the pressure in the air had changed. By the end of our phone-call we were certain of it, that thing that kept escaping me before: The precise moment of saying "I do!" had changed everything.

We are anti-consumerists. The cycle of most American products now for sale looks wrong to us. The sweatshop factory, the over-shipping, the over-packaging, the saturation advertising, the credit and purchase and—the waste. We don't like globalized retail. Our opposition to this totalizing world has led us time and time again back to the commons where our free speech is threatened. Free speech in public space, and not just the Internet—that is our foothold. This is the landing area for re-taking our culture, where our resistance must start. It's the last place where sometimes the logo is slowed down. If they corporatize and over-police our commons areas, then Consumerism's triumph is assured.

Activists who resist Consumerism don't often link it to First Amendment rights—but we do. Consumerism is the great censor now oppressing us. Of course, television is famously accused of having its impact, but we see the problem as the mental and emotional delivery systems of the products themselves. Our strategy: First, secure the streets and parks and beaches—public space that is designated as such. And second, expand the places where First Amendment rights should be enjoyed, but which have become privatized. Push back the advertising, go into traffic jams, open up pockets of culture in the big boxes and float a different boat on the "sea of identical details." Amen!

To our surprise, the ritual of the wedding ceremony—long associated with the public space of sacred meeting places, banquet halls, of street parades and musical venues, picnics and parks—has become effective activism for the Church of Stop Shopping. But it is only powerful if the marrying is real, heartfelt, the partners very much in love. We do find a natural link from declared love to social change. We have married all kinds of people, from fellow political pranksters to Citigroup executives to criminals on the lam—in bars, on the Brooklyn Bridge. And then two beautiful women named Filthy McNasty and Snatch in the Smoochdome at Burning Man. We even guest-ministered at a wedding in a right-wing apocalyptic church in Charlotte, North Carolina. Always, always—the ritual of love holds its power. Always—amid flowers, vows, and tears, something so seriously moving overwhelms any outside trappings.

Corporate marketing's repeated effort to mediate our life passage events is the Devil showing his hand. The marriage ritual is no exception and many are highly commercialized. Still, after years of pressure, we still have a moment in most weddings that is not corporate-sponsored and simply cannot be. All the marketing falls away. I see it again and again as I stand there and the two lovers look into each others' eyes and stop noticing the crowd of friends and relatives enveloping them, and even the two of them, stepping into marriage, are surprised at the landscape that opens up at that moment. The "Yes, I do—I will do my best to be with you, in an acknowledged couple, in a marriage, I will be with you."

Now Savi and I study weddings. When we walk away from a good one, we know something happened there that we must not forget. For a moment, a key secret was in our hands. We don't fully understand it yet. We interrogate each other—where else does this kind of thing happen? It seems that when the two lovers have been asked the final question from the community, "Do you take . . . to have and to hold . . ." and they have a few seconds in which they seem to be so intensely alone despite having invited the people who know them best, their dramatic aloneness sweeps us away.

Let's go over that again. The two are alone, but surrounded by this community concocted out of their love. The two are alone when they near the moment. Between the end of the final question from the pastor and the beginning of their answer they see into each other's eyes and imagine all the cities where they will live, the oceans they will cross together, the decades of time and the thousands of hours of loving and dreaming side by side. In Anna and Matthew's case, they may have imagined a third person, Hugo, their son, who is now busy growing every day and living with his parents in Washington, DC. When they come out of their kiss, they remember that we are all standing there, cheering. And we feel their brave aloneness come into our own bodies and we all feel like we can do anything.

The next morning, as the judge, Savitri, and I walked away from The Tombs, Savitri and I agreed: If the life-saving change in the world ever happens, it will have to come from something like what we witnessed between Anna and Matt yesterday. The judge changed the charges from "Trespassing" to "Obstructing the Sidewalk," reduced from a crime to a misdemeanor. However, even though we didn't cross into the Starbucks physically, perhaps the police were more correct to call what we did "Trespassing." When the two lovers were face-to-face on the freezing center of the intersection, we received such a bolt of expansive energy, we turned and yes, we did penetrate those chain-store walls. Oh! We put the nipples back on that mermaid! The Exorcism, hundreds of hands on the windows of the place, must have felt so powerful to the cops that they just had to take the preacher to The Tombs. Maybe a charge of "Spiritual Trespassing" might have been more accurate. I remember shouting, "Those children in Ethiopia hear us! They hear us assuring them that they will not be hungry! Yes! They are HERE. They are HERE with us. They are walking through the Starbucks and it will never be the SAME!"

The instant community of the wedding party that day, then feeling those two lovers so exposed to us in their confession of love, but so alone in their vow, greatly expanded the public space within us as we walked from their "I Do!" toward the coffee chain. Matt and Anna had seen so many years and miles in each other's eyes, their expansive imaginations went right into our bodies. We felt the presence of Starbucks' victims easily. Those hungry children seemed not far away, because the bride and groom had vowed to cross such great distances together. We felt like we were flying with a fine anger. Now we are free! We can do anything!

In our Sidamo action we were in a park, then a street, then a sidewalk: three jurisdictions of public space, each with its own layers of laws. We carried through all three the visionary seed of the "I Do!" moment and the public part of public space was greatly expanded—it gave us a psychic path straight to the transnational corporation's property edge. This is what we must be able to do in public space, a kind of expansive "trespassing." It is from such public-space outbursts that all the radical change we ever have had in the United States originated, from the Boston Tea Party to Civil Rights to ACT UP.

Despite invoking the privileges of private enterprise constantly, Starbucks advertises itself as public space. A principal strategy of Consumerism is to bring all public institutions—public space and, of course, the government—into the market. Everything we do must have a price and all exchange must afford profits to hidden investors. Consumerists disdain city parks, for instance. Such public spaces are considered an under-exploited market. All kinds of people go there, and they are out of control. Gift economies start up—flea markets, massage chairs, jugglers and musicians. Such public-space activities are continually under attack in New York City. Legally they are very similar to political protest and the whole array of First Amendment–protected free expression.

Starbucks has patterned itself not just on the old-style beatnik café, but on public space generally. The company's visionaries invoke the concept of "The Third Place"—a mystical sounding phrase that means, simply, a "commons," where a citizen can go and not be at home (the first place), or at work (the second). But that is what parks, libraries, and the other publicly supported spaces were meant to be. Therefore it is in the interest of the corporations to encourage the under-funding of such traditional public projects, and also countenance police harassment of the kinds of gift economies that arise there. Meanwhile, Starbucks is a company that sponsors activities in parks, schools, libraries, and streets, trying to affix its logo to objects that cross into public space.

In particular, when the public whips up an event that is intensely energetic—possibly creating a new cultural direction—the most interested parties, hoping to supervise, are the corporation or police. In our neighborhood in Brooklyn, we have the band shell at Prospect Park—

and arguably our most intense local activities take place there. The night Manu Chao's band took over: transcendent. Manu Chao is the most political band we've had at Prospect Park this year. One of his homes is Barcelona, where he has actively defended neighborhoods against tourist development and American chain stores. However, in Brooklyn, the principal sponsor—you guessed it—was "Starbucks Coffee," as a banner directly over Mano's head at the top of the band shell proclaimed all night long.

This is a time that we must return to radical theater to move forward with free speech. So sometimes we do trespass. We do take the action onto the property of the offending Starbucks, whose public space becomes private very quickly if anything is uttered or photographed or painted or juggled and, especially, if in doing so some political opinion is ventured. Now we add to the shouting, picturing, painting, and juggling a new activity that they can't control, one that holds such promise for future activism: the wedding ceremony, the precise moment of "I Do!"

Lick-a-lujah, Lamer-lujah

SAVITRI D

The Catalonian radicals found us at the baggage claim. They had invited us to Spain to participate in a festival called The Influences at Barcelona's Center of Contemporary Culture. They took us to Starbucks right away. It sits there, all alone, on a strange little tourist peninsula, jutting out into a grand plaza on the edge of the old city. The Starbucks sign, the great green logo, is huge, much bigger than the plate-glass windows that front the place, much bigger, in fact, than anything in sight. We stood there for a while, observing, watching the trash barrel fill up with cups and overflow. Barcelona is just not a place where people walk around with coffee, unlike, say, New York, where coffee is little more than a portable stimulant. The disjunct between café culture and Starbucks became increasingly clear as we watched every to-go cup pile up in the trash can just a few steps from the door. Lumpy mounds of white cups marked a perimeter, inside of which could be a textureless anywhere, and outside of which rose the sexy, storied Barcelona.

Later, at the hotel, we slept off the long day of travel. I woke up in the middle of the night. Billy was gone. From our open window, at least, the city was quiet. A truck pulled up to the gated kiosk across the way and delivered the morning papers, and some nineties techno music whispered from the rock club down the block. Billy came in a few minutes later. His eyes were wild.

"That Starbucks is like an alien," he said. "Like a gigantic spaceship shipped in from another planet. And who invited it? Did the people of Barcelona say, 'We want a Starbucks? Hey, hey, hey Howard! Please. We don't have enough coffee in Barcelona! We don't already have the best coffee in the world so, please, Howard, please!'

"Yeah, and when do they get to say, 'Go away, Starbucks'? How would that happen? Maybe the city itself will just reject it, like a heart transplant."

When we woke up the next day it was clear what we had to do. We would induce a mass organ rejection. We would take the Starbucks into our bodies and let our bodies reject it.

We would lick the Starbucks, eat the Starbucks.

We explained all this to our translator provided by the festival, Nuria, a young Spanish woman who spoke English with an Australian accent. She shook her head, not sure if we were serious. "I don't know. Yuck!" she said, sticking her tongue out.

Fifty or so people met us in the courtyard of the museum that was the center of the week's activities. We sat in the shade of a large glassy building and talked through the action:

Go to Starbucks.

Lick and chew the Starbucks.

Take it into your body.

See if your body rejects it.

When Nuria relayed these directions, they were met with some murmurs and groans. "There is a little confusion," she said. "People think—do you actually you mean lick, actually lick?"

"Yes!" Billy yelled. "The building, the walls, the windows, the sign, the equipment.

Lick-a-lujah!"

Billy demonstrated on the bullhorn, then he got down on his knees and started licking the courtyard. The crowd's enthusiasm rose out of some disgust, but they were game, I could tell. We all stood up together. Lick-a-lujah!!!! And Nuria's translation: Lamer-lujah!

And so we paraded from the museum courtyard and out into the street, past graffitied walls and into the narrow canyons of the old city, the densest section of which lay between us and the Starbucks.

We turned into an alley full of hookers in tight athletic clothes leaning on shops full of hanging meat and mobile phones. We clapped and shouted, two and three and seven abreast. Lick-a-lujah! We marched. The Starbucks sign revealed itself just as we emerged from the narrow and nearly carless streets of the old city. The mermaid hung there like an unwieldy airship, demanding our gaze and denying us the satisfying traction of beauty or meaning. Just a distended logoblimp, ready to be popped. "Lamer-lujah!"

Billy dropped to his knees a few feet from the door and lifted his palms in prayer: "What is this strange life form? What is this? What is it doing here? And why does that mermaid have no nipples?"

Catholicism is strong in Spain, of course. The church, the priest, the collar—these are powerful symbols and the sight of this crazed American in holy garb on his knees in front of the Starbucks drew people close. Traffic piled up on either side. Billy's face was a scarlet pumping cartoon. We were all excited.

Billy took a deep breath and crawled toward the entrance. He licked the bottom of the door, then the handle, and then as he lunged inside we swarmed. Several of us took our posts along the picture windows, licking the outside while the others, too many to count, went in and licked the counters and the chairs and the inside of the windows. It was like a Hieronymus Bosch painting come to life. Dozens of bodies writhed around, their mouths open, their tongues grazing all available surfaces. I saw Billy whispering a little apology into the ear of an amazed barista and found myself in long, flat eye contact with an American girl in a thick red sweatshirt. I was licking the window just a few inches from her face and she was, impossibly, ignoring the chaos around her, fiddling with her iPod, scraping the foam off her whateveruccino. She closed her eyes and tipped her head to the right. I could see Billy through the window, behind the counter. He was licking the machine. Then he put his whole mouth on the steam nozzle and started sucking.

A smiling ten-year-old boy with one eye on Billy sidled away from his parents, who sat quietly reading the *International Herald Tribune*, their hands groping at cups and muffins absentmindedly while a beautiful girl with pink hair chewed on their table. From outside it was soundless, dreamy and far away, a fantastic human aquarium. I started licking in earnest and even the street sounds faded. I couldn't hear anything. Billy was crouched below the counter and people were starting to dance. I ran inside.

Billy had climbed onto the counter and was offering communion with the silver milk pitchers. People were licking each other by now. We were seconds away from a full-on smash-up ecstatic riot when Billy said: "Now! Now! Let your body tell you. Do you accept or reject this devil chain store? Will you allow the alien corporation Starbucks to come into your body, into your neighborhood, into your town? Do you accept the devil chain store?"

"No no no no no!"

"Do you reject the devil Starbucks?

"Sí sí sí," the crowd cried. "Lick-a-lujah!"

Billy danced and shook and fell from the counter, tumbling out the door, his suit splattered with obscene milk stains. I knew the cops couldn't be far away, so I led the group one way and let Billy escape down a side street with just a handful of people. They shouted up at the open deck of a tour bus.

Everyone was elated and clearly wanted to go to the other Starbucks. I thought that was a bad idea. A young woman from Brooklyn assured us that the cops were different in Barcelona. They don't care about stuff like this, she said—but I have learned to trust my gut when it comes to cops and chain stores and told them one was enough. We regrouped by a Christian charity table whose staffers thought Billy was a "real" priest and asked if he had ever done any missionary work. Before he could answer, the cops, four young men in stiff white shirts and serious black hats, appeared.

They hustled Billy and me away from the group, demanding our passports. A reporter from *El País* was with us, and made herself known to the police. She stood by with a photographer and a Catalan lawyer friend. About five others, some with video cameras, stood on the sidewalk a few feet away.

The cops told them to turn the cameras off. No one did and the police got mad and started yelling. The policeman in charge got a call and stepped away from the car. Our lawyer friend told us not to worry, things really had changed. These police are too young to have been Fascists, he said, the older ones are much crueler. He said, "It's different now. Ten years ago I was arrested for speaking Catalan. Just down the street. By Plaça George Orwell." The lawyer told us that George Orwell Square was the first place where the city installed surveillance cameras, to stem the thriving drug scene. Now, he said, just above the George Orwell placards there is another sign: "Beware! Surveillance cameras in use."

The captain came and told us that McDonald's and KFC had called, claiming they were under assault by a crazy American priest. "Was there another one dressed like Billy?" he asked. "Are there more than one of you?" No, we told him. "Okay, but you were at the Starbucks?" We admitted straight out that we had been inside the Starbucks, just moments ago, performing a special communion. But none of us had been anywhere near the KFC or the McDonald's. "So none of you were at McDonald's? Since then?" No.

Amazing. Do these chain stores have a script? Does being a hostile, predatory culture-smasher just lead to automatic paranoia? And what exactly is going on here anyway? Are these other stores really claiming to have a "crazy American priest" at their counter, or are they just afraid he's on his way? Are they hoping for some American-style pre-emptive policing? And is it also possible that the desk captain on the other end of the phone might very well be old enough to have been a Fascist? He would want to shut down dissent, silence the threatening voice. Keep people hypnotized and locked in the gestures of buying no matter what.

The Church of Stop Shopping has been barred from chain stores by full-on militarized riot cops. We have been locked in, locked out, arrested, charged, banned, and escorted to the edges of towns by police who seem to work for the transnationals, who may not be actual Fascists, but admire the costumes and psycho-posture of the old-time Fascists.

We stood around for a while. It was getting hot in the sun and the action adrenalin was definitely on the wane. The cop was on the phone again. Finally, he hung up. He walked over and handed us our passports. He just kept shaking his head; his whole body rhythm was completely defeated. "Please don't go back to Starbucks," he said, and with a hopeless flick of the wrist, sent us on our way.

We had a great show the next day. Almost a thousand people crowded into the spacious hall and the Center of Contemporary Culture supplied hundreds of wireless headsets for simultaneous translation. John, our interpreter, was a tall and handsome Catalan with a shiny, freshly shaved head. We removed all the curtains from the sound box, lit it from the inside, and put him in a white suit and a collar. Reverend John. A comedian.

During the show, the calls and responses got bigger and bigger until by the end the whole room was shouting "Amen!! Amen!!" A little later, at the bar, we were told that everyone, including Reverend John, thought Billy was saying, "Hey, man!" So every time he said, "Amen!" they said, happily, "Hey, man! Hey, man!" It felt good.

The post-show discussion was longer than the show. The questions were not so different from the ones we are asked in other places: Do you think theater is a viable political tool? Why do you disrespect God? Is Reverend Billy a celebrity in the States? If so, can he still be taken seriously? Are you conscious of how dominant the heterosexual white male is in your show? (To that last one, of course, we said yes and that we wished the choir could have come.)

An angry American artist in the audience asked if we were aware of our own hypocrisy: Did we know we were using the very same manipulative methods that commercial culture uses?

Then, thankfully, the conversation shifted away from hypocrisy-hunting and toward the work: How do Americans actually feel about George Bush and corporate culture? What does a healthy neighborhood look like in America? How can we stop shopping?

We didn't talk about the action at all that night, but at some point someone played a very rough video of it. The shots of Billy sucking on the steam nozzle and giving communion to a throng of tongues elicited wild cries from the audience. I was still up in the air about the action. I knew it felt really good, but that probably isn't the right measure.

I thought about a group of unemployed Argentine workers I had seen portrayed in the film *4th World War* as they stopped an eighteen-wheeler carrying gasoline. They believed that Consumerism, and especially the globalized economy, spreads like cancer. Their solution was to block it out, even to the point of doing without petrol and other conveniences. They built walls and fortresses around their communities on the urban outskirts, put nails on the highways, fires on the roads. They did not accept the necessity of this system, nor believe in the "inevitability" of the market. They fought neo-liberal globalization in the most basic, rudimentary way—they cut it off, locked it out, and deprived it of oxygen wherever and however they could.

Those Argentines chronicled in the film established a division, making it clear that what lives inside the barrier they erected is different from what lives outside the barrier, and I think it is fair to say what lives inside their community simply could not survive outside in the global neo-liberal economy.

So what would "inside" look like in the United States and in Western Europe?

Is it possible that we are so saturated by Consumerism that the only "inside" we can look to and trust to be free is the inside of our own bodies? The billions of cells, the tissue, the bone?

To lick the Starbucks is to expand that inside, that radical interior.

We probably can't make a larger inside as our friends in South America do, by erecting boundaries. What we can do is trust and assume the unassailable intactness of this one "inside" that remains to us and insist on its rapid, euphoric expansion. Start small. Leave a few cells on the counter. Later we can plant trees in the aisles at Wal-Mart.

Our point of contact with the power structure is the transaction, the exchange of money for goods or services. At one time there may have been a more balanced relationship between goods and currency. Value may have been grounded in the logic of resource, manufacturing, and work—the corn I buy for the price of the beef I butchered. No more. Now I can go buy a forty-piece glassware set for $7 or a scrap of T-shirt designed by a rock star for $99. Sometimes in the same store. Value is no longer a function of work, time, and necessity. The relationship we have with the market is suspect and unbalanced.

I say, create a parallel point of contact with the market, one entirely unrelated to the terms it has determined. Licking the Starbucks might seem whimsical. In fact it is not. Leaving something other than your money in a chain store is powerful. Expanding the autonomous self into retail space can spark a movement. Refusing to take into your body what the corporation wants you to take into your body and instead forcing your body into the corporation's space? This action creates a point of contact beyond the dollar-for-product exchange. A mysterious market has a fingerhold!

I call the elaborate mechanism that would keep America America "The Commodity Wall." It protects the market from us and it is not quite a wall—more like an interface, or a phase change. It is the slippery surface coated by advertising. It is the ionic imbalance of the super-mall, the sickening overabundance of brands and logos, the cops outside McDonald's, the overplayed hit single. The Commodity Wall takes a number of forms and can even disguise itself as art. Lives and dreams are staked to it; parents and politicians take their cues from it. Sometimes it adds to the confusion by stimulating the reflex of actual necessity, but more often it plays into a desire it invented just for you! Whatever form it takes and whatever it is doing here, we have to remember that just on the other side of it, millions of people are fighting for their lives.

Any chance we have to push against it must be taken now, whenever we can, however we can. I want to contaminate The Commodity Wall, puncture it, teach my spit to burn a hole in it. If we lick Starbucks long enough, we will taste Guatemala.

5. Coney Island: The Mermaid in the Window
SAVITRI D

The Scene

In 2005, New York City proposed a massive strategic rezoning of Coney Island. By 2008 the plan was well on its way, and developers hovered nearby. A man named Joe Sitt had systematically purchased enough land along the boardwalk to transform the area into a flashy tourist destination replete with luxury hotels, retail entertainment, and a "brand new identity for the Coney Island brand," as promotional materials promised. All he needed was for the city to amend the zoning. Beachfront real estate thirty minutes from Manhattan? The arrival of condos and chain stores seemed imminent.

The city's basic idea was to turn the fabled amusement park into an economic engine for the rest of the area, and while many of us feared the rezone and subsequent development would ruin the Coney we loved, we also knew that the people who actually live on Coney Island needed a rezone. Coney Island includes the largest tract of public housing ever built in NYC. Unemployment and crime rates rival the South Bronx and the rate of AIDS infection is twice that of the rest of the city. They needed the change. It had been decades since anyone had made a meaningful investment in the lives of Coney Island residents.

Over a two-year period city officials met with representatives from a wide range of community groups, residents, and land and business owners. Together they developed a highly imperfect plan that nevertheless seemed fair to as many people as was imaginable. The amusement area was protected, even expanded, and there was a general sense that things would improve with the rezone. Then, at the eleventh hour, just as the rezone was entering its final public review process, we received a phone call from Dick Zigun, the unofficial mayor of Coney Island and founder of its annual Mermaid Parade.

"They changed the plan!" he said. "They changed the plan in the middle of the plan! After I went public in support of it! They're cutting the amusement area to almost nothing! We are ready for a fight. Will you and Billy be King and Queen of the Mermaid Parade? You have big mouths. We need you to shout and make a scene."

Right away we said yes, without knowing whether there was any realistic chance of "saving" Coney Island, and without quite knowing what a saved Coney Island would look like, but knowing we couldn't just ignore the situation. I was sure of that, but the more I thought about the parade the less I knew how to approach it. The Mermaid Parade is all fun, handmade, human scale—it celebrates the beginning of summer, the opening of the beach for swimming. It's definitely not the kind of day you want to spend haranguing people. What were we supposed to do? Ride down the street with crowns on our heads shouting "Save Coney Island"?

I called Dick and asked him some really basic questions: Who can stop the rezone? City Council. Does anyone really support the plan? People who want jobs, unions. Is there an organized opposition to the plan? No, not really, we were all at the table until now. Is there a counter-proposal that makes sense? The plan we just developed for three years. So Dick, what do you want us to do? What's the goal?

Dick described an upcoming land-use meeting that would set in motion a public review process culminating in a vote at the City Council. Dick wanted us to get enough people to that land-use meeting, which was scheduled five days after the parade at 6:00 p.m. What do you mean by enough? I asked. "The auditorium seats seven hundred," he said. "That's what I mean by enough."

Five days after the parade—that was too long for flyers and press from the parade to do much good. Somehow we needed to tie the parade and the meeting together.

On Becoming the Mermaid

I love the ocean, love swimming, but I'm not like one of those so-called "water people." I don't really relate to mermaids, maybe because I am a runner or because a burst eardrum in childhood made going deep underwater a little uncomfortable. But I needed a costume and a plan. So I began a long journey into mermaid world. I started reading everything I could about mermaids, looking at pictures, the Peloponnesian mermaids, Gaelic Selkies. I recited ancient poems and lyrics, tales of swimming women and sirens, lovelorn sailors chasing whales. I started directing my imagination toward the sea, the pearly caves, the spiraling columns of fish, long dragging tendrils of seaweed and glimmers of sunlight. I still couldn't quite "see" the Queen Mermaid, couldn't feel her magic.

I was building up the parade part of it pretty well, though, making cardboard skyscraper puppet heads and gluing moss and glitter to parasols. I found a bunch of nets outside a remodeled Chinese restaurant—props for the little divertissement the choir would enact around us on parade day. Mermaids vs. Developers! They would take turns netting each other and escaping and netting each other and escaping—improvising dramatic and hilarious antics. This simple back-and-forth—legible from any distance—could accommodate as many people as we could convince to join us. The mermaids could come in any form practically, the developers would wear hard hats and carry blueprints, and those without costume could stumble around inside the cardboard skyscrapers.

Slowly but surely I constructed a costume: a long beaded gown, a silver tail, an elaborate Victorian headpiece. Everything was very fine, very formal. No one would mistake me for anything but a queen. But it was just a costume. I still had to do something.

One night I was up late trawling the Internet for a good example of a mermaid tail and came across a DIY video of a lovely teenaged girl sitting on the floor in a kitchen with a piece of bright blue spandex and a mono-fin, a sewing machine by her knee. Occasionally a pair of legs appeared in the furthest part of the frame, a sister or mother walking through. The girl is very still and concentrated. She speaks deliberately, in the style of DIY videos: "Okay, first we are going to make a template out of cardboard. Try to make the two sides of the fin symmetrical, just free-hand one side and then you can fold it over and trace it. The cardboard won't be the basis of the tail so you don't have to worry about bending it. Next we are going to trace this shape onto the spandex. Make sure you do it about an inch outside the tail to make room for the seam . . . just like this . . ."

DIY videos are generally fascinating, but this one has a special charm. I couldn't look away. The muscular legs appear again just as the girl puts the finishing touches on the tail. This time they stop and watch as the girl wriggles her way into the tail. She lies on the floor like a beached dolphin, flicking her legs back and forth to demonstrate how she would swim were she in water. For a moment it is all very quiet, the bare legs at the edge of the frame, and the mermaid tail swishing. The camera cuts to black.

The credits include a link to another video. This second video starts with a long shot of the surface of a lake. Suddenly the camera dives into the water as if it is chasing something. I see movement in the dark water, a glint of silver, then I see it's the girl, wearing a silver mermaid tail, her hair loose down her back. She is swimming mightily through rocks and fish, the light streaming down from the surface. Her expression, her whole body, is calm; the world moves around her. Then she darts off behind a rock and the camera, suddenly tentative, follows. We drift into a field of greenish light. She is floating slowly to the surface, trailing tiny bubbles behind her. The video is about four minutes long, and as far as I can tell it's a continuous shot. I watch it five or six times before I turn on the sound. I recognize her voice from the how-to video:

> I've always dreamed about the water. I always wished I could come back to life and be in the water, a water creature. I don't know why. Ever since I can remember, the place I most wanted to be was under the water. It's like a secret, so beautiful the way the light shines, the way I feel so weightless and free. I tried scuba diving, but I didn't like the equipment. Now I just work on holding my breath. I'm up to about four minutes at one time. When I'm down there I don't think about my everyday life, I just swim like I've always been swimming, under the water, a mermaid. I guess that's what I really am, not an ocean mermaid, though, a lake mermaid. I don't know if they have those. If they do, that's what I am.

I thought about the mermaid girl for days, how seriously she took being a mermaid. I imagined her practicing her breathing, mastering free diving techniques online. And who was making the video anyway? Was it the same person who wandered through the kitchen? Does she

Savitri D and Reverend Billy on the beach at Coney Island, 2008. (Photo by Eric H. Brown.)

eat only fish at home? Are mermaids vegetarian? It occurred to me that I was becoming obsessive. Maybe Method Acting was the way to go, the way to a good idea: I am the Mermaid Queen. I am the Mermaid Queen. What would the Mermaid Queen do? How would she sleep? How does she hold her head? How does she feel about the rezone? What will she say to her subjects at the parade?

Nine days before the parade I lay down to take a nap, once again puzzling over the parade, the meeting, the meeting, the parade, how to attach these two events. I should go to both, I should be the queen at both, maybe I should be the queen the whole time, I thought. I could schedule a lot of meetings as the mermaid, organize a rally at City Hall, gather other mermaids and go see the mayor. I was falling asleep. I could have a flotilla of mermaids in mourning, arriving at the meeting on a ship. I could canoe from Coney Island to City Hall and back, in mourning! All in black. But that was too sad. And if we were in mourning it was too late! Plus I didn't have a canoe and those East River currents were fierce, and it was summer and people are flaky. This had to be something I could do with almost no help, alone.

I couldn't move the meeting. My body, in some form, would have to be the connection. I could stay in costume, wander the city, the lost Queen Mermaid, her home destroyed. Or I could camp out at the meeting place. Maybe I could camp out in one of the windows at Coney Island, so people who loved Coney Island and went there would know there was a threat and also a way to get involved. But is living in the window enough????? Oh, and I could fast. Yes, that's it, I could fast. No food, no more fish, no more. It suddenly seemed obvious, inevitable. Mermaid Queen refuses food! A hunger strike.

On Parade Day

The last thing I ate was a cupcake shaped like a breast. It had a white chocolate nipple and fluffy coconut frosting. I washed it down with some Freak Show beer. We walked out to the lineup. Everyone stared at me. I was so fancy.

We rode in a wicker carriage, pushed by some Coney Island old-timers. I waved and shouted as the *Mermaid vs. Developers!* scenario played out around us. Occasionally the wicker carriage would hit a curb and tip over backwards, and Billy and I would lie there on our backs, looking up at the blue sky, laughing, waiting to be righted. Our handlers were unbearably tender, cradling the backs of our heads as they picked up the carriage.

I love the Mermaid Parade because the difference between participants and spectators is so slight. There are moments when you almost can't tell what is parade and what is audience. As it moves toward the boardwalk and the beach, and mermaids and seahorses merge into bathing crowds and roving dance parties, the distinction melts away completely. A good number of people in the parade make their costumes out of things they find in the closet, as evidenced by delicately engineered props and tails made of duct tape. It's almost devotional. How many hours did that one girl spend gluing seashells to her umbrella? And how did those kids save up enough money to rent a truck for their "ship hop"–themed pirate float? Did that guillotine really work?

The funny thing about a parade is how everyone is looking at you, and how they wave back when you wave, as if you are waving at them specifically and not just in their general direction. After a while it seems like everyone is waving at everyone else.

There were moments during the parade when I drifted off, even as I waved and smiled and acted queenly. I was imagining five days of fasting, and I was a little scared. I'd done juice fasts and other "cleanses" but going five days without calories was another thing. Would it be hard? Would I get sick? Would anyone come to the meeting? Billy was shouting into his bullhorn. The choir swarmed around us. Monica was dressed as an evil green Starbucks mermaid. Gaylen, in a hard hat and work boots, beat her with his blueprints. She pretended to die, then resurrected herself and trapped him in a giant fishing net. Camera crews appeared in front of us, thrust microphones to our mouths. "What do you think will happen to Coney Island? What do you make of the development plans?"

The crowd at the parade was thick. There were so many happy people. The New York joke was really on; people were laughing and they didn't know why. Maybe it was the robotic space animal with the ten-foot penis, maybe the perfect choreography of "Marine Antoinette." It was all a little out of control—not dangerous, but definitely wild. That's what that rezone was banking on, that energy.

In spite of the joyous atmosphere it was clear the fate of Coney was on the minds of many. The development, the prospect of a cleaned-up, fancier amusement park was not welcomed. Was this the last year for debauchery and fun? Would next year's parade be a more buttoned-down affair? Would there even be a parade next year? Would there be any rides? Would there be a Coney Island?

I fell in love with Coney Island in winter, on a cold day when the boardwalk was deserted. And in truth we go there more in winter than in summer, stroll by clusters of chess-playing Russians, exercise fanatics, salty dogs smoking. We stop and talk to the guy and his daughter combing the beach with metal detectors. It's quiet out there in winter, just the sea gulls and the roar of the subway trains pulling in and out, the electronic ping of their doors opening for no one. That desolation I love is exactly what the rezone is trying to eliminate. They want people out there spending money all year long. They want, understandably, jobs that last past Labor Day.

At the end of the parade we walked down to the beach with drummers and dancers. We cut a red ribbon with a pair of gigantic scissors, officially opening the beach for summer. There were a thousand cameras. Billy said a prayer: for safety, for fun, for freedom, for freaks. Baskets of fruit appeared at our feet, watermelon and pineapple and grapes and mangos. We made an offering to the sea. Billy and I were throwing the fruit as far as we could; the kids swimming out at the breakers started throwing it back. Pretty soon it was an all-out war, the sky spinning with flying fruit. I felt my first hunger pang.

Life in the Window

I moved into the window at Coney Island USA, home to the Freakshow and the Coney Island Museum, around sunset. Renovations of the storefront, which until only months before had housed an army recruitment center, were almost complete and the Freak Bar was open and crowded. By nightfall on parade day I was ensconced, surrounded by cardboard skyscrapers and a painted backdrop that told my story:

> I am the Mermaid Queen, I have come here again, to the earthly capital of my magical realm. I want to celebrate the opening of the beach and bless your human safety in the ocean. I want to bless Coney Island. But this year there is something else on my mind. I am told your govern-

ment is threatening this place, threatening to take away this playground, this magical place where for more than a century I have reigned. So I have decided to stay on land for a time. I will not return to my pearly castle beneath the water. I will not eat again until you, my faithful subjects, join me at the meeting and insist that this people's playground, where we indulge the fantasies of our spirits, be protected. I will not eat! I will not return to the sea! I will not abandon you until we declare our demands to the city together. Save Coney Island! Go to the meeting!

Michael and I activated the Mermaid Cam; it beamed me perpetually onto the Internet. I called a few people and asked them to sign in to the chat room so we could work out the kinks. They told me what they could see and hear, how long the delay was. Barbara kept typing "you're in a fishbowl." The dance party on the street lasted well past midnight, and I drifted off to sleep on a blowup mattress, my mermaid tail curled up beside me. The Mermaid Cam stayed on all night, and I woke up with the hot sun at dawn.

I was startled to see that hundreds of people had visited the Mermaid Cam during the night. Some had left messages. What are you dreaming about, mermaid? Where is the mermaid? Oh, there she is, sleeping. They were mostly love notes to Coney Island, expressions of longing—"Coney Island is my favorite place in the world." "I've always wanted to come to Coney Island." "Please please don't turn Coney into another Disney World."

The fine weather continued and the Freakshow carried on around me. Sword swallowers, blockheads, and the snake lady strolled through between acts. They stopped by and said hello to the chat-room audience, gave little curtsies. I started to lose track of things. It is harder to mark time without meals; mornings and afternoons get muddled. I was hoping that what I had heard about fasting—that the first two days are the hardest—was true because I definitely did not feel very good and didn't know if I could handle feeling that bad for another four days. By noon my stomach had stopped growling and started cramping. I tried concentrating on other things. I drank water in small sips. Quilty and Urania came for a visit. I decorated the window with cardboard waves and made signs to hold up in the window: "Do you Love Coney Island? Go to the meeting!"

By Sunday afternoon word of the hunger strike had spread; news crews appeared outside the window and shot segments for the evening broadcasts. I was talking to radio audiences as far away as Australia. The hunger was making it hard to concentrate. I slipped through the interviews, held on for dear life. Some friends came to visit. Cars drove by, with people shouting out the window, "We love the Mermaid Queen!" Laughing children banged on the window. Traffic on the Mermaid Cam kept growing.

By noon the next day the Mermaid Cam had gone viral, and the stream of Web comments was going by so fast I couldn't read them in real time. I started scrolling through and reading random comments. People from all over the world were writing in about Coney Island: Singapore, Moscow, New Zealand, a note from Dover, from Buenos Aires: "I visited Coney in 1977, I'll never forget it!" There were thousands of messages from New Yorkers: "I was on the Wonder Wheel during the blackout and watched the riots from a hundred feet in the sky. It was the sirens that lit things up." "I met my husband on the boardwalk. He fell down and broke his thumb and I was the first person to ask if he needed help." "My brother and I spent every day on the boardwalk when we were kids. Sometimes we could sneak onto rides." My father wrote in to tell me that my grandmother escaped the Luna Park Fire with her skirt aflame. The gate she ran out of was about fifty yards from where I was sitting.

I was really hungry two days in. They said it wouldn't get much worse. It was pretty bad. My stomach was cramping and I felt like someone was stabbing me between the shoulder blades. I drank water and stretched, stretched and drank water. I held up signs in the window and joked around with the freaks. The webcam continued to stream.

Around 3:30 a gang of randy teenage boys took over the chat room, bullies trying to make me cry. They called me a slut and stupid and said I wasn't a real mermaid. They said it was stupid to try and stop the city, stupid to care, a lost cause, what a joke. I started to get frustrated. There were hundreds of them swarming me. Didn't they know I was starving and vulnerable? "Show us your tail," they said, "your mermaid ass." I considered abandoning the chat room, but that would have been a victory for them. I had to stick it out. The insults continued. "Head on keyboard head on keyboard," kept scrolling by. I found out later that head on keyboard, or HOK, signifies a "win" for chat room takedowns.

I was about to give up. I mean, how many times could I say, "But it does matter!" Then my defenders appeared and struck back at every stupid comment.

By nightfall I was adjusting to the fast. Very suddenly it was less difficult and small sips of water seemed to quash the rumbling. The glow-stick man appeared, staking out his spot for the third night in a row. I marveled at how democratic New York is. A guy can go to a wholesaler down by Redhook and get a few boxes of glow-sticks and then stand out here on a patch of concrete about one foot square and do a brisk trade. Would he put a kid through college with those glow-sticks? Maybe. Was he building a village in Senegal selling those glow-sticks? Maybe. He was the reason we were doing this. That guy wouldn't be allowed to do that in front of a fancy hotel or condo, and he wouldn't be able to do it in the new retail spaces (mall) the new version of the rezone would create. People wouldn't be able to invent their futures at the new Coney; they'd be stuck with minimum wage retail jobs and no guaranteed hours.

The people from the ramshackle Tiki bar across 12th Street kept offering me margaritas. A woman with an enormous torso, round in every direction, and tiny stick legs walked over holding a marbled plastic cup with a two-foot straw. "Honey, have a drink," she said. "It's on us." This was the third time I'd turned her down. "You know I can't, I'm fasting," I said. She smiled and nodded. "Oh I know you are, but we thought you might be ready for a drink by now." I laughed, she laughed. My head hurt.

Fasting is great for dreaming, but that night I tried to be awake at midnight so I could spend a little time with people on the other side of the world. Coney Island is so famous, everyone seemed to know about it, people who had never been here, never even been in the US. It's a fantasy place. I got an email from Moscow. The pleas continued, "Don't let them destroy Coney!" I heard from people whose own boardwalks had been "updated," who had lost an old carnival haven to Abercrombie and Fitch and the Gap. A nine-year-old girl from Brighton, UK, wrote and said, "People need some fun that isn't shopping."

The last forty-eight hours of the fast went by quickly; the fasting got easier, not harder. By the end I felt elated, even hyper, and I knew we had a lot of local momentum. Billy stayed with me most of the time; he sat at a table in the Freak Bar working. Some friends visited. Every now and then a harried TV news reporter would appear to "follow up" on the story. The Mermaid Camera rolled on and as the meeting got closer people started to call and say they would be there.

Going to the Meeting

Dick borrowed an antique wheelchair from Serpentina, the snake lady, and recruited some people to push me over to the meeting. I was feeling weak. I had dropped some weight and was getting klutzy, banging into objects, dropping things. My eyes shined like a baby's.

I put on my couture gown in the bathroom. Some of the burlesque performers were going to the meeting with us, big buxom blondes with teacup dogs. The girls loaned me lipstick and touched up my tail. I signed off the Mermaid Cam and we left for the meeting. We quickly discovered the wheelchair was too delicate to actually roll me around in, so I walked along next to it. I could get in it for the last block or so, within eyesight of the meeting. It felt great to walk, to be out in the air. We stopped at the handball courts and tried to get people to come over to the high school. "But it's not six o'clock yet!" They said, "We have to finish our game." I was terribly worried that no one would be there, and in fact, when we arrived there weren't many people, though TV trucks were lined up with their satellite dishes saucering into the sky, and I got rushed by cameras like a movie star when I rolled up in the wheelchair.

I tried not to worry. I had done what I could and after all it wasn't quite six o'clock. Most people were rushing over from work. The guys carried me up the stairs in the wheelchair and parked me in a wonderful ray of evening light. Billy was passing around the bullhorn to community members, people who lived and breathed Coney Island. I sat in the chair and acted weak and hungry—even though I wasn't acting. The community was still talking to the media when five passenger vans pulled up, one right after another. The doors opened and out spilled what must have been the entire city planning commission, dressed identically, in business neutral, with low heels and soft briefcases hanging at their sides. The bureaucrats. They filed in quietly with their heads down, no contact, no comment. The PR unit hung back and wrangled the media, cheerfully handing out business cards, starting the spin. A second fleet of vehicles pulled up and released the creative types, designers with flashy haircuts and Italian eyewear. They smiled at us as if we were their fans, shook hands with a few of the politicians standing on the stairs, then streamed inside to unleash their Power Points. My heart really sank when the union buses showed up. Legions of men poured off rented school buses into the parking lot. They'd come in from Jersey and Long Island on the union dime, with free meals and T-shirts a part of the deal. First came the yellow shirts, then the purple shirts, and finally another group wearing red. I shook my head. These were family men, they wanted to work. Their hard hats bore the marks and abuse of years on construction sites. A union captain handed out signs as they walked in the door: "JOBS NOW." Of course they should have them, but the last-minute rezone plan, which stomped on the compromise plan that would also have developed jobs, was not designed primarily to serve the interests of workers. That seemed so obvious, and yet it looked like we would be far outnumbered.

True, there was a pretty constant stream of people coming from the subway. Some of them must have opposed the rezone. I went inside, signed up to speak, and sat down toward the front of the auditorium. It was a lovely room with huge windows, endless drapes, and oil paintings of unrecognizable important men. The city had a table on the floor in front of the stage and a couple of screens for their presentation. A nice kid I recognized from Critical Mass (the monthly traffic-calming bicycle ride through the city), was running the sound system. He gave me a little wave and thumbs up. The room already felt raucous. People were talking too loud and shouting across aisles and to my great relief the room was already almost full.

Around 6:20 the presiding bureaucrat banged a gavel and called the meeting to order. A woman representing the city started her presentation. The first slide of a watercolor Coney full of shoppers and happy yuppies caused the room to erupt into boos and jeers. The woman carried on. More pictures of pastel-wearing tourists, more catcalls, more booing. The presiding bureaucrat silenced the room, threatened us all with "removal," and asked her to carry on. And she did. But the room never did stop responding, and was never silenced. I'd say six hundred people were there when the public comment period opened around seven o'clock. We were in for a long night. Sometimes they carry the meeting over to another day. Would I have to keep fasting if they did that? Or could I eat at the end of the meeting? I asked Michael and he looked at me like I was crazy. "You can eat tonight," he said. "You can eat anytime you want."

Dick and Billy were the first people called on to comment. Dick gave a galvanizing speech about the city abandoning the community after all their effort and good faith. He talked about the importance of the amusement zone, how we needed a place that was just for fun. He was forceful and clear. The room was enthusiastic. He definitely went on for longer than two minutes, but no one tried to stop him. Billy was next. He took the microphone and jumped up on the table. "FREAK-A-LUJAH!" he said. "FREAK-A-LUJAH!" The crowd screamed "FREAK-A-LUJAH!"

He continued: "Coney Island is our dream state, the site of our magical imagination. Here in New York City we're only a subway fare from the fantastic. We can all come here, we can all be here. On a hot summer night we know where it's happening. Freak-a-lujah?"

"FREAK-A-LUJAH!" the crowd replied.

"Coney is a democratic space. It discriminates against no one. We don't have to shop and we don't have to buy. Coney Island is not for sale. What we have here is the promise of freedom. Life, liberty, and THE PURSUIT OF HAPPINESS! This is where we pursue our happiness. Amen? Freak-a-lujah?"

"FREAK-A-LUJAH!"

The proceedings had ceased to resemble a planning meeting. The presiding bureaucrat got angry and asked for the police to come inside. "If anyone," he hissed, "and I mean anyone, uses this meeting for—this meeting will be civilized and orderly—do you understand? Do you understand?"

"FREAK-A-LUJAH!" The crowd shouted spontaneously. More laughter. While the freak factor at Coney is certainly high, there was no shortage of middle-class people and professionals expressing their opposition to the plan. A couple dozen middle managers from the city sat quietly in the front rows, absorbing the near hysteria of the crowd, the emotional and articulate comments by locals, Coney lovers, and experts of many kinds: historians, environmental engineers, small business advocates, people from the amusement park industry, preservationists.

The meeting went on and on. Predictable patterns emerged. The people in favor of the rezone, as put forth by the city, wanted jobs, and were willing, as a bloc, to accept the rezone without amendment because they felt any criticism of the plan would jeopardize or slow down the arrival of new jobs at Coney Island. The people opposing the rezone, or pressing for amendments to the rezone, were largely concerned with preservation of the amusement area, the real economic potential of the city's plan, quality of life, and the longer-term impact of the rezone. Not surprisingly, those who were most willing to sacrifice the character of Coney Island and least engaged by questions about what kinds of businesses would be developed, were those most desperate for jobs.

The FREAK-A-LUJAHs petered out as the night wore on, and we all became exhausted. I took pleasure in the specialized language of the amusement park, a man talking about his father walking the "hills" every morning, and the many, many stories of long-lost Coney: "I went to Steeplechase Park every Saturday when I was a kid," or "In those days we used to hide out under the boardwalk, looking for pennies and nickels people dropped." By ten o'clock that night the crowd had thinned considerably, but the testimony continued. Finally at about 10:25 it was my turn to testify.

It was hard to say anything that hadn't been said already. And if you opposed the rezone, you were definitely seen as opposing the needs of the unemployed. Some supporters of the plan issued territorial challenges to those of us in opposition: "You people aren't even from here, what do you know about what we need?"

I didn't respond to that directly, but I tried to broaden the debate a little: "You decided to draft one enormous rezone, but at stake is the one and only area in the entire city zoned strictly for amusements. Coney is a resource that belongs to this entire city. Every borough needs and uses Coney Island . . . So hold a hearing in every borough, at least hold one in Manhattan at an hour people with jobs can attend . . . Here it is, 2008. The housing market is crashing, the economy is in the toilet, for the first time in fifty years not a single new mall has opened in the US and the only idea you have for the future of Coney Island is retail entertainment?! Tell your bosses down at City Hall, tell them we have some problems out at Coney Island, but building a mall is not going to solve them. We need a rezone, but not *this* rezone. The rezone we need will be good for most of us, and it won't be based on a dying economic model. Shopping is over."

We walked back to the Freak Bar. People were drinking beer and re-hashing the finer points of the meeting. There were enough people there, that was my assessment. The city had to know this wouldn't be easy for them. The city had to know there was an opposition, and that we were not just one kind of people. Everyone was being nice to me. I was still the Mermaid Queen. I was spaced out and wanted to get in the ocean so I could eat.

We walked out to the beach. I waded into the surf, dove past the waves and fell into the dark water, shaking off days of discomfort. I floated to the surface, stared back at the shore. The Wonder Wheel hung from the clouds amid the pulsing lights of Astroland. Behind the park the silver ribbons of subways traced the elevated track, coming and going, so quiet, so lovely, flickering jewels in the night sky.

The Mermaid Queen Hunger Strike was an instant folk story. The New York *Daily News* had been in my house taking pictures within two hours of receiving our media advisory. Children brought me gifts. Jokers came by and taunted me with goldfish in little plastic bags. Tens of thousands of people sent me emails, and I'll never know how many people watched the Mermaid Cam.

I look back at the decision to be a spectacle in the window and it seems not at all whimsical, rather more like an inevitable solution to a particular set of organizing problems—how to connect a parade to a meeting, how to politicize a parade without raining on it, how to get people to go to a boring meeting. But I am aware that the solution came not only when I started viewing it as a set of theatrical problems—What is the drama? How can I make it to the end of the "play"? Where is my stage? Who is this character? What does she want?—but when I succumbed to a real act of imagination and inhabited a character. It was only when I *became* the Mermaid Queen and suspended my own disbelief that the hunger strike occurred to me.

The last effective real hunger strike I can think of was Bobby Sands and nine other men from the Irish Republican Army demanding to be recognized as political prisoners by the British. It was 1981. I was nine years old and remember the emaciated faces of young men wrapped in blankets, leaning on cold tile walls, how they died one by one. There are other examples going back in time—Mahatma Gandhi, so many of the great suffragettes. These are heroic people, heroic acts. I called on those real strikers for strength, because fasting, even when you know it will end in five days, and not in your death, is challenging. It feels like a powerful act, like an essential act of resistance, a mighty statement of sovereignty, the body as weapon. There have been times when hunger strikes galvanized movements and brought down governments. But not lately, and not in our culture. Now, even when activists declare "real" hunger strikes and threaten to go the distance, no one pays much attention. No one takes them seriously.

Maybe in the age of suicide bombers and school shootings no one cares if you die as long as you don't take them with you. Death is devalued along with everything else. Or maybe dying for something you believe in is too sincere an act for a cynical age. Maybe people are too far from a real knowledge of hunger for it to make sense, or maybe it doesn't work because people no longer believe an individual act can change anything.

I think people responded to this particular hunger strike because it was both real and not real. I was really fasting, but "I" was a "mermaid." I wasn't actually threatening to die, and in fact I never could die, because I wasn't real. The death I threatened was palatable, unthreatening, and even better, people could even play along and "save" me by going to the meeting, or writing to the mayor. Had I done the same thing as myself, as an individual citizen, I am pretty sure no one would have paid much attention. This says as much about the deprivation of our imaginations as of our politics, and maybe the two are connected. Maybe reinvigorating our imaginations, our sense of play, is the way, at least a way, back to our politics. We start with fairy tales and pretty soon we are marching to the sea. Crack open the imagination, inspire naïveté, stir up dreams and memories, and find the seed of another imagining: You mean we might be able to wrest a beloved place from an unscrupulous developer? Or a corrupt government? We might actually save Coney Island?

At the close of the 2008 season Astroland, the largest amusement park at Coney Island, having failed to renew its lease, packed up its rides and shipped off to the Caribbean—some say Mexico. Thousands of people came to see it off, some from as far away as Florida, and I don't think I've ever seen so many sad people in one place.

Over the following eighteen months the Coney Island rezone plan was approved at every official level: by the community board, the

Brooklyn borough president's office, the city's land-use committee and finally the full City Council. Significant concessions had been made regarding size, scale, and placement of hotels and retail, and the city retained the C-7 zoning for an amusement park and made clear its intention to obtain as much acreage within the amusement zone as possible. In November 2009, Mayor Michael Bloomberg announced that the city had purchased 6.9 acres of property from the developer Joe Sitt and would begin taking bids for rides and amusements almost immediately. We rejoiced.

On Memorial Day, 2010, Billy and I rode the F train out for the opening day of Luna Park, an impressive new amusement area featuring glorious, shiny rides from the world-renowned Italian manufacturer, Zamperla. I hadn't seen Coney so crowded in years.

There is much to loathe and regret in the process and the outcome of the rezone. In particular I was disheartened by the degree to which the legislative process favors property owners, even in New York City, where the vast majority of the citizenry are not and never will be property owners. And in spite of the encouraging signs, Coney Island is still threatened, particularly its historical buildings, many of which face demolition and "renewal." But it does seem less and less likely that Coney will turn into the sanitized tourist destination we all feared; it won't resemble Times Square any time soon. We have the recession to thank, of course, and the tireless work of mostly unlikely activists, but there is something mysterious at work there too, protecting the spirit of the place. And after all, when you stand on the beach looking at the ocean, well, it's the ocean and, for a moment, anyway, you can imagine that it almost doesn't matter what's behind you.

6. Long Island: Police Theater of Hofstra

Warm-up for Interruption

REVEREND BILLY

The American Sociological Association's Section on Collective Behavior and Social Movements wants a Stop Shopping show for their conference and it's being held at Hofstra University in Long Island. That means a couple hours down the freeway, a forty-five-minute show with singers: leave at four o'clock, back by midnight. Not much money, but not so difficult to do. We gather at the rent-a-van place near Penn Station and off we go, a dozen of us, with our robes, our makeup bags, and our musical instruments.

We don't drive often and the thirty-mile trip strikes us as unreal. Just a bear of a traffic jam—inching along, no hope. People in the SUVs around us are having séances, voice lessons on the cell, doing homework with the kids in the backseat—this is their everyday culture. We are stupefied. "This is Long Island," the lady at the tollbooth says. "It's like this here. You could say Long Guyland is a Long Parking Lot, but it's not funny for you, I realize that. I'm sorry to make light—you're stuck in it. What are you? A little church? It's not Sunday. Yeah anyway, traffic that doesn't move, that's the way of life here! It's how we live."

When we find the exit to the campus we are relieved. The highways are so clogged, we thought we'd have to cancel. We get there just in time and our nice host lady directs us through the last few blocks to the student activities complex by cell phone, gives us our parking sticker, and takes us to our dressing room. Then she says, "Sorry, it's kind of a meeting room." She leaves us there and is off to join the sociologists.

Savitri mentions that we had been given assurances we would have a regular dressing room, but the nice person doesn't know anything about that. Well, OK!

We have about forty-five minutes till curtain, so we start getting dressed right away. I look around and get into the corner and shimmy out of my civvies. I have my Billy polyester double-stitch pleat pants pulled up and am looping the white belt when—whoops! A student marches in and says, "We have this room reserved." The singers and all of us look at each other. Savitri says, "I think maybe it's been double-booked. Should we talk to our producers?"

"No! We are coming in now!" So Savitri goes out looking for who's in charge and we grab our clothes and wander out into the cafeteria area.

We break up into three groups and embark on an old college routine when you have a show in a lecture hall, etc. that has no dressing room—you go find a bathroom. Meanwhile we're doing yoga stretches and singing practice scales in the hallways, getting ready for our performance on the fly. I'll be doing my "If I Can Dream" sermon, so I have to sing, and I'm stealing glances at my outline of the sermon, eight themes in a composition book. Savi and I thought this would be a good sermon choice for the sociologists. "If I Can Dream" is a meditation on the theft of dreaming, the depoliticizing of songs by celebrity culture, in a nutshell. A good one for this audience.

People start claiming mirrors in bathrooms. And a couple of singers are stretching against the hallway wall. Gina and I go downstairs. Much of the building looks closed for the day—it's summer, after all—and it's darker down on this floor. The men's room is locked. The women's room is open and there's a powder room with big lighted-up mirrors with a door separating it from the toilet area. We nod and set up the hair and makeup, placing the sprays and creams on the counter and getting out the hair blower. "The higher the hair the closer to God!" I shout, getting my energy nice and crazy, starting to feel that preacher feeling, smiling, shouting, singing.

We are warming up, getting in costume, and I have my sermon laid out on the counter. We will be ready in time for the collective behavior, social movements sociology professors, just in the nick. A couple times we motion people past us to the women's room, and we keep doing scales. Once in a while, my Elvis impersonating for the sermon, or a particular phrase—I belt it out. Then I do my guttural workout, in which I sound like a bullfrog.

Our voices warmed up, we go up the steps in the empty activities center and see what looks like a board meeting going on in a glassed-in area. All the little pizza stands and T-shirt shops—typical of this kind of center of campus—are closed now. We can hear the professors, a good-sized crowd, beyond one of those light-brown rollaway partitions. The singers and Savi and I file into an area of cafeteria tables, with the nice host lady returning to help us with the countdown to curtain. No glitches. Everything going well. We wait for the MC to introduce us. The choir seems in good shape. Savitri studies the scene, checks in with Laura, Gina, and Moses. She is giving them the usual coaching: "We're not sure of this sound system. Really connect with people, give Billy some support in the sermon. Katrina, do you know the cue for 'Can I Shop Enough for Africa?'" But she is giving more than just the details—her calm quickness, the tone is livening us up.

Nervous about my sermon, I am re-reading my notes. Finally I put the composition book back in the bag—there comes a moment when it's better to get up there and count on the timely arrival of the Holy Spirit. Or on my improvisatory experience from hundreds of scene classes. And there's a little known overlap between the spirit of the lord and the improv for the horde. So, preach it Billy. God, I really love to preach.

The singers are doing the little nervous jumps, staying loose, then somebody goes into a deep stretch. The usual gig-banter. Valerie and Laura striking up a whispered harmony from the song "Pushback," feeling their way into the song. Wonderful being with this family just before curtain—"How's my hair, Stefani?" "Rev," she replies, "the brand is intact"—in that pause before forty-five minutes of high energy. "We've got a churchful of intellectuals over there," someone says. Yep. "Super-shrinks." "Book-writers and essay-publishers and footnote-hawkers, God bless 'em." "No wonder they want some preachin' and singin!" "Oh yeah, but are they ready for a SOUL TO CATCH ON FIRE!" "Well, amen," says James Solomon Benn, who has as many different "amens" as Eskimos have snows, being the son and grandson of preachers.

I start my last pre-curtain warm-ups: an exercise where I focus suddenly on an object nearby while simultaneously gesturing at the same object—creating the same focus in the hand and the eye for a split second, then throwing the same focus to an object far away, then on the floor between my feet. This would look insane to most passersby, but to the singers it's old hat, because it's a famous warm-up and we've all been in plays all our lives. Then I go into my laughing routine. That seems even crazier. Forced big guffaws. Savi hushes me, finger to lips—the collective behavior, social movement sociology professors, those shrinks of whole crowds, whole nations, these decipherers of dreams and neuroses—they are just a few feet away in an open room.

Then it feels like a car accident is happening and you know what it is, you watch it, you are completely still, you cannot move, and the collision is seconds away. An elderly and rotund man is walking toward me with a smile on his face and he has four policemen—or shall we say, college security types—marching resolutely behind him. "Reverend—what's your name, let's see your identification."

"Can this wait? We're going on stage in thirty seconds. This is my costume."

Savitri is trying to catch the guy's eye. "We are legally contracted to be here."

Now he's grabbing my arms and I'm lifted and shoved as the choir starts moving in, but the uniforms block them off. The old guy says, "What are you doing here? Huh, buddy?"

"I'm performing."

"Like hell you are."

Missed Cues, Stolen Script

SAVITRI D

A nice lady directed us into the campus over her cell phone. I didn't care much that she was nice, only that we had finally escaped the horrendous traffic that turned what should have been a forty-five-minute drive into a three-hour nightmare that almost ruined my life. Long Island. Power ballads on the radio and a van full of singers are good for a few laughs, but by the time we pulled in to the parking lot, the bloom had left the rose.

It was early August. The Hofstra campus was flat, hot, and deserted. We rushed from the van to the student activities building and jumped on the stage for a hurried sound check. Everyone was hungry and a little short-tempered. Check, check, check. It sounded like another language—more like "tegue, tegue, tegue." I asked the tech kid to turn everything down. He looked at me and asked why. Uh-oh. Tegue tegue tegue. Gina requested more vocals in the monitor. He ignored her. I shook my head and asked if he had a spare extension cord, and as soon as he went out I ran over and tweaked the board myself.

Though Hofstra has a Center for Civic Engagement that aims to instill democratic participation in its students, and its theater faculty includes professors who write about radical performance, we were there to perform for an event not sponsored by the university per se: the annual gathering of the branch of the American Sociological Association that studies social movements and collective behavior. Great, we said, when they asked us. They'll know how to shout Amen! and Changeallujah! And maybe we can learn something from them, maybe they can tell us about consumerism in America. Maybe someone will write a great paper about the show or offer us some insight into our work. The money, enough to cover transportation and give everyone $100 for the day, was not much of an incentive since pretty much everyone was taking the day off work to go. I mean, the check just meant that we weren't losing money to do the gig. All I'm saying is, we took the gig because we thought it would be good to perform for the ASA Section on Collective Behavior and Social Movements.

Before any show, in any space, I look around and wonder how to overcome the conditions, good or bad. A perfect stage has its own kind of limitations, and I usually prefer funky setups, but the bad sound and surgical lighting in the food-court cafeteria at Hofstra were daunting. I took a deep breath, and heard my first acting teacher saying, "Don't get fussy! All you need to put on a great show is a piece of time and a lightbulb."

A lot of performers thrive in bad situations; it's all just a challenge to which they can rise. "So you're so drunk you can't see us?" "So you can't hear a word we are saying and you don't speak English?" "So the spot light is in your eyes?" "What? We are on at three o'clock in the morning?" "Bring me my boa!" I took a plate of cookies and vegetables from the buffet and went to find the choir. They were scattered in the hall. Stefani asked what she should do with her bag since we no longer had a green room. "Put it under the stage," I said. "No, wait, give it to me. Let's keep some stage magic here. Stay out of sight." I looked at the clock: nine minutes. I took all the bags and walked toward the stage. When I got back I gave a five-minute call.

I could hear Billy hooing and haaing down the hall, Laura singing scales. Quilty was doing handstands against a brick wall. Our host, Professor G, asked if we were ready. "Yes! We sure are!" I said, "We are ready." He smiled and asked if we wanted an introduction. "No, that's okay. We'll just start high-stepping in."

The choir stood in a circle waiting for me. I raced through the set list, James said a prayer, we laughed a little, then got serious. We had a show to do. We always slow down to zero for a minute together—no matter how late we are. The passage from regular life to the stage is important, and disrupting the ritual can have a serious impact on the show. People make the transition differently. Some get very quiet, talk too much, wish they had gone to the bathroom. Others have to look at their hands or make eye contact. Some count, pray, talk trash.

I was walking toward Billy with a water bottle—last-minute hydration. I saw three men come in the front door beyond him. "Oh, that's funny," I thought, "Cops! What are they doing here?" The campus seemed so deserted. The cops were walking purposefully. I looked behind me to see what they were walking toward and then I knew, and in a split second I felt everything go wrong. Billy was between us. They grabbed him, pushed him face-first against the wall. Billy, already deep in his pre-show hyper-focus, was stunned, even scared. I jumped in. "What's going on? Take your hands off him." Billy was struggling, pinned against the wall. Quilty had the presence of mind to get out his camera and start shooting.

"Back off lady!" said the cop, the plainclothes guy, the one in charge. He put his finger to my chest.

"You back off!" I said, wiping his finger off my chest. "Don't touch me. What's going on?" Billy was wriggling around trying to get free.

I bolted to the cafeteria. "Hello! Excuse me, can someone help us? We're being arrested over here."

A roomful of heads swiveled in my direction. Nobody moved. Silence. "We . . . are . . . being . . . arrested over here!!!!!" I said again, louder. By now the cops were dragging Billy out the door. The sociologists were glued to their seats. The singers were confused. "This is not the show!" I said. "We are being arrested. Please help us!"

The choir and I followed Billy and the cops down the wheelchair ramp. Professor G and the host lady appeared. The head cop started grilling us. "We have reports of a pervert priest in the bathroom using foul language and bothering some girls." Gina, who grew up in Alphabet City, was not intimidated. She shot back, "What? I was there the whole time. That did not happen at all. Billy and Adetola and I were in a bathroom downstairs doing our hair before the show. In the powder room. Please."

The host lady, astonished, said, "Why weren't you in the room I assigned you?" And Gina, dismayed by our host's accusatory tone, came back, "Because someone came and kicked us out of there." The host lady didn't believe Gina. She said, "Well that was your room! I reserved it." Gina, containing herself, said, "Look, we were in that bathroom downstairs, nothing inappropriate happened at all, two girls came in and we said we were doing a show and getting ready, Billy was warming up his voice making oooohhhh ahhhhs. Please! Oh my god. Nothing inappropriate happened at all!"

I was glad Gina was there because I could barely speak. I turned to Professor G. "Can you please explain to the officer that we were invited to do a show here? And that we are, were, about to go on stage?"

The cop seemed genuinely surprised to discover this. "Is that true?" he asked Professor G. Professor G nodded and the cop paused. "Well then, can you vouch for him? Because I got reports."

Professor G, disconcertingly impressed by the "authority" of the police said, "Well, sir, [sir?] I wasn't actually there."

"Okay great," I said, and turned to the cop: "Officer, we are guests of this university, contracted to perform here. This woman assigned us a space. We got removed from that space by some students. To get ready for the show, we made use of what we thought was an unused bathroom on the bottom floor of the building. The men's room was locked. We are very sorry for the misunderstanding. Reverend Billy is a well-known performance artist and I am sure he would be happy to apologize to anyone, as would I. We really just want to do the show we were hired to do." I was trying to get Billy unarrested. It wasn't going very well. The cop's face was completely immobile and Billy was handcuffed nearby. The uniformed cops were pressing him against their squad car, shouting at him, "NO, actually. This is PRIVATE property and we don't have to tell you anything!" Billy was unnerved. He was thrashing against the door of the car. He didn't want to get in. The choir stood in a huddle, visibly upset.

A professor named Kelly Moore walked up and talked to the uniformed police: "Officer, can you stop being so rough? Would you please relax?" Then to Billy: "Billy, try to calm down. They are arresting you. You're arrested." We knew Kelly from the East Village, Reclaim the Streets, and the community gardens. She was experienced with police and tried to deescalate the situation. She got much further than I had. Somehow she managed to climb into the backseat of the squad car with Billy. We all felt better knowing at least he had a witness. They drove away.

A woman appeared at my elbow to inform me that a man who had negotiated with cops at some peace rallies was here. Maybe he could help? I smiled. "Help with what?" Professor G stood very close to me and said something about when Billy gets out and whether we will shorten the show or do it as planned. I shook my head: I don't think so. I said, "We are leaving the minute Billy is released." I walked into the cafeteria where, unbelievably, a number of people were still waiting for us to take the stage. I picked up the microphone: "I regret to inform you that this evening's performance has been canceled. Reverend Billy has been arrested for warming up his voice and pumping up his hair in the wrong room. If any of you would like to join us at the 'campus police station' we would appreciate it. Sadly, this is the security climate we live in. Good night."

A small group of the sociologists followed me out the door and across the highway to the "police station," a small brick building with a little strip of grass and an overbuilt sign announcing its importance: "HOFSTRA CAMPUS POLICE." Inside were a long counter, a few desks, and a couple of holding rooms. It felt like a car rental agency, the kind that is some distance from the airport. The arresting officer, apparently a lieutenant, stood behind a desk staring at a clipboard. He was a thick five-foot-six with burned red skin and stubby fingers. I was willing to bet he started out with the NYPD, then switched to the Nassau County force, and then retired to Hofstra Campus Police. I guessed he was pulling two pensions and a decent salary and was happy not to wear a Kevlar vest in the summer. And the Ford Explorer they threw in when they hired him didn't hurt, either.

I overheard a deputy telling Gina that the "girls" they talked to were cheerleaders attending the nation's largest cheerleading camp, which happened to be held on the Hofstra campus, and that there were about one thousand of them there.

Gina said, "Oh, you're kidding. You mean to tell me there are a thousand cheerleaders on the other side of that hedge?" The deputy nodded, smiling.

I said to the deputy quietly, "Let me ask you something. What exactly did the cheerleaders say?"

"Lady, I'm afraid I can't tell you what she said."

"She? I thought there were some of them. It was only one of them?"

"I don't know. They were talking to him." He jabbed a finger toward the other guy, a guy in his twenties who exercised just enough to look like he exercised, the kind of guy who gets loud around pretty girls and whose handsome is definitely assisted by his uniform. I suddenly saw it all: this guy was standing outside the student activities building and a couple of "cheerleaders" walked by. He said hello, they all said hi, and the girls twittered and giggled, so the cop gave them a good smile, then they giggled more and whispered to each other as the cop stood up tall, and really pressed, filled out that suit, so one of the girls walked over and said, "Officer, um, excuse me but, OMG there is totally a priest in the girls' bathroom, and he's, like acting really weird . . ."

Or maybe that's not at all what happened. Maybe there really was a scared girl, maybe someone with a trauma in her past, or maybe all those stories about priests just make people paranoid. A girl opens the door to the bathroom and all she sees is a priest with big hair making faces in the mirror, so she freaks and runs back to camp where she tells a counselor, who tells a cop, who arrests Billy. Up to the part with the arrest, you can't entirely reject the scenario. A teenager probably should report a strange man shouting into a mirror in a women's bathroom; security should investigate. But they didn't investigate. They just reacted.

Gina and I talked softly at the counter, rolling our eyes, "This setup is ridiculous," I said. "A campus, some cheerleaders, a priest, and police???? It's like a B-movie plot." Gina nodded.

I asked the deputy, who was looking at our website, "What's your policy with the real police? I mean, when do you have to call them?" He looked at me sideways. I went on, "When do they get involved and what are the charges here anyway?"

The head cop walked in. He completely ignored me, didn't even make eye contact. "Why are you holding him?" I asked. "Are you charging him with anything?" No response.

I walked outside and called 911. I told the dispatcher, "This is a call for immediate assistance on the Hofstra University Campus. We are being harassed by Campus Police. They are holding my husband illegally. He is handcuffed. And they are being abusive. Please send help right away."

The 911 dispatcher connected me to the police. "We need help, please! I am at the Hofstra Campus Police station and this is a serious call. Please send someone over here right away. These officers are out of control." She asked me to repeat where I was. "I am at the Hofstra Campus Police Office. This is an emergency. Please." She said she was looking to see who was in the area. Something in the tone of her voice was not encouraging. I smiled wanly at the scholars on the grass. "I called the cops," I told them. They looked at me like I was crazy.

Back inside, the lieutenant was on the phone. "I called 911," I said. "I called the police." He shook his head. "I know," he said.

"Why are you holding him?" I asked again. "Are you charging him?"

"I got complaints" he said. "Believe me, I got 'em."

"Do you want to take a statement from another witness? Because I got two of them right here," I said gesturing to Gina and Adetola. "And by the way, exactly how many cheerleaders was it? I'm just wondering because you said 'people' and that guy over there said 'girl,' so I'm just wondering how many of these cheerleaders actually complained."

He looked at me. "I don't have to tell you anything."

Normally, at this stage, I do not hassle cops. It never helps. Once a person is in custody, I am very polite. But this guy, the so-called lieutenant, was not even a real cop, he was a campus cop, a glorified security guard. To make a real arrest he would have to turn Billy over to the Nassau police. And somehow I just knew that was not going to happen. For one thing, there were about a dozen sociology professors on the lawn outside the window and for another thing, the deputy was still looking at our website. I heard him telling the lieutenant about all the press we got when Billy was arrested for reciting the First Amendment in Union Square. "It was in the news, even in Russia. I mean, it was really big news."

Everything changed when the lieutenant said, "Look, miss. What am I supposed to tell those cheerleaders' parents? They are paying a lot of money for that camp." I recognized his shrugging remark as something like a justification and it was as close as we were going to get to any kind of explanation.

"When can we leave?" I asked.

"When he signs this," the lieutenant said, holding up a letter: "I _____ willingly agree never to come to the campus of Hofstra University again."

"Great," I said. "That's great. I'd like to sign it too. Can we all sign it?"

"Side door," he said with a jab of his thumb. "Ten minutes."

I hustled the choir to the van. Eight minutes later Billy and Kelly came out. Billy climbed in the van. Kelly leaned in the window. "I'm really sorry," she said. "I'm really sorry for all of this." I thanked her and we pulled out, our tires sticky on the asphalt. The sociologists gathered behind her on the grass, watching us leave. They all turned at once as a Nassau County Police car rolled up in our place, its sirens calm, its windows dark.

Welcome to the Future

What happened to us on the Hofstra campus is exactly what often happens to us in super-malls. But Hofstra is not a mall. Hofstra is a university. So what happened? For years we have been hearing from professors and students all over the country about the commercialization of higher education. Who hasn't noticed the Coke and Pepsi wars on campuses, the rings of fast food, the ubiquitous coffee chains. In some institutions students are even referred to as "customers" and we know that educators have developed a fundamentally different power dynamic with students as a result. But it's still a *university,* right? The core of its mission is still education and discourse.

We went to Hofstra to perform, to do a short show: seven songs and a sermon, maybe a little credit card exorcism. We didn't go there to do an action. We didn't know that the situation would demand one, and I never would have guessed that under the circumstances we would fail to come up with one. We make it our mission to open up seams on the edges of things, break open space. At Hofstra the tables were turned. It was a campus cop who edged into the seam, our seam, and broke open our space, reminding us that no matter what, we can never claim the parochial safety of the arts, can never just be merely performers again. We are the interveners, and we are woefully unprepared to be intervened upon.

A twenty-year-old student misread a room chart and we lost our dressing room. Someone told us, "We need to use this room," and instead of finding the student activities coordinator and demanding another room and a key to the men's room, we rolled with it, we said, "um . . . that's cool." That, amazingly, was our big mistake: We were flexible. In a security-skittish, corporatized environment, you must always be exactly what you say you are. You must perform your classification and live up to its expectations or things are sure to get hairy. Be an artist demanding a dressing room and all will be well. Be merely human, responsive, mutable, and you might get arrested.

We are performers. Hired to put on a show. We got shunted from room to room, treated badly. This is why artists have riders and contracts. This is why we ask for a secure space and a dressing room in our contracts and why artists travel with managers to enforce the rules. But it wasn't our contract that got Billy out of jail, and it wasn't the imminent arrival of the real cops, or the halfhearted clamoring of a handful of upper-middle-class academics on the lawn. It was our website and the two dozen stories about our last arrest in prominent news outlets displayed there. It was a campus cop, a lieutenant, asking himself if he would risk the publishing of this story as a kind of Keystone Kops comedy in the papers in Minneapolis and Los Angeles and London and Moscow. It was a cop making a call, weighing the empty complaint of a teenaged girl against a likely media blitz.

We were flexible at the wrong time. When the cop approached Billy, we should have switched out of performance and into action, and then we should have turned the action into a performance. Usually when we encounter police we already know the play. We write the play. We cast the police in a role and they hit their marks and remember their lines. Cops, shoppers, passersby, managers, workers: these are stock characters in our plays. Things fall apart and come together differently. Sometimes a worker at a Starbucks will hand us a training video or ask to take our picture; sometimes a vigilante threatens us with violence; and once in a while a cop knows the First Amendment. It's not all predictable. But it's predictable enough.

Hofstra was a surprise. "Action" was the furthest thing from our minds. Police??? What? The breakdown was all about expectations, ours and the audience's. The conference of collective behavior and social movement sociologists was expecting a certain kind of show. Without authoritative cues from us they could not switch to another set of expectations and view the arrest and its aftermath as a "show"—even though, on the surface, it bore more than a passing resemblance to the intervention as show that we have done for just such gatherings on numerous occasions.

At Hofstra the cops took charge of the story. And we never got it back. If we had been more agile, or even slightly prepared, I think we could have turned it around, taken control of the story and won the day, though technically the outcome probably would have been the same. Billy still would have been arrested and banned from the campus. But there is a big difference between performing the crime and being assigned the crime.

What happened at Hofstra was like an episode from our future, a perfect manifestation of corporate fascism. What a remarkable, sophisticated fabrication! Why, it looks just like a college campus! Look at those leafy trees and the lovely lawns and those dignified brick buildings. Parking lots, pathways, hallways with bulletin boards, a theater with a shop and an open space where people laugh and play hackysack. Oh, and a wonderful library, too. And did you know there is a world-class aquatics center? Everyone is doing such a terrific job and everything seems, well, perfectly normal. But be careful! Watch yourself. Watch the others. The slightest deviation, any adaptive impulse, that pesky urge to spill, to share, to experiment, to make mistakes, be human: that sets off a series of overcharged and irrevocable responses. Oh, it's fascism. The whole place is mechanized! This is how it feels. Banal. Terrible. Like discovering you are eating prop food. We came here artists and we were leaving criminals. We even signed a document saying we would never return.

When did it all get so brittle that a fairly minor mistake in the midst of the setup for a dumb joke (did you hear the one about the priest, the cheerleader, and the collective behavior sociologists?) could erupt into this messy a situation? What led to this arrest-first-talk-later mentality? Why didn't the cop just ask us what was happening? Or look around and surmise that there was a show, that Billy was an actor? Why did the cop feel compelled to violence? Why was their violent behavior normal, even acceptable, to most of the academics? Professor G said it was because of school shootings, the generally fearful climate on campuses. But I suspect that school shootings and violence are as symptomatic as the over-reaction we experienced.

We were assaulted by cops just a few inches from a food court full of chain stores, in the midst of the biggest, most profitable cheerleading camp in the country. Retail environments, with their lack of feedback and human connection, are incubators of isolation, alienation, and crisis. And that's what happens when public space gets dismantled, when the First Amendment is abandoned, when the primacy of openness gives way to the primacy of profit. University campuses are not meant to be commercial spaces, and the difference is not only superficial. Making a campus free is not just a matter of agreeable landscaping and reliable wifi—openness reaches all the way into how we communicate with each other, the complexity of our engagements, our body language.

One thing I knew for certain: we would have to let it all go. Priests and cheerleaders and collective behavior sociologists and hedges and cops and women's bathrooms are funny, but the only thing anyone was going to remember was the priest and the cheerleaders. "Oh, Reverend Billy? He's the guy who had the thing with the cheerleaders, right?" We didn't want that story floating around and we didn't want charges to suddenly appear in our mailbox. So later that week we asked our lawyer to send a letter to Hofstra, requesting an apology and asking the administration to take a look at their security procedures, hoping more than anything to get the lieutenant's actions on the record. At least if someone else got the same treatment they would know it had happened before.

A week or so later Professor G emailed, admonishing us, saying the school was litigious and that sending a letter from a lawyer had basically destroyed the possibility of any dialogue. He said he wished we had talked to him first. And that's the last we ever heard from him, or Hofstra. And I haven't been back to Long Island since.

7. NYC, SF, and Alberta, Canada: Vicki's Dirty Secret

REVEREND BILLY

I stared from the stage. They're *doing* it! Here was that famously over-cultured species of human, the New York audience, after taking their seats with the usual "all right-I'm here-now-what?" I might as well have asked them to leap off the edge of the canyon and fall into the space above a river, and these urbanites would have said, "Well, all right, here goes!" From their seated positions they agreed to my suggestion: that they turn themselves into wild forest animals.

A minute earlier they had picked out of a hat the species-names of tamarack evergreens and peregrine falcons and caribou and rainbow trout and snowshoe hares and common loons and grizzly bears. These were creatures from the forests and wetlands east of the Rocky Mountains up near the Arctic Circle. And now, here before us was an audience-turned-ecosystem—gyrating, fluttering, meowing, stalking silently.

One lady ticket-buyer was making whispering sounds in front of the tenor section and she seemed fully committed to her animal. She was face-down on the floor, in a sculpted bronze and black dress with a crushed linen jacket. You could imagine that she was a sophisticated lady, in her former life. But here—in the Spiegeltent set up at Manhattan's South Street Seaport in the balmy late summer of 2006—she was curving and re-curving with a sort of secretive smile—a snake!

I got the signal from Savitri and proceeded to the next chapter of our church service turned dance-play: "All right, now stay in your species, stay with that life you're living—but you sense something is wrong in your forest. A new kind of darkness is approaching from the south. It is a great army of whining chain saws and growling trucks steadily threshing the forest, the thunderous thud of very old trees, the ground splitting on the force. You are one part of a great wave of terrified animals running and flying and crawling."

I glanced at Savi. We were asking a lot of this audience: simultaneously to be terrified animals while receiving instructions from this preacher-ringmaster. "And look! Oh my God! Look! What is *that?* Striding through the forest with a great unappeased hunger! Their hips are swaying invitingly from side to side, knowing smiles, dancing with the unbelievable chain saws, marching sexily through the clear-cuts, billboards made flesh. Oh no! HEIDI KLUM. GISELE BUNDCHEN! RUNWAY GIANTESSES WITH AN APPETITE FOR WILDLIFE!"

The sophisticated lady in the bronzy ensemble hissed with savage alarm. Savitri gave the signal and our angels appeared from behind the curtain—the brazen drag angels of the Church of Stop Shopping Gospel Choir! First out, the Broadway gymnast-hoofer named Pacho, followed by the noted Radical Faerie Donald Gallagher, and finally Dr. Ben Dubin-Thaler, a cellular biologist with a Ph.D. from Columbia University. They sported not much clothing. They were very close to stone naked. And they made imperious forest-killing angels, swinging six-foot-long silver cardboard chain saws at our wild congregation, which retreated like a herd of wildebeests who had been sipping from a lake of Red Bull. They screamed and retreated, knocking over chairs . . .

"But animals of the north! Black-footed ferrets and hawk owls and leopard frogs! Look! Watch your back! What is coming from the other side of you, from the arctic to the north? It is the sound of melting ice, the rising of the waves. The permafrost is opening sinkholes, glaciers gone, drifting polar bears . . . you are trapped! . . . caught in a pincer movement of apocalypses . . ." (Now *that's* doomsday preaching!)

Meanwhile, Barbara Lee of the soprano section was on stage with a deadly serious mission. Barbara is a heartily substantial woman—we wouldn't waste apologetic words like "Rubenesque" on this African queen. Barbara was silently holding up high above her glaring eyes a Victoria's Secret catalogue, open to a double-page of Flavia de Oliveira languorously lying on a white sand beach.

Now I knew we were close to the moment of the full-on WHOOP. But look at this spectacle: New Yorkers exorcising their unresolved feelings about global warming in this self-willed public embarrassment. I will wait for the whites of their eyes, I thought. Savi was studying the mayhem of screeches, wails, and air-clawings.

One more time: "Listen up wildlife! Vicki's voracious angels on their runway of devastation coming at you from the south. And from the north—the flooding from the arctic. Take in what is happening here: This is global warming's cause and also its deadly result! You need to find something in your scream! Life itself must hear you! Is this the end or is this the beginning? You cannot escape! So—Rage! Pray! Evolve!" The well-dressed audience-animals rushed at our drag angels. Pacho, Donald, and Dr. Ben shot concerned glances toward Savi, as if to ask, "Was personal injury part of this?" My lady snake was growing legs and snarling.

Then a white woman in a brown business-suit-style dress walked up the aisle. She stood before Savitri with a distraught look on her face. For a moment I wondered what animal she portrayed. She was our producer. And she was terrified of a contract-breaking performance, that these animals might attack the Victoria's Secret store in the mall a mere seventy feet away. These forest creatures might snarl and chew the lingerie to shreds. She gave Savitri a note and left with a weepy shout. Two sullen male producers, her bosses, stood in the back of the tentful of politicized wildlife, frowning at the pandemonium.

A year before, a man known as Terry Gross when he is legal counsel for the *New York Times*, but called "Lightning" when he is legal counsel for Burning Man, drove Savitri and me to a dark ristorante in North Beach in San Francisco. He introduced us to Lafcadio Cortesi from a group called Forest Ethics (FE), and Frederick Hahn and Nick Morgan, officials from the Grateful Dead's Rex Foundation.

This group of men entered the place laughing and were never far from laughing. They didn't hurry to get down to business. Eventually, Lafcadio began talking about the sourcing of the paper for Victoria's Secret catalogues, published at the rate of *a million catalogues per day.* The glossy paper for the catalogues was supplied by the International Paper Company (IPC). And this company was on an extraction free-for-all. It was clear-cutting the boreal forests in Alberta, Canada, on the eastern slopes of the Rockies, with such murderous thoroughness that Lafcadio's descriptions brought two things to mind: World War One and the mountaintop removal strip-mining in Appalachia.

IPC was using giant ground-hugging chain saws called "Feller Bunchers" that shaved whole hillsides of forest within hours. The forest was razored at the roots and felled, then chipped, pulverized, and made into shippable wood-paste right there on the spot. The process is so extreme that migrating caribou herds were detouring off their ancient migration routes, not crossing rivers at the annual fording point. We sat there quieted into weary postures, looking up at the ceiling, at the floor, slumped.

"So," he whispered. "Forest Ethics started a campaign called Vicki's Dirty Secret." Then he jumped up and began to pace in the restaurant. I got the feeling that we were here at the place for a reason. This was not unexpected. Victoria's Secret, Lafcadio shouted, "is a worldwide enterprise teetering on a wispy bit of lingerie and, and, and long legs! There's nothing *actual* about it. The scale of it! This catalogue we snuck into the bathroom to look at when we were fourteen! It is entirely a sustained public titillation. In the process of raking in billions, the only non-virtual part is a handful of sweatshops, and the rape of mountains' worth of temperate boreal forest, a massive carbon-dioxide-scrubbing forest, a most diverse and crucial wetland ecosystem, teeming with life, called by scientists the 'lungs of North America . . .'"

Lafcadio closed with some good but hard-to-believe news. FE had gotten the images of the Canadian devastation in front of a vice-president of Vicki's owner, Limited Brands of Columbus, Ohio. The knowledge of the eco-cide, the images, the feeling we shared in that restaurant that afternoon, had worked their way up through the ranks. Now, Lafcadio sensed an opening. A tipping point was approaching. In response to FE's campaign, Limited Brands was secretly looking for paper-supply solutions. They were even considering setting up suggested new pulp recycling factories, which had never been done before on the scale they would require. And yet, the possibility was in sight.

The punch line for us: "Would you help with a New York City campaign in the coming year? We think that extra push in New York might put us over the top." In later meetings back at the Forest Ethics office we heard some of their ideas for the Church of Stop Shopping: the choir somersaulting on trampolines on a flatbed truck going down Sixth Avenue, singing in the air, past the Fox and CBS buildings. Ah! Those fanciful first impressions—collaborators imagining what we might do. It's an important upside of our project—that people feel liberated thinking up operatic spectacles for the Church of Stop Shopping.

When Savitri and I returned from San Francisco, we talked to the Canadians in our choir, then called the activists living in the midst of these clear-cuts in Alberta. Over the next few weeks at our home in Brooklyn, we would get up in the middle of the night and walk around the block thinking about it. That's always got to be part of it, the troubled soul part. The cause must insist. The mass murder needs to be taken personally. As the old spiritual says, "God's gonna trouble the water." If Savitri and I were not to feel the soul of that western rattlesnake writhing under the blade, then our sophisticated New York lady wouldn't ever be possessed.

At this time, 2006, the Stop Shopping Church experienced a general shift in our resistance to Consumerism, something beyond the "stop shopping" that drew us to the staged rituals of holy cleansing at the cash registers of Disney, Starbucks, and Wal-Mart. The debilitating impact of corporate marketing on the psyche of the individual, especially on children, was always key for us. But now that psychic field had spread to cover the planet itself. In the era of climate change and mass extinctions, we saw Consumerism's attack on the life of the Earth.

Certainly this Victoria's Secret campaign, as it took more and more of our waking day, felt like it was beyond environmentalism as we traditionally understood it. We were no longer working any single category of activism. We did not have a single "issue" campaign here. This was more like all of activism. It contained all the issues because it was saving life as such. Our Vicki's Dirty Secret campaign would feature more than the largest forest in North America and New York City. The two lead actors were: The human beings dedicated to killing the earth and the human beings wanting to save it. This was the activism of survival.

And so the forest came to the city. It took some practice. Lots of walking in Prospect Park. But we did begin to hear the whistling of the wind through the trees on our paved island. We did feel the craggy roots grabbing the sides of aging skyscrapers and wolf packs leaping up to the balconies over Central Park. We did feel all that death and life quietly raging across Manhattan, whose chauvinism toward the outside world sometimes resembles the arrogance of the human species to the world of other life.

The emotional consensus of our decision-making in the Stop Shopping community was making its way forward. When a campaign picks up steam, we feel coming toward us that first action in which we cross the line. We're ready to be foolish, to cross into the Sacred State of Exalted Embarrassment!

We had that opportunity with the twenty-fifth anniversary of Victoria's Secret. The celebration was planned for the old hulking Armory on Lexington Avenue. A nice long runway could be erected in there for the models in their angel wings. The buzz had it that Heidi Klum would reveal her flat stomach, only eight months after giving birth! This was an ongoing office joke at the Forest Ethics office at One Haight Street: the cliff-hanger of Heidi's tummy. Would the millions be satisfied with the angelic skin, flat and inviting between the hip bones? Ah, the camera would linger . . .

We re-conned the huge red armory building with Dan, an FE associate assigned to our part of the campaign, and our feverish imaginations were buoyed by Spider Man and Bat Man and other anthropomorphized forest creatures. We imagined swinging in through windows on long ropes, dropping down through skylights, rushing the runways, startling the millionaire angels in their nighties and wings. But Dan made clear there would be no arrests. No invasions. This was not our movie to make. When the anniversary night came, the entrance to the place was surrounded by tailored canopies, awnings, velvet ropes—and cops. We gathered at a nearby deli in a downpour worthy of a blustery Rocky Mountain night and marched singing to our doom. There was, in fact, a "March of the Light Brigade" ambience to our portable church service this night. Then we got reinforcements. A second activist group created from radical coeds of local universities strode out of the night—the counter-angels.

Here was some skin shining in the rain, the garters and stockings and leather halter-tops that didn't make us think of Vicki's angels at all. Clearly, these were women with actual sex lives, seducers and seducees emerging from a happy trail of dirty beds. And they were brandishing it, with strap-on toy chain saws. So now we had a feeling of sexual pride, a pride parade with the power of smelly, smiling sex. This made the rain feel better. The gospel choir and the rockettes of orgasm marched to our spot opposite the armory's long red carpet, a rectangular fenced-in area tended by yet more police. How military the defense of Consumerism is!

The stars pulled up to the bumper, baby, in their long black limousines—but the resonance of that song faded in the rain of militarized 2006. The celebrities were enveloped in anti-paparazzi swat teams. The bouncers seamlessly meshed with security officials of various mysterious ranks. People in uniforms with badges marching toward our bellowing—they all insisted that they were "real cops." "Well, we're real angels," our actresses shrieked. "Get back in your demo pen," the possibly-cops said, and then we were bathed in *Live at Nine* light.

One expensive couple walked down the red carpet trail toward us, tall and striding, both with iPhones aglow and a large umbrella unfurling overhead. The man pointed at us and seemed to inquire about us from a security guy. We cavorted with our comic anger. But what could they hear from my bullhorn? Something about forests? Climate change? The bouncer/cop had been told to advise these Underwear Royalty that they would not have to walk near us. But the two had an unexpected response: They walked toward us squinting, as if amazed that someone would be out in this downpour. They came fairly close to our steel fence and listened to a sermon about clear-cuts and lingerie.

The looks on their faces were of high-end befuddlement. The couple came from the Darwinian victors' world of the Wall Street textile rich and to their minds there was a natural order for all things. Human labor and natural resources issues would have to be worked out in the distance by subcontractors, somewhere beyond the ocean, thank you. This was at the height of the Bush bubble and the main thing they communicated as they turned away, walking to an idling Town Car, was "Are you people still doing this? I guess you always will . . ."

And thus began a series of actions around Manhattan that featured our church not so much whirling memorable shapes in the air before the facades of power, as shouting ourselves hoarse inside the NYPD's "demo pens"—the hollow-poled metal fencing arranged around protest areas that after 9/11 replaced the friendlier light-blue sawhorses. As a matter of personal policy, we have always resisted this limitation. Savitri never goes in. She tells police, "You can put me in the pen or arrest me, I will not step inside."

Her decision is partly because we hope for (non-corporate-sponsored) wildness to return to public space, and so we must bring back our intuitive feel for the First Amendment. Police fencing compromises the "peaceable assembling" that makes free speech possible in public space. When we are shouting from inside these police barriers, with the boys and girls in blue lounging around the edges with an occasional German shepherd, the effort to say something becomes what Savi calls "police theater." For many citizens, this is no longer public space. The protester becomes a generic "protester"—upset about something, generically upset about everything.

So in FE's original excitement about involving us in their bid to save the boreal forest, the trapezes and weightlessness, the high color and memorable shock of the new—it was forgotten that these original visions, if pursued as dreamed, would risk all of our arrest. Add the need for police permits, disallowing of electronic bullhorns, presence of fencing, dogs, and guns—that mind-set of preemptive blame kills any drama at all. We are made predictable and we are silenced. The boreal forest in Manhattan is silenced.

We were effective again when we found our way to the Spiegeltent, a new and unusual performance venue that had come to town. This old cabaret/circus tent would be where the sylvan majesty of our subject would really see the light, free of Forest Ethics and demo pens. FE were nice people, but we couldn't be "protesters for hire," trying to flash the forest to the public from inside demo pens. We would need to be pure volunteers again to return to the original prankster visions that stopped us with the caribou on that afternoon in North Beach.

Where is the charged theatrical place? Where does a shout ring out into history, into our collective conscience? Where does an expression of distress re-frame the eye of the passerby, and where is it that right and good are shockingly clear? The Greensboro Four at their Woolworth *whites only* lunch counter, the Capitol lawn under the AIDS quilt, the sea turtles trapping the WTO delegates in their hotel in Seattle, the young man with his flowers stopping the tanks in Tiananmen Square, Gandhi's march to the sea . . . ?

The charged air around these acts, which makes them immediately recognized by us as iconic moments, always waits for us. As the life of our community becomes corporatized and corrupted, it is a citizen's job to look for the opportunity for such a moment. It is around us, but it is never the same as it was for Rosa Parks on the bus, or Mario Savio on the police car, or dancing for the martyrs in the South African soccer stadium. For us it may remain elusive, moving, but it is always nearby. And that is a faith that we must share, even if the charged moment where political freedom becomes clear can seem to be absent from the landscape for decades.

And we want a boreal forest to rise in its vastness in the middle of Manhattan. How do you do that? We want forest-beings to attack the mannequins in their garters and teddies. What's the picture? What do people see? The caribou need to move again, across Fifth Avenue, blurring with yellow taxis and adrenaline. The activism of survival must find its theater. An ancient stream of caribou will cross the river!

The Spiegeltent was set up at the South Street Seaport, a cheesy little mall on the East River under the Brooklyn Bridge. The mall's claim to fame, enough to get it on the tourist bus-stop list, is the docking there of two beautiful tall ships. Beyond that, the seaport is conventional shopping, chain stores and tchotchkes, all the "I (heart) NY" T-shirts you can eat. What intrigued us was the Spiegeltent itself, one of a small number of antique tents from a century ago, which are circular wooden affairs with a round floor seating two hundred, ringed with raised hardwood booths and a varnished beaux-arts bar. The oak panels of the booths were topped with panes of beveled glass. A crew of six traveled with the crated tent and only these skilled artisans were allowed to erect it. Marlene Dietrich sang "Falling in Love Again" in the old von Stroheim film *Blue Angel* in one of the Spiegeltents, and in the six or eight of them still standing in festivals around the world, performers probably all claim Marlene's echoes. We felt drawn to the old tent. We agreed to perform in September and October on Sundays. We shared the tent with a post-modern bawdy circus, the kind with giant bowling pins and whips, torches and ropes, a portable trapeze and an outlandish bathtub. All these were stored haphazardly between the tent flaps and the edge of the pier, hard by cramped dressing rooms on wheels. I saw the painted face of some kind of sexual clown poke his head out of his dressing room, hung-over and dismayed to see a cheerful church choir warming up their harmonies.

Overhead, the amazing Brooklyn Bridge plunged out over the churning East River. All the singers and musicians loved the Spiegeltent. Our first sound checks and credit exorcism run-throughs went joyously. You could tell our particular shake-and-bake shamanism would go well in this place, the way we burst into song and dissolved in laughter all the time. The circle of windows above us was stained glass; plaques of luminous colors moved across the floor as the sun moved.

We thought we could hear the young vamp's voice: "Falling in love again / never wanted to / what's a girl to do / can't help it . . ." Somehow as our warm-ups picked up steam, we glided and rolled and jumped up in strange improvisations with the ghosts of circuses past. So, when we took the stage before a full house, Savitri took that wildness up the mountain. She began reading descriptions of the beings of the boreal forest—foxes and dragonflies and mountain trout. The circus people glanced over at us—what's with the gospel church? The whole tent howled with wolves under a trapeze moon.

The producer thrust the note into Savitri's hand. Savi was off the edge of the stage to my left, just beyond the band, on the uptown side of the tent. On my right was Barbara Lee, holding the catalogue pages depicting a skinny white girl up high. At our feet were the writhing, flying, hopping, singing and stalking-quietly living things from the faraway mountains. The producer stood quite close to Savitri, waiting for an answer to the note.

I watched Savi read the note and she looked at me with a complex expression that had in it both a detective's thoughtfulness and a director's authority, but undoubtedly told me to get back to the performance's finale. This all happened in seconds. Our sophisticated snake lady was shedding her skin, growing back arms and legs, and rising as implacably as evolution, assuming now a orangutan's crouch in her thousand-dollar dress. She was my audience bellwether, my leader of the animal revolt, and her atavistic fantasy was wearing off. She was becoming human. I was losing my boreal forest.

"Children please! You are caught between two devils! The giantesses of Victoria's Secret from the south and a wall of salt-water from the arctic! You are evolving valiantly! The trees are gone and the sea is a tsunami flowing south across Canada. But the earth never dies. You are resurrecting. You are the real angels! Rise up everyone! The forest is reborn and whatever animal you are—we're going to fly and crawl and sprint and hop right out of this tent and pay a visit to the Victoria's Secret next door!

"The boreal forest has within it the power of Resurrection! And this is something that a corporation that makes billions of ugly bikinis can't possibly resist! Onward resurrected forest creatures! Onward to Vicki's Secret! Follow me, slither and thrash and worm your way right past the bar and take a right in the mall!"

Amen! We had the forest coming so nicely back to life. And our move toward the door—we were so ready to finally take global warming seriously. We had some direct action in us—ready to hold a guilty corporation responsible. We had it all set up. A writer and a photographer from the *New York Times* were waiting in front of the store. And more to the point, the Vicki's surveillance cameras would be humming and we would perform for the Victoria's Secret management back in Columbus, Ohio.

Then the producer from hell took my pulpit from me.

"YOU CAN'T GO TO VICTORIA'S SECRET! I DON'T CARE WHAT THEY DO TO YOUR FOREST. YOU CAN'T DO THAT AND YOU WON'T. YOU WON'T DO THAT. NOT IN THE SOUTH STREET SEAPORT! MAYBE SOME LINGERIE STORE DOWN THE ROAD! NOT HERE! WHEN YOU EXIT FROM THIS TENT YOU WILL NOT BE WOLVES OR BUTTERFLIES OR . . . OR . . . BADGERS. WHILE YOU ARE HERE IN THIS . . . YOU CANNOT GO INTO THE VICTORIA'S SECRET WITH YOUR ANIMALS! YOUR ANIMALS MUST STAY INSIDE THE TENT!"

Oh! I see. We *are* animals. We were play-acting, but now we are wild animals in the eyes of mall security. More bad-tempered men in dark clothing were gathering back by the bar. I turned to Savitri, who like everyone else was staring at this woman. I looked back at the wilted wildness of the audience. After this flash of diversionary hysterics from management, we were reverting to the usual docile audience again. My forest creatures began to sit down. They shed their boreal characteristics and started resembling obedient consumers.

Savitri turned and said something . . . What? She said it again: "Pray."

I understood the direction. I felt the same way. The thing to do now was to move into this new over-scolded world, walk quietly into this hush of judgment, and pray. Praying is always powerful when it is sincere, when we are really talking to someone, with a power. Those who are not praying, but who suspect the prayer is about them, can be neutralized by this, the thrown voice of a spiritual cry.

The producer's interruption was the anti-prayer by a local bully deity—the super-mall god—threatening us. So our direct action could be right here inside the tent, a bunch of animals praying in a circus tent.

"Let us pray." Like many times in my life, I said those powerful words without knowing what I would say next. But in the slow motion on the bridge to the next "beat" of the performance, the song "Falling in Love Again" came singing its way into my mind, in that frozen clearing of a stage left by the producer and her fury. The Spiegeltent's own song came back into my prayer.

Falling in love again / never wanted to / what's a girl to do? / can't help it.

Maybe we all saw the singer, too. I did. Marlene Dietrich singing with her legs saucily apart in the turned-around chair, with that young but knowing smirk. We all started singing the pop ditty of so long ago.

Falling in love again / never wanted to / what am I to do? / can't help it.

"All the life in this community of life, the forests that we honor here today. All this life adds up to the creator, and that is who we want to talk to today at the end of our worship-show. You animals that we have been living with, we want you to live and we want to survive with you, yes we want to live, too."

The very hummable tune continued to spread through the audience. Will you, gentle reader, venture a hum?

Falling in love again / never wanted to / what's a girl to do? / I can't help it . . .

After going through the practice of mountain beings, and then the panic of the producer, we enjoyed the lullaby-like song, many of us holding hands or laying our arms on a lover's shoulders, and swaying back and forth.

The lullaby rhythm gave way after a while to a much more up-tempo reading of the *Blue Angel's* lament, because the Not Buying It Band started up, especially Eric "The Professor" Johnson, the drummer, a native of New Orleans and Chicago. We repeated the riff again and again and it got hotter. "Falling in love again" sounded more and more like George Clinton and Parliament.

Savitri was just smiling. The horns kicked in and we climbed the mountain toward something akin to James Brown. And I gave my wireless mike to people in the front row and the mike went from diva to diva. Anyone who wanted to sing—harmonizing or soloing—they busted out.

Then the microphone ended up in the hands of a young banker in a pinstriped outfit. The mike was forced on her by her friends. I watched it unfold. The friends knew how she could sing and also knew that there was bashfulness to overcome. I remember that this woman had been an owl in our forest-show, hooting, big-eyed, standing motionless on a chair. And what she did with our song has become legend. She Aretha'd the thing. After a time she had everyone clapping and she took her jacket off and she was walking up and down center aisle, gesturing and jumping and full of life. Her name is Tola and she has since become a soloist in our choir. "Falling in love again," by the time she was finished, was a glorious survival anthem.

"We know that remembering the earth isn't something we do easily in the center of a metropolis. But we are the earth, each of us. We are animals and birds and trees, and if we remember who we are, yes, it is like falling in love again. Earth-a-lujah!"

At the end of the show, I told the producers in back with the slack faces: "We won't come back."

The singers and musicians and friends of our show gathered after the gospel choir sashayed out of the tent. We gathered because we knew this was a special one and wanted to be together for a while. And a decision had to be made. So we talked, and what developed was an impromptu town hall meeting. The *New York Times* left their Vicki stakeout—the mall officials may have threatened them, we don't know. I found myself adding, "Let's perform somewhere else next week. We don't need these money people and all their fear."

The producers wanted us to continue our run and said so. Officials from the mall and from Vicki's were standing around the edges of our meeting.

Addressing the producers, Savi said, "We have never had this sort of interruption during a service, and we should move on. This show had a serious kind of make-believe, a careful thing to create in a performance. You stopped it because of your conservative politics. You have mixed feelings about us and that's fine."

A young man raised his hand and he spoke: "What happened here today was an experience that does not take place very often. The way that we tried to act out the life in those mountains, and then we were interrupted and then made our way back to our prayer that then some-how became a hot sing-along. The fact that it did happen here, with your church, or, your mountain, under these conditions . . . please come back! We need that gift of falling in love again!"

We stood there together, having our thoughts. It seemed that the decision to return had been made, and we did. But the first thing we did after that meeting was put a call in to Canada, to some friends way up in the woods.

Over the next year, we performed "Retail Interventions"—cash register exorcisms, in-store parades with our drag angels with the strap-on chain saws—inside Victoria's Secret stores not only in New York, but across the country.

Earth-a-lujah!

Post Script

Unlike so many activist ventures, this one has a happy ending. Forest Ethics and Limited Brands finally negotiated an agreement that promised significant changes in how Victoria's Secret procures its paper. Each year, the percentage of trees felled for the glossy lingerie catalogue is reduced, and the use of recycled paper increases. We were credited with entering the picture at a critical tipping point, entering Vicki's stores, performing our dramas, and handing out information about the clear-cuts.

The threat to the boreal forest now takes the form of tar sands oil exploration. We stare at photographs of giant toxic pits. Oil companies try to keep the birds away with cannons and flares.

Lafcadio has moved on to the Rainforest Action Network (RAN), which worked with us on our effort to get J. P. Morgan Chase out of the business of financing "mountaintop removal" strip-mining. This campaign, in 2010, for which we sculpted little mountains in the lobbies of twenty Chase branch banks in New York City, was also successful. However, as soon as Chase moved to pull out of mountaintop removal, UBS of Zurich and PNC Bank of Philadelphia were reportedly moving to pick up their market share.

Our consumption of paper is ultimately what encourages clear-cuts. Our consumption of energy creates the market for dirty coal. Our consuming must change. In late 2010, it is still not something politicians or major environmental groups seem able to talk about. Such behavior-change is apparently out of the question, as they struggle to get their consumer economy going again. But until we change how we live in that basic way, there will always be a new attack on the great boreal forest, and on all our wildness.

8. NYC: Radicals in the Park

A Shout from the Pavilion

REVEREND BILLY

Dedicated to Debra Bernhardt

Where is our commons?
What do I own with you and you with me?

It is our Pavilion, our reviewing stand,
On the uptown end of Union Square in New York City.
It is that place in the passing of American time
And we are the workers parading by it.
We see Paul Robeson singing on it
And Dorothy Day praying on it
And Emma Goldman shouting above a sea of fedoras . . .

The Pavilion is designed by the First Amendment.
Its wide-open rotunda, its colonnades and symmetry—
It is a body of a building made for wailing, beseeching,
    demanding . . .
We cannot sell this place and let all those heroes die standing up
In a tastefully framed photograph on a restaurant wall.

Can we parade backwards and silence the Lucy Parsons in us?
The Joe Hill and Angela Davis and Upton Sinclair in us?
The decades of tens of thousands chanting and marching?

What is our commons?
What do we all own at once?
Can we actually send this Pavilion back
As if our city is just a big box store
With a return policy for our own history?

We accepted the gift of this place that they risked their lives to
  create
By using its freedom every day.

Where is our commons?
We take a breath to shout the question forward into time
To keep the gift going . . .

Union Square Campaign

SAVITRI D

The campaign to save the Union Square Pavilion involved a wide group of people. The "we" referred to herein includes the primary organizers and decision-making body of Save Union Square, a coalition that included: Mark Read, Benjamin Shepherd, Deanna Zandt, Cathryn Swan, and Benjamin Cerf; Jason Jones and Winnie Fung of Not An Alternative; Marisa Jahn and Michael O'Neil, both staff members of the Church of Stop Shopping; Reverend Billy, and myself. Many other individuals and groups contributed invaluable resources along the way. These actions took place between May and October of 2008. This is not a comprehensive survey of the work we have done in the park. —SD

Union Square Park sits right at the center of the five boroughs of New York City, but was named for its position at the junction, or union, of Old Bloomingdale Road, now 14th Street, and Eastern Post Road. As a heavily trafficked crossroads and major subway hub, it is a diverse confluence of the city's residents and visitors. Seventy-five percent of the people in the park on a typical day do not live in the area. On a given afternoon you might see break-dancers, Christian missionaries, T-shirt vendors, skateboarders, an animal adoption group, and some truant teenagers all within twenty yards of each other. It's a good show.

Union Square is our commons, a social and almost magically inclusive space that is increasingly threatened by the shopping culture that grows around it. In 2003 the local business association proposed elaborate renovations that would include a high-end, for-profit venture inside the park, at the pavilion on the north end of the park. As construction loomed in the spring of 2008, we became immersed in the conflict surrounding the pavilion. Months of meetings, demonstrations, interventions, and online organizing followed. It remains one of the most instructive campaigns we have ever undertaken: an active investigation of the relationship between street activism and lawsuits, the limits of the ritualized struggle for police permits, the spatial demands of defending public space, the nature of the freedoms we were fighting for, and the activist history we belong to.

We dedicated ourselves to Union Square because it is the city's most emblematic commons—both as symbol and reality. As it is our stage now, it was the stage for our predecessors. We are fighting for their legacy and our future. The fight for public space is the fight for democracy itself.

A Radical Legacy

Union Square has been a natural gathering place for as long as New York has been a city. George Washington and the Continental Army rested in the grass along its western edge after driving the British Army back down the East River during the American Revolution. After the fall of Fort Sumter in 1861, four hundred thousand people descended on the park in what was then the largest gathering ever held on American soil and it was from the park that Union troops amassed and departed throughout the Civil War. Vibrant military parades and patriotic gatherings took place at Union Square until the end of the First World War and spontaneous gatherings of thousands were common well into the 1950s. This tradition has clung to Union Square even in more recent years. New Yorkers poured into the park on September 11, 2001, and the days following, building impromptu memorials and erupting into communal song.

Crucially, Union Square possesses—and represents—a populist and progressive legacy New York cannot afford to abandon. In 1882, Labor Day was celebrated for the first time in United States history and a grand parade celebrating workers moved through Union Square Park. At the time garment factories and light manufacturing surrounded the park, and shift change brought thousands of men and women to the park for much-needed fresh air and sunlight. The union movement grew quickly and in 1886, when the Federation of Organized Trades and Labor Unions called on workers nationwide to strike for an eight-hour workday on May 1, ten thousand workers marched in a torchlight procession to Union Square. Strikes were common in the park and along its edges, and in 1910 the garment workers started a picket line that lasted fourteen weeks in the bitter cold.

By then, the park was ringed with cheap cafeterias, where working people could get an affordable lunch or an unemployed person could sit out a cold day for the price of a cup of coffee. During the Depression, unemployed workers gathered in droves, looking for work or company or attending the free, ad hoc lectures given by professors from all over the city in what some have called the Poor Man's University. Across the twentieth century famous radicals like Emma Goldman, Paul Robeson, Dorothy Day, Lucy Parsons, and Norman Thomas spoke to great crowds in the park and Union Square became closely associated with socialism and communism. A rally of one hundred thousand people at the first National Unemployment Day Protest in the 1930s resulted in a riot and set off a years-long tension between local store owners and the people, who claimed the public space as a place for free assembly. The presence of Communist Headquarters (where Babies-R-Us now stands) and the active presses of the *Daily Worker* fueled the building tension. Local merchants formed the Union Square Association (USA) in 1932, claiming capitalism as the truest form of patriotism and urging people to resist the Communist presence in Union Square. Gradually the NYC labor unions consolidated and became more conservative under Samuel Gompers and moved their big parades and gatherings to Fifth Avenue; Labor Day in September replaced the old May Day. The Red Scare stilled the political spirit of Union Square and the radical movement suffered there, as it did everywhere, but the soapbox atmosphere survived well into the 1960s.

The park has always been an expansive, open area; today wide pavement (where Union Square's famous farmers market sets up four times a week) rings the raised park ground of grassy lawns, bench-lined walkways, and abundant trees. There are no buildings, save for the graceful, all-weather pavilion standing on the park's north end. The structure started out as a reviewing stand in the Civil War era and was upgraded into a stately stone pavilion in the late nineteenth century by the landscape architects Frederick Law Olmsted and Calvert Vaux (creators of Manhattan's Central Park and Brooklyn's Prospect Park). Olmsted and Vaux designed the northern end of the park as an assembly area, formalizing the purpose for which it was already being used. They incorporated the reviewing stand into their design; for well over a century, it doubled as a performance site and, called the "women and children's pavilion," as a shelter for families visiting the park year-round. By the 1980s, the city's parks department had let the pavilion fall into decay. Even a hard-won 1999 national historic landmark designation did not improve the park or the pavilion's upkeep; unfortunately, such designations do not offer funding or protections to locales and their structures.

Save Union Square

The igniting event in 2003 was the establishment of the Union Square Partnership (USP)—an organization dedicated to the area's economic growth—which formed through a merger of the Local Development Corporation (a for-profit enterprise) and the Union Square Business Improvement District (a quasi-public agency). Soon after, the USP announced an elaborate renovation plan for the park. The city had already promised $2 million for rebuilding the park's playground, but the USP flatly rejected it, opting, instead, for an anonymous private donation of $7.1 million that would refurbish not only the playground, but also the walkways, the trees, and the paving stones. Without designating or naming the eventual leaseholder, the donor—unknown to this day—stipulated that a for-profit enterprise would occupy the pavilion. A plan was developed for a white-tablecloth restaurant with four-star aspirations. The vision included a catering kitchen and expansive outdoor seating and would certainly make any other use of the pavilion impossible.

Local residents and users of the park who make up the thirty-year-old Union Square Community Coalition (USCC) objected to secret private interests controlling—and indeed, privatizing—plans for Union Square. When USP renovations began in March 2008, the Coalition sued. The lawsuit claims that the restaurant project went forward illegally, without required review and approval by the state legislature. In May of that year, the judge, Jane Solomon, issued a stop-work order for the construction of the restaurant, but allowed the rest of the work in the park to continue. Scaffolding went up, clay roof tiles were removed and stacked carefully along the pavilion's rooftop. Big trucks, work trailers, and piles of materials surrounded the pavilion, while a tall cyclone fence kept everyone at a distance.

We got involved.

We are fighting the restaurant in the pavilion at the north end of Union Square because the square is the most important public assembly area in the city. It is a crucible of radical change, a through-line to previous social movements and actual, effectual citizen-driven change. But even if that were not the case, even if the pavilion and the surrounding assembly area were not at the center of our progressive history, we would fight the restaurant there. Union Square has more restaurants and less public space than anywhere in the entire city. We don't believe that parks should be profit centers, even if the profits go directly into maintenance of the park, which, in this case, they would not. Parks are necessary in this city as a simple respite from the pressures of commerce and urban density. Privatizing parks sets a dangerous precedent, divorcing citizens from their own resources and furthering the misguided notion that everything must pay for itself, earn its keep. We also don't think the fate of our public resources should be decided by anonymous donors or conditional grants. Any efforts to privatize public resources or turn public lands and holdings over to individuals, organizations, or corporations for potential profit must be transparent and aboveboard.

When Judge Solomon issued the temporary restraining order, we knew that the injunction would not hold forever. Leaders of the USCC told me we had at least six months and possibly a year to increase public awareness and expose what looked more and more like a dirty landgrab. A number of other groups had already worked against the renovation, significantly influencing the design but failing in their efforts to take the restaurant off the table. Almost all of the typical procedural options available had already played out at community board meetings and public hearings and we knew we were showing up at the eleventh hour. Still, we felt optimistic about our chances; the restaurant plan did not seem inevitable.

We organized Save Union Square 2008 (SUS) as quickly as we could. The meetings drew individuals from all over the city, some representing organizations, some not. We were activated for different reasons. Many were concerned about the threat to public assembly, some were worried about their livelihoods, and others were disturbed by the process itself. There was a fairly wide range of skills in the room: bloggers, street vendors, designers, environmentalists, students, professors, visual artists, historians, activists, preservationists. There was a great deal of passion for the park and many of us were discovering Union Square's fertile history for the first time.

New York City citizens are burdened with prohibitive permit requirements for parading, assembling, and speaking. Political activity in New York is most often relegated to metal protest pens and two-by-two sidewalk marches in marginal areas. The demoralizing trend toward confined and super-controlled protest that began in the late 1990s has only gotten worse. As we fight with police over arbitrary borders and whether we will be allowed within sight of our opponents, the issue at hand—the cause that brought us to the streets in the first place—gets lost in the negotiation. As a result, activism is often reduced to a bureaucratic struggle for a permit that might eventually grant us permission to stand inside a pen like a herd of shouting cows. And even with permits, and even in pens, arrests are common. All of this has had a highly deleterious effect on movement building, community organizing, and political dissent in the city. There are fewer and fewer people in the street.

On top of these procedural hurdles is the unfailing tendency of the New York Police Department (NYPD) and private security guards to quash all protest seen as interfering even remotely with commerce. This takes the form of protected sidewalks, the oft-spoken, "don't disturb the customers" and "don't block the doors, please!" but also more subtle tactics like the elimination of seating areas, tightly choreographed pedestrian flow in heavy shopping areas, the subtle pressure to shop when among shoppers. These strategies are employed by the business improvement districts (BIDs) that manage a significant portion of NYC's public space. The Union Square Partnership has as its mandate the well-being of commerce and business in the Union Square area, getting "eyes on windows"; it is a *business* improvement district, not a *community* improvement district, and the restaurant is a perfect manifestation of their idea of a healthy public space.

At our first SUS meeting we defined our priorities: Above all, the park should remain public and for the people. In the process of saving the pavilion we wanted to define and amplify the intrinsic value of public space; we wanted to help people visualize, imagine, and connect to the history of the park. We wanted to publicize the role of the USP in the restaurant plan and redefine the BID as an agent of commerce as distinct from community. We hoped to stake a physical claim to the park. For many Americans the concept of "privatization" is so normalized that opposing it requires a rudimentary, from-the-ground-up explanation. If we were able to do that forcefully we could connect the privatization of Union Square Park to struggles against privatization in other parts of the world, effectively tying this deeply local battle to larger global movements. We also felt it was important to illuminate the trend in NYC toward privatization and overdevelopment of parks in wealthy areas and neglect and criminalization of parks in poorer communities of color.

We identified our targets: the Union Square Partnership; its corporate members and executive board, including co-chair and celebrity chef Danny Meyer; City Council member Rosie Mendez, who signed off on the deal; the NYC parks department and its commissioner, Adrian Benepe; and Mayor Mike Bloomberg.

We defined our public: those we really want to talk to, as people who use the park, but also a broader group who may not spend time in the park but understand its importance. As always we were aware of the audience of history itself, which would ultimately have to fit these events into the much larger story of Union Square Park.

The Actions

When the fence first went up around the pavilion in the spring of 2008, before we were even involved, we got a number of calls. Judge Solomon's injunction had not yet been issued and the extent of what was happening was still unclear. "They're cutting down the trees! Come quickly," people shouted, some of them in tears. Within two days, as scaffolding went up the back of the building, the parks department removed a dozen hundred-year-old elm trees. Enormous chunks of trees lay about in what had once been their own shadows, while just budding branches and boughs were fed into chippers, turned to mulch, ground cover. Things looked grim.

We had a show at the Highline Ballroom that weekend and I talked to the audience about what was happening in the park. I invited them to write messages on hundreds of cotton strips I'd torn from an old sheet, asking them to write something about the park, the pavilion, or the trees—and after the show about fifty of us walked the six blocks to the park and painstakingly sewed hundreds of them to the fence with bright red thread, the needle and thread linking us to the seamstresses and garment workers who fought so hard for their rights in that very space. The messages were simple: "I love these trees!" "NO restaurant" "I kissed my girlfriend on those stairs" "I cried here on September 11" "Parks for the People." The streamers were gone when I walked by the following morning. We repeated the action two more times over the following week, arriving in the afternoon and sewing until we ran out of light. Each time the streamers were cut down by morning. The remnants hung on, trails of red thread and what must have been, by then, close to a thousand scraps of blue and white cloth. Images of the streamers showed up on the Internet for weeks, posted mostly by people just passing by with cameras and phones: "I made love here." "My grandparents sat in this park." I kept thinking of the person whose job it was to cut them down, reading the messages, the briefest of stories, one after another, with an accumulating awareness of the place, its intimacies, and all that had gone on there.

That first month of the campaign was revelatory. Everyone had a story about Union Square. A man in his nineties named Jim found us in the park and told us how he rode down to the park from the Bronx every day during the Depression: "There was thousands of us just hanging around waiting for those professors. I learned French down on the south end, and History right there by the fountain." My own Uncle Hans had gotten wind of our work and called to tell me that my great-grandparents met at a union dance right in the park. The closer we looked at the history the more we felt ourselves connecting viscerally to remarkable events: Emma Goldman speaking to thousands of young women about birth control in 1906; huge crowds standing silently while Sacco and Vanzetti were executed; a block over, audiences in 1963 climbing through the window of the Living Theatre to see *The Brig* after authorities had padlocked the doors. We started compiling photographs, and pored through books, archives, and the documents sent to us by preservationists and historians as we tried to come up with a strong, evocative visual language for the campaign. We wanted to bring the park's stories into the present moment.

After much deliberation we decided to make life-sized cutouts of historical figures who had spoken at the pavilion or been in the park during many eras. We found iconic images of Emma Goldman, Lucy Parsons, Dorothy Day, Norman Thomas, Paul Robeson, and George Washington, turned them into line drawings, projected them onto sheets of cardboard and began the strangely satisfying process of hand-painting each one. The idea was to educate people about the park, and also to suggest that these people, these heroes, were watching us now. The figures stood in pairs, their arms linked and their outside arms available to link with live people. We envisioned standing in a circle around the construction fence, arm-in-arm with the past.

Savitri D, Mark Read, and Reverend Billy moments after dropping the "NOT FOR SALE" banner in Union Square Park, 2008. (Photo by John Quilty.)

We were working toward a major public event in the park on a Thursday afternoon in early June, in conjunction with the USP's annual cocktail party and "community report" at the exclusive W Hotel on the northeast corner of the park.

We fired a salvo the day before. At maximum pedestrian rush hour Wednesday afternoon, I met Billy and Mark, a member of Save Union Square and longtime activist, by the newsstand on the park's northeast corner. Thinking we would certainly be spending the night in police custody, we showed up with full bellies, wearing warm clothes, and carrying solid ID, quarters, and proof of residence in our back pockets, without bags or phones, and with lawyers on call. We were ready to be arrested. Friends with cameras were planted around the pavilion and in the second-story window of the Barnes & Noble across 17th Street. Mark carried a huge canvas banner tightly folded in a backpack, a rope already strung through its grommets. We squeezed through a gap in the fence and walked fast, steadily, through the construction mud and straight up the scaffolding on the backside of the building. We dropped the banner as fast as we could, a fifteen-feet-square fire-engine red canvas with "NOT FOR SALE" painted on it in enormous white block print. Below us pedestrians wove by, smiling up at us, watching the spectacle. People still at work stood in windows watching while Billy led onlookers in a call and response: "UNION SQUARE NOT FOR SALE! UNION SQUARE NOT FOR SALE!" Across the street a couple of cops sat in their cruiser with the windows down, low in their seats, barely visible, the bright white paper of deli sandwiches gleaming in their laps.

Mark and I saw park security guards emerge from their trailers behind us, but we couldn't tell if they were coming for us, or if they even knew we were on the roof. We decided to bolt, and raced down the scaffolding across the muddy field and back through the gap—not in jail, like smoke, free. We stood in front for a while admiring the banner and talking to people. When you think you're going to get arrested but don't, time gets peculiar and light, and everything feels wonderfully untethered for a while.

We went to a bar around the corner and ran over the next day's events—it was prop-heavy and would take a lot of setup time, but it was worth it. We were going to take over the north end of the park and fill it with imagery and bodies, things we made with our hands. We had a feeling a lot of people would come, the word was out. Pictures of the

"NOT FOR SALE" banner were sweeping the Internet.

The next morning, thirty sets of life-sized historical figures lined a pathway and members of the choir dressed in period costume were standing beside them on soapboxes orating. Valerie, a dreadlocked singer in the choir, played Lucy Parsons in a finely cut, yellow linen dress borrowed from a Broadway costume house. I was Emma Goldman in a woolen cape and old-fashioned spectacles. Some characters read and quoted directly from speeches; others gave brief first-person accounts of their time in Union Square Park. The crowd wandered among them, learning a bit about each character and then Billy MC'd a series of short speeches on a high platform constructed to look like an old-fashioned reviewing stand.

Across the street at the USP's presentation of its "community report," Kurt, a former Billionaire for Bush, dressed in his best business casual, checked in with the clipboard girl at the door of the second-floor conference room of the W Hotel. The room had thick, silencing carpeting and cushioned chairs, mostly empty. A bored bartender stood behind a long banquet table at the end of the room serving up booze and soda in plastic cups, gesturing people to the already ravaged hors d'oeuvres. Once the meeting was under way Kurt started asking probing questions like, "So, and I hope you don't mind my asking—why are we even bothering with a playground? Or let me put it this way: Since we had to give up all that space for the playground, is there any profit potential there?" The irony was lost on the room. When we looked at the tape of his intervention made by his "date," we could see it actually was hard to tell he wasn't part of the crowd, which illustrates just how far you have to go to overwhelm a ritual as practiced as a business meeting, even one described as a "community report." Kurt would literally have had to throw money around and froth at the mouth for anyone in that room to understand that he was being satirical. The only person who even blinked was a watchdog from a citizen's group who politely asked him if he "was sincerely suggesting that the BID find a way to charge admission to the park."

We wanted to crowd the USP that day, swarm them, make a spectacle. We were all over them outside, inside, on the Internet. We tried to be audible and visible and unavoidable. We stretched the crowd—the hundreds of us who had come on purpose and many other passersby we recruited—along the length of the fence and recited the First

Amendment, the cardboard historical figures multiplying our numbers. The Rude Mechanical Orchestra, a radical grassroots marching band, led us across 17th Street to the hotel with boisterous New Orleans jazz. Billy climbed up the traffic light and shouted, "KEEP PUBLIC PARKS PUBLIC" into the second floor where the meeting was taking place, while we filled up the picture windows on the ground floor, three or four thick and chanting very loudly: "KEEP PUBLIC PARKS PUBLIC, KEEP PUBLIC PARKS PUBLIC." The cardboard cutout figures danced along the windows, and traffic started to back up. The police had to be close, the hotel security team was going nuts, and we decided to end on a high note before the NYPD showed up and started making arrests. Billy led a call-and-response First Amendment—"Congress shall make no law," down through "the right of the people peaceably to assemble and petition the government for redress of grievances." And then, "Free speech, Free speech, Free Press! Free press! REDRESS! REDRESS!" The NYPD moved in right on cue, but we were already on our way out.

Energized by the success of that first action, we started going to Union Square every Wednesday afternoon hoping to become a regular presence in the park. We felt we had to compete with the USP's normalized presence there. The construction had pushed the farmers market to the western edge of the park and it was so crowded that we had to set up our card table in a cramped slot between the back end of a flower stall and a walkway that cut across the park. We hung the clean white "Community Improvement District" sign on the cyclone fence and stood the historical figures all around us. We had flyers, petitions, a soapbox, and a grab bag of coats and wigs and other costumes. We invited passersby to stand on the box in a hat or a mustache and recite the First Amendment, or read excerpts from famous speeches.

Representatives of the farmers market appeared, unabashed, and asked us to be quiet as we were disturbing their customers. We laughed and said their customers were actually secondary to the purpose of the park, but that we were happy to share the park with them. We tried to be nice but made it clear we were not going to be quiet; we were there to talk. Crowds gathered. The conversations were heated at times. People described their perceptions of the space, its uselessness: "It's just a bunch of kids hanging out anyway" or "What's wrong with a restaurant?" "You should have seen this place in the '70s!" "Oh well, if it's

Danny Meyer, I'm okay with it. Danny Meyer is such a good guy, he would never do anything bad. He saved this neighborhood." Or "It's so inoffensive, I mean, compared to the Iraq war, like, why aren't you protesting that? Or that monstrous hospital they are planning over in the West Village?"

We developed conversational tactics: If people didn't care about the restaurant, we tried to persuade them the process was suspect. If people didn't care about history we tried to explain the scarcity of public space. If people thought the issues were minor, we explained that we would have nowhere to address any issue soon enough. After a few weeks, we got more comfortable and stretched out; the farmers adjusted to our presence and even started giving us cookies and cider. Some days we leafletted our way through the market, walking around in costume talking about the pavilion in loud voices. We got hassled by the parks department a lot. They would arrive and tell us to stop, using proprietary language: "You can't do that, not in my park." "You can't hang that on my fence." All in the same low-level management jargon used in almost any retail environment. We tried to discuss the park as a commons, a shared resource, explained the First Amendment over and over. Large groups gathered around these debates, but the regular NYPD remained very hands-off. Surely the USP and parks department had made it clear to the NYPD they didn't want arrests; they weren't going to give us that press story.

I wanted our next action, in the height of summer, to demonstrate what the pavilion could be used for. I envisioned a picnic in the construction zone. I wanted to go inside among the bulldozers and the tractors with a hundred people and lay out blankets and hampers and have a big meal. We talked about it. It would never work. Or at least not inside the construction zone, where everyone would be risking arrest. There just weren't enough of us.

We needed to attract new people to the cause and thought maybe it was time to have an event in the other part of the park, beneath the trees on the grass. We dreamed up a patriotic picnic just before the Fourth of July. We would gather inside the park with watermelon and cupcakes, bunting and balloons. We would stage a country-fair-style auction and Billy would auction off the park, tree by tree, bench by bench.

The plan seemed fine, but tame. We needed to push against something too. If part of our challenge is to expand the pool of participants by inviting people who might be cautious or wary of police, then we must also give them a way to stretch just a little bit. Certain actions are opportunities to integrate those who will with those who won't. Dividing actions into stages, or acts, is the simplest way of providing both non-confrontational and confrontational actions. Moving people from an un-arrestable action in one place to another more confrontational action in another place gives them a chance to test their own comfort level, stay behind, duck out—or get super involved. It's generally a two-act model with a physical transition gradual enough that people can back off, disappear, or witness passively from a distance. We are often surprised and delighted by who ends up front and center in Act Two.

Act One, the picnic, under a gentle canopy of trees near the big fountain, unfolded as planned. The balloons and bunting really did seem festive, and bright wedges of watermelon made the day look hotter than it was. The choir sang and Billy climbed up on a soapbox and began auctioning off the park, starting with the small trees and ending with, of course, the pavilion. "Can I get two million? Can I get three million, three million ten?" Kurt, dressed like an executive again, offered to buy the whole park and we fell on him like piranhas, exorcising his demon soul. At the end, Kurt was wonderfully contrite—a banker on his knees, clinging to his *Wall Street Journal*.

Now to Act Two. We told the hundred or so people gathered that we were going to deliver a gift to Danny Meyer at his exclusive high-end restaurant, The Union Square Café, a revered New York City institution. Danny Meyer stood right at the heart of the restaurant plan; he has placed restaurants in other city parks and operates among the power elite of the city. It was time to pressure him directly.

We marched from the center of the park to the Union Square Café with five big rolls of sod and seven trees about the height of an eight-year-old. We walked up to the restaurant and Mark and I opened the door and went inside. "Hi, we have a delivery for Danny Meyer," I said. The maître d' looked at me quizzically so I said it again, loudly, "We have a gift for Danny Meyer and if he isn't here we would be happy to leave it for him." "What is it?" he asked and we shouted, "IT'S A PARK! A PARK! A PARK!" I unrolled the sod I was carrying. The crisp room filled with the smell of wet earth; the maître d' looked horrified. Two undercover cops, high-level detectives in shiny sports jackets, were pushing through behind me. "But Officer, it's a gift! A park for Danny Meyer!" I said. They had me firmly by the elbows. Mark, just to my left but still free, started shouting about the pavilion. The diners were staring at us over their appetizers, spoons mid-chin. As the detectives pulled me out I got a glimpse of the outside through the picture window—what a sight! The sod was unrolled and the trees were in place, a hundred people were gathered around the miniaturized park, many in sun-colored hard hats. Billy was preaching loudly and people kept opening the doors so the words could drift inside. Others held flyers up to the windows. The cops were stymied. There were far too many people to arrest. They gave up. Laura, a longtime singer in the choir, pretended to meditate on a strip of sod by a tree.

Harvest in the Square

We kept up our presence in the park on Wednesday afternoons throughout the summer, but didn't plan another major action until September, when we took aim at the USP's major fund-raising event of the year, The Harvest in the Square. It's a perfect example of what our parks are increasingly used for and why we are fighting the restaurant. For the gourmet event, where dozens of celebrity chefs cook their signature dishes and offer sample servings, the western half of the park is cordoned off, tented, and secured, and fake walls are constructed to create a private space that only ticket-holders can enter. Tickets start at $125. Early in the evening there is a VIP donor cocktail hour. Dignitaries speak, famous people mingle—it's a self-congratulatory schmooze-fest and we were pretty sure every one of our targets would be there. We guessed they would be protected by the tent, out of sight, and that our best hope was to make a lot of noise. We instructed people to bring pots and pans and wooden spoons. We procured tall white chef's hats and aprons and told people to dress in kitchen whites. We called it The Citizen's Chef Brigade and we advertised it broadly, knowing it would agitate the USP.

A number of police were already there when we arrived. They hassled us immediately, told us we couldn't use the bullhorn, and talked to us as if we were naughty children. The lieutenant actually told me to behave myself. He threatened Billy too: "Listen you just better not start shouting, you better just be quiet . . . or I'll . . . look, just keep it down would ya?" Billy played along, bantering cheerfully while the rest of us put on our hats and aprons. We started as far away from the tent as we could and paraded indirectly toward it, winding our way around the park banging and shouting, back and forth, while Monica, the choir's longtime Action Captain, led chants she had taped into her frying pan. The closer we got to the tent, the harder we banged. It was wonderfully, maddeningly loud.

We gathered at the most porous part of the tent, where people inside could see all seventy-five of us. "The park, the park, the park is no diner! We don't need no restaurant! Say NO to Danny Meyer!" People inside drifted over to look at us. The cops escorting us were clambering over the fences to talk to plainclothes cops huddled inside. It was clear the inside cops were calling the shots; they were so mad their faces were red. Everyone was frustrated by the noise, the clanging and banging; it was really hard to think straight. We got louder. Billy stood on a bench preaching into the tent. Chardonnay-sipping yuppies smiled uncomfortably. More cops arrived. Some young boys started folding the flyers into airplanes and sailing them through the gap between the tent walls and its roof. A whole new set of cops showed up and within two minutes Billy was arrested. The volume was really making the cops crazy. They were losing their cool, telling us to shut up. We added recitations of the First Amendment to the din as we followed a handcuffed Billy to the van, where three-quarters of us swiftly split back around the edge of the tent. By the time the cops realized arresting Billy wasn't going to end the action, we were directly behind the stage where the speeches were taking place. We held the pots and pans high above the tent walls and banged and clanged. The boys continued gliding flyers through the cracks. We kept it up for about twenty minutes, then headed to the entrance for a finale. On the way over, one of our leaders, Ben, got arrested for throwing a flyer over the fence. "That's litter buddy! You're coming with me!" the cop said. We enjoyed one last banging-and-chanting session near the entrance and stopped before there were more arrests. A few of us lingered near the entrance and handed flyers to people as they went in.

Half an hour later, two of our number, Mark and Marisa, entered the tent, a little dressed up, as if on a date, advance tickets in hand. Mark planned to stand on a table and make a speech, but saw an opening when the dinner jazz combo took a break. He walked over to the stage, picked up the microphone and delivered an impassioned speech about the value of the pavilion and the USP's efforts to make a profit center out of it. At first people thought he was part of the show, and they listened and nodded. Then he started raising his voice. "The USP is no friend of the park and no friend of the people," he said, demanding that everyone who loved the park leave with him, exhorting them to abandon the frivolous party and go out into the real life of the park. A few people were still nodding, genuinely caught up in what he was saying, but others had connected him to the "protest" outside and a lady with a clipboard started waving her arms at the sound man until flummoxed security guards rushed in, grabbed Mark by the collar, and escorted him out the back, by the dishwashers and the trash. Marisa left flyers on every table.

The Straight Event

A few weeks later, on a cool October evening, we commemorated the tenth anniversary of the designation of Union Square as a national historic landmark. We made a massive outreach effort to unions, educational institutions, activist and artist groups, and neighborhood organizations all over the city. We hoped to connect the landmark designation to the pavilion and the restaurant plan, and highlight how important the pavilion is to so many kinds of people. The extensive "coalition-building" experience was not new to us. We definitely spent more time than anticipated assuring our partners that we wouldn't "misbehave" or "upset" anyone or be "rowdy" or even "rude" and reminding them that being on a list of endorsers regarding the preservation of the pavilion didn't mean endorsing every thing the other cooperating groups had ever done before. Most of these groups were unwilling to participate unless we had permits, so we went to the community board and the police station and filed for assembly and sound permits for the first—and I hope last—time in our history. They took more than eight weeks to secure.

The evening was made up of many pieces. We organized walking tours of the park and set up a drawing station where people envisioned possible uses for the pavilion. Later we made a calendar out of the drawings and sent one to all the City Council and community board members. We erected huge displays of historical images borrowed from the Tamiment Library at NYU, workers on strike, the incredible gatherings and parades that took place there. We provided detailed information about the restaurant plan and the history of our opposition to it. We took full advantage of the permits and stretched our displays deep into the southern end of the park.

A number of historians and labor leaders spoke about the history of the park, its value to the city, and the legacy of labor. As they spoke I started thinking how the theater of events like these is almost invisible to me: It's the performance of not performing, or of only performing. I kept thinking I should be doing something. But what? For once I wasn't constantly monitoring the police or gauging the likelihood of arrest; all I really had to do was keep the generator running and get the right speaker on deck. I have to admit the sanctioned stage, just a few yards from where Billy was last arrested, felt diffuse, uncharged. Somehow the permit made the event almost too stable. Where would its threat come from? Where was the drama?

Then our choirmaster, James Benn, sang the old Yip Harburg tune, "Brother Can You Spare a Dime," and the park really came alive. The meaning and the words were the threat, the drama of history was the threat. We felt the presence of Depression era crowds, out-of-work men and women crowding the nickle-a-pie cafeterias, looking for a lifeline. James and his beautiful tenor voice made people stop on their way and listen as the song unwound its tragedy, our tragedy. The markets were crashing again and that level of unemployment didn't seem so far off.

Say, don't you remember, they called me Al; it was Al all the time.

Say, don't you remember, I'm your pal? Buddy, can you spare a dime?

Billy started preaching, leading us back to something like hope, with real authority and a great rousing sermon. I ducked away to take a frantic call from the big final act. "Where are you?" I shouted into the phone.

The Gathering Storm, a fifty-piece, high-school-age brass band and stepping team from East New York, were an hour late and unreachable and I had pretty well given up. But here they were, calling and from only three blocks away! They turned onto 14th Street just as Billy's last chorus of "Amens" started. I signaled to Billy to keep it going a little longer and he stretched it out until their purple and silver bus, aged but still charging, pulled into the loading zone. The bus doors swung open.

I grabbed the microphone and told everyone to turn around and have a look behind them just as the band poured off their bus. They were decked out in shiny purple and silver sequined jumpsuits and hats, and they must run late a lot because getting off the bus—which they matched perfectly—was part of the show, totally choreographed. Two young men with tails and tasseled hats stood at the bay doors of the bus and handed out instruments and accoutrements. Seven dancers in leotards led the way onto the plaza, followed by horn players and percussionists and finally, the gleaming Sousaphones. They filled the park, weaving and kicking and collapsing into circles and squares and lines and pyramids. It was pure NYC Theater. People wandered by with their mouths hanging open, traffic jammed on three sides, and the choir stood in small groups, expressing various states of awe and excitement. The band played for about twenty minutes, then drove into a syncopated percussion number and a final dramatic full stop. Then they turned and, led by high-kneed drum majorettes, danced their purple sparkling way back onto the bus and were gone, back to East New York, to homework and little sisters and dinner and school the next day.

I was elated, but a little let down, too. I longed for the smell of damp sod filling up the restaurant, the historic figures dancing in the window of the W Hotel, the pots and pans banging in the background of the park commissioner's speech. The night was good, really, it went just as we planned. But it's not enough to produce spectacle now; things have to take another step. I thought of all the times we had rolled up to just such affairs with the choir, jumped out of vehicles, sung songs and then marched the crowd into a Wal-Mart or straight out into the street. Next time I would ask The Gathering Storm to lead us to something, take us somewhere.

Contested Space / Lawsuits

The lawsuit filed by the Union Square Community Coalition in April 2008 created the space for our laboratory of activism, making it possible for groups like ours to have impact either on the plan itself or on the perception of the plan. Our interaction with the court case has been minimal, but it bought all the time in which these actions operated. We don't see the lawsuit, or work on it, but it's always there, a painted-on shadow. We see construction creeping up to the edge of the pavilion, we see the scaffolding on the building, the foundations being expanded. We watched the trees get killed and new paving stones laid down. We see the farmers market moved around, the vendors adjusting to space constraints. At the center of it all stands the pavilion, off-limits to all of us, out of use, but contested. And that is our stage.

Working with Save Union Square was not the first time that park served as our stage. Our experience in Union Square the year before we started SUS primed us for that fight.

On June 30, 2007, Billy and I awoke to a disturbing article in the *New York Times* about a proposed new law that would require anyone taking pictures or shooting video in the city to have a permit. Everyone would be subject to a permit process, and anyone shooting on a tripod for longer than thirty minutes would require a $1 million insurance bond. This policy was the last straw for us. We had already been fighting draconian parading and assembly laws that left us all vulnerable to police harassment and severely limited our ability to gather or engage in public space. The film permit requirements would give the NYPD yet another way to harass people, to stop people for no reason. We were upset.

It was the last Friday of the month—the day cyclists gather for Critical Mass, a monthly, un-permitted, decentralized, self-organizing, traffic-calming ride. It has left from the north end of Union Square for ten years and has defined the relationship between the NYPD and protest movements since 2004. What was once a lighthearted, family-friendly environmental and bike-safety event has become a highly policed, criminalized ritual. Hundreds of people (including Billy, myself, and many members of the choir) have been arrested and/or ticketed while participating. The vast majority of charges and tickets are thrown out in court, but not before massively inconveniencing their recipients. The result has been that fewer and fewer people show up for the ride. It sometimes used to draw more than a thousand participants; we rarely see more than a hundred now.

Billy and I headed to Critical Mass separately. I arrived first and was, as always, infuriated by the police presence: there were fewer than thirty cyclists and approximately fifty police, many of them high-ranking brass. I started thinking about the impact the proposed film permits would have on our ability to film protests and police activity, long our only defense against police misconduct. I began reciting the First Amendment directly at the police, from about ten yards away. I walked as close to them as I could, repeating it over and over: "Congress shall make no law respecting an establishment of religion . . ." I circled them. I was loud. They were annoyed and moved away from me. I followed. They told me I had to stand back and I asked them how far. I asked them to show me how far. They pointed to a line about fifteen yards away from where they were standing.

I stood at the line. Billy arrived and joined me. We recited it together: ". . . the right of the people peaceably to assemble . . ." Billy had his big white megaphone. The cops came over and told us to be quiet. We ignored them, maintaining the established distance. We were starting to get to them. They moved about ten yards farther away. We moved with them, maintaining the distance they had delineated. Cyclists continued to gather and briefly outnumbered the police, then a fleet of scooters arrived and the cyclists were once again the minority. A cop walked over, waved a finger in my face, and said, "I'm warning you." We shrugged. The cop walked away. Billy turned his back and started saying the First Amendment away from the police, toward a crowd of curious onlookers. The same officer came over and put cuffs on him unceremoniously.

Billy was arrested. The civil rights lawyer Norman Siegel was present at the time of the arrest and quickly issued a statement: "Reverend Billy has the First Amendment right to recite the First Amendment." It was the July Fourth weekend.

News of the First Amendment arrest spread around the world, appearing in papers in Singapore, Russia, even Cairo. Not surprisingly, the charges against Billy were dropped almost immediately and Norman Siegel and his colleague, Earl Ward, filed a suit against the city for wrongful arrest. By the time we started our campaign against the restaurant plan nearly a year later, we had been in court four times.

What's in a Domain Name?

It was not the last of our legal troubles. In April 2008, Michael O'Neil, the media manager of the the Church of Stop Shopping discovered that the USP had neglected to register their own domain names—unionsquarepartnership.com and unionsquarepartnership.org. We quickly claimed both and started studying their website, a window onto USP's sterile vision of the park. Its slightly offbeat sherbet color scheme, slide shows of happy shoppers and lovers on the lawns, aerial views of markets, and well-placed shots of "ethnic" people, resemble a tourist brochure or an orientation pamphlet for a university campus. Our friend Vera called it, "The New Fake Europe." Marisa began constructing a mirror website, an exact replica of the USP's site, only telling the real story of the USP and the restaurant plan. She mimicked the colors and design, but in place of smiling tourists and gleaming new solar-powered trash barrels, posted pictures of destroyed trees, construction, the banner drop, and cyclists being harassed by the police.

The main body of the site was a short video clip in which I impersonated Jennifer Falk, the executive director of the USP. With a slightly regretful face, I explained what was really going at the north end of the park: "Hi! I'm Jennifer Falk, executive director of the USP and I'm here in Union Square to issue a heartfelt apology. We made a mistake. My former boss, Mayor Mike Bloomberg, has a plan for this city. My only regret is that it took me so long to see through it. We are withdrawing our plans for a restaurant in the pavilion on the north side of the park." It was all very convincing. I looked just harried enough and my jacket was just expensive enough to make it all credible. All outgoing links from the fake site went to either a calendar of our upcoming actions, or straight to the petition against the restaurant at our site, which by then had thousands of signatures.

We thought of the fake site as a fairly minor aggravation, something to unleash at a moment when the USP was already feeling a little pressure. In early July, the day after we entered the Union Square Café with sod and trees, we sent out a fake press release from the USP, in which the USP declared it had changed its mind about the restaurant. The release directed people to the fake site where "Jennifer Falk" appeared on video apologizing. The site didn't generate as much interest as we thought it would. Some blogs picked it up, but only a few thousand people visited it and we sort of forgot about it. Until, that is, I received a takedown notice about seven days later. I filed a counterclaim and offered to put a disclaimer on the site, but refused to take it down. This put the onus on them to prove wrongdoing, and the only way for them to get the site down would be to file a lawsuit.

In early August I received an email announcing that I was being sued in federal court for copyright infringement and a week later, a thirty-page document came by certified mail. Our Internet host also received the suit and, pending a decision by the courts, it blocked the site. To my great relief my name was alone on the suit. I was glad not to bring Marisa and Michael into it, even though they deserve most of the credit for the site.

I knew we could use the suit against the USP to our own ends, but only if we had activist lawyers. It would be a major pro bono commitment. I felt sure it would at the very least generate some chatter in the media, and any platform to talk about the restaurant plan and the USP was welcome. I also knew the case might be valuable for others—that it could expand protections for parody and satire on the Internet. So we started looking for lawyers in earnest. In mid-September the Electronic Frontier Foundation (EFF) agreed to take the case and we began the significant work of fighting the claim.

Lawsuits are costly and time-consuming and I was advised by the team (Corynne McSherry, Matt Zimmerman, and Michael Kwun) at EFF to keep an open mind about a settlement. Activist lawyers like the EFF take on cases they think can be won, help clean up case law, or set a strong precedent. A case like ours presented an opportunity for all three, but the odds of a flat-out win were barely even; they told me their primary goal was to get the site back up as soon as possible.

There was a great deal of back-and-forth between lawyers on the case. It was clear that the USP would get their domain names no matter what, given the strong precedent on the matter of "cyber squatting" or holding names hostage, usually for profit. The case hinged instead on the copyright claim and whether we would be able to have a site that mirrored theirs so closely. They alleged copyright infringement of the "look and feel" of the site.

The notion that a yellow and purple stripe and an off-the-shelf font in white across the top could be copyrighted was a stretch or, as our friend and sometime attorney Terry Gross said, "an outrageous expansion of the concept of the logo." At first the USP acted as if they were going to go all the way to court with the suit, but once the actual process began and they realized I was being represented by seriously determined groups of lawyers like the EFF, as well as two highly reputable firms in NYC, the USP made it obvious quickly that they didn't have the stomach for a real court battle and agreed to our terms. Their sole demand was that they acquire the domain names unionsquarepartner-ship.org and unionsquarepartnership.com.

We would be able to talk about and publicize the terms and conditions of the settlement, and to keep our site exactly as it was with a small disclaimer. We only had to promise not to use photos taken directly from their website or impersonate the executive board in videos without a visual or audio disclaimer. The name of our new mirror site could not include the names of their board members or the words "union square partnership" alone. In a time-honored tradition we chose unionsquarepartnershipsucks.com for the site and just like that, it was all over and we put the site back up. A few press releases went out, they generated some Web traffic, I did a flurry of interviews, and that was that.

We have to take advantage of weaknesses and be as opportunistic as possible. If a corporation like the USP doesn't register their own domain names, when any twelve-year-old can tell you that is the very first thing an organization must do in order to qualify as an organization, we are obliged to take advantage of their error. Being sued is not necessarily something to be afraid of, but not a situation I would spend time trying to create without a very precise reason or desired outcome. For a group like ours, there are too many unknowns in lawsuits, too much of the work is in the hands of other people and experts, and being tied up in court depletes our resources and keeps us off the street. All those days we spent talking to lawyers and preparing documents are days we could have been doing things in Union Square Park. I am glad we pushed back and held the line, glad we didn't just sign the sites over right away and give in to the USP's bullying, but is having the website unionsquarepartnershipsucks.com operational worth it? I don't really know.

Activism in the courts takes place at a highly fitful pace and runs very much on its own schedule. It is, above all, a technical process, and its dramatic force is cloaked in opaque language. It is an interesting, rarefied world, visited by many: victims of grave injustice, activists from the street, people with stories. But it's not necessarily vibrant or dynamic, and the outcomes of court cases are not always easy to read or translate to a broader public. Still, it is important that we take them as far as possible. Push forward fearlessly with the First Amendment and retrench and defend it whenever we can.

We sued the city for wrongful arrest, but instead of admitting they wrongfully arrested Billy, they eventually gave us $23,000. The USP sued me for copyright infringement. They never had to prove that, but they got their domain names back, I got to put our site back up, and I am free to talk about the suit however I want. In neither case do we have a clear, uncomplicated narrative. They aren't real wins—and the first headlines for both are still the best: "Reverend Billy Arrested Reciting the First Amendment," "Activist Sued by USP for Parodic Website." The final outcome is not as powerful as the initial story. The energized moment of confrontation at the outset may be the only part of the story we choose to tell, and it's up to us where in the course of those events we shine the light—we make the play.

The long-term impact of court cases and lawsuits on community struggles is worth paying attention to. When a situation gets clarified into a court case, honed down to legalese and the work of experts, it often disappears from the community into the justice system. Then, so often, the only interaction the community has with what had been a personal struggle is raising money to fund the lawsuit. I think that's a problem. It's not that anyone should stop filing these lawsuits. Obviously we can't afford to stop. They are almost always a last resort, the only wedge still holding a door open. But it's important to keep another aspect of the campaign active, even if it just seems like theater. The outcome of a struggle may, in substance, be determined by the courts, but regardless of what happens there, win or lose, there are other outcomes to every struggle: the agency the struggle gives the community, the legacy of a movement, the practice of participatory resistance. I really believe all court cases should be accompanied by other kinds of organizing—on the street, in real time, in public space. The health of democracy in the long run depends as much on the practice as it does on the outcome.

The Civil Rights Movement makes this so clear. It fought multiple cases in the courts all over the country, and put new laws on the desks of legislators. The decisions, the actual civil rights, were being made behind guarded doors, but the streets were crowded with public theater. That was how the story got told, the information passed: the lunch counters of Greensboro, Rosa Parks on the bus, crowds marching across the bridge in Selma. When it came time to resist the war in Vietnam, people remembered the public theater of the Civil Rights Movement.

Even today those actions are talked about in organizing meetings all over the world.

Every day I read remarkable stories coming out of the courts, incredible victories and bitter losses, but there is no public theater to marry these cases to, no way that I can participate in the struggle, win or lose. So when that struggle comes to me, when my community is threatened, when my park is sold off, will I know what to do? Will I have a way to resist other than letting the story drain into the courts, wait patiently for a result, and then accept the decision? Or will I stand in the street and shout across the rooftops: "Hey! People! Something is happening!"

And let's not forget the relief our "opposition" feels when unruly change-agents like us are finally well behaved, under the controlling gaze of legal protocol and the supposedly fair but nonetheless oppressive influence of the courts. I remember the first time a lawyer told me I probably should not get arrested while a lawsuit was pending, not only because it wouldn't "look good," but because it would make me harder to reach. We have to maintain the threat of action outside the system. And yes, justice may prevail, but even if it doesn't, we still win something when we play the story out in public space.

Our effort must be visible and memorable. The struggle for public space must take place in public space; it must be active and inclusive. Early in this campaign we determined that the restaurant was an insidious way for the city to control public assembly. The restaurant plan may or may not be a result of an organized, methodical effort to squelch dissent, but it is safe to say that the ideal conditions for consumerism are almost never the same as the ideal conditions for a civic democracy. If they can't shut public space down with laws and permits, they will shut it down with shopping.

Freedom is not a resting state, as Thomas Jefferson—or Janis Joplin—more or less said. What defines a public space ultimately is its active use by the people. We must use public space! Any gains we make defending Union Square from commercial encroachment come from being in the park, doing what has always been done there. The fastest way to reclaim public space is to go and get in it. The law that protects us there, the First Amendment, won't save you from being frisked, harassed, or even arrested. The only real authority in public space is public action. Bodies in space, talking and listening: The freedom starts there.

Sermon of the Wild Commons

REVEREND BILLY

This is the text of Reverend Billy's performance with the choir at the Highline Ballroom, in the meat-packing district of NYC, in the summer of 2008.

(A dedication, stately.)

Greetings, children! There never was a place like Union Square, at Broadway and 14th Street, for bringing together all the issues at once. Go stand there, between the Lincoln and Gandhi statues, and within an hour or two you can bet everything progressive that can possibly happen and the conservative reaction to it, will bristle up your skin.

The historic momentum of the place comes up constantly in another public "incident." The fourth Starbucks opens on the square and is opposed by a Fair Trade parade. A mysterious subcontractor cuts down old trees, and urban druids fly to the scene. Then a phalanx of cops rises on mopeds, and a brass band from Chicago called Hypnosis is pushed toward the curb, and a thousand new Americans shout "Sí, se puede!" and the Green Market makes a comeback in the shadow of Whole Foods. George Washington rises impassively on his great horse out of the din of the America that he created. His bronze right arm has been held aloft for a century, pointing out a glimmer of Heaven or Hell on the horizon.

(The message proper begins.)

Welcome to our Fabulous Worship at the Highline Ballroom in New York City's lovely meat-packing district! Welcome to you, the faithful stopshoppers, and to the newcomers, too. It is June first and we find ourselves on the hot cusp of summer.

So we are now six months away from that moment in the theological calendar of the Church of Life After Shopping, that confrontation that sums up our work, when at five o'clock on the morning after Thanksgiving, the choir and I face the cold at Macy's front door. There we try to hold back with singing and preaching that socially sanctioned door-busting herd of shopping sinners.

(Looking upward at the Highline ceiling like an astronomer pointing to constellations in a planetarium.)

Oh, I'm talking about Black Friday, or I'm talking about Buy Nothing Day, depending on which church you belong to! But for us, up here on this stage—that screaming festival of two-legged wildebeests with credit cards runs toward us six months in our past, and also six months in the future.

If we look out across the radius of the orbit the earth is spinning around the sun, there is our other self, where we were and where we will be. We are here on this whirling wet rock called Earth, and out there—oh, we are out there in cold space, trying to wrestle Christmas.

Back here, in feverish late spring, we are traveling, shifting; we make new relationships and visit old friends, too, and bask in strolling dates through the long, sweaty days, or follow the path of most resistance to some outrageous kink. This is a time of a loosening of imperatives, passionate encounters with ideas, with lovers, willful confusion and the acceptance of the new! Let's call the whole thing BURNING. Amen?

In the park, the birds are crying on the branches—drunk on the sex and ecstatically circling twigs and horsehair toward the hot spot of the nest. The leaves plunge up and the roots plunge down and the air, the rocks and leaves—all of it is sensually moving with a willful plan.

Oh! Absolutely nothing in this green fire has a logo on it! Life itself, lo and behold—life is not corporate-sponsored! No one gave Life permission! It's growing, changing . . . CHANGE-A-LUJAH!

(Walk to a new part of the stage to start over. To the choir:)

Thank you sexy gospelers. Amen!

Alright, let's talk about parks. What are they? Well, parks are wild public space. Wild? Wild, you say? Well, there is always a cultural struggle between letting a park stay in its natural state, or to civilize it—manicured and fenced and fertilized to within an inch of its life. In today's sermon we're plugging for the wild park. Amen?

Let's start with a wide-open definition of the wild commons. We are wild when we are making our own way without the judgment day of someone's fundamentalism, of the kings and cults and corporations. NO! We Stop Shopping!

This wild commons is protected within the freedoms of our First Amendment. The First Amendment is a force field of those forty-five words, the five freedoms: worship, speech, press, peaceable gathering, and protest. Let's sing it!

(Choir sings First Amendment Song:)

"Congress shall make no law, respecting an establishment of religion, or prohibiting the free exercise thereof; or abridging the freedom of speech, or of the press, or the right of the people peaceably to assemble and to petition the government for redress of grievances."

(Take a beat, walk again to a new spot, look up, use the planetarium stars and planets again.)

On Buy Nothing Day—way over there a half a revolution away—we know what we are opposing: the Christmas frenzy of hypnotized buying and excess and indebtedness.

But here at the burning time of late spring, we pursue something unknown under the protection of the First Amendment. When I try to write a sermon at this time of year, from inside that burning green life, I end up with mysterious contradictions. I stare at my old typewriter. There are phrases I have written that don't make sense—like "necessary eccentricity" or "zero tolerance for zero tolerance" or "we want the funk, gotta have the funk." It's the season of George Clinton, what can I say?

We used to have a song, remember choir? "We've gotta be surreal, gotta exorcise, gotta be impossible sometimes to understand." What does that mean? It's circusy here in the middle of the park, the edge of spring and summer, under the protection of the First Amendment—it's the Cyclone at Coney, it's screaming, changing, mutational, it holds something we never saw before to be self-evident . . . something happens that is impossible, but maybe it makes sense later, *it saves our life!*

We can keep that wildness alive by gathering once in a while in a non-corporate public place like Union Square. Then what? A big belief gets a shout? A new idea comes out of nowhere? An unexpected kiss? We don't know for sure.

It's all of life's mystery. Let's call what we have here The Fabulous Unknown. We've got an honorary transplanted Union Square inside the Highline today. We've got life rising in us. I'm feeling a nice chaotic intimacy in the air. Amen?

Spring becomes summer. Burning green. The Fabulous Unknown!

(Shift, up a step.)

I use the word "fundamentalist" to describe the kings and cults and corporations, those companies that surround our parks and want so badly to get in.

Because we live in the age in which fundamentalists can simulate their wild opponents, let's make sure we know what they are. The identifying characteristic? They have the answers to all questions.

They say: "Listen, little consumer. Life looks pretty scary. It begins you and it ends you and it doesn't explain why. Well, you don't worry. We have all the answers for you. *All* the answers. For instance, you want to know how to have freedom, democracy, all of that? Just don't you worry. Buy something and you'll know."

And so Union Square, like many commons around the world, is surrounded by these promises from Staples, Barnes & Noble, Starbucks, McDonald's, Toys "R" Us, Virgin Megastore, Whole Foods, H & M, Deisel, AT&T, Radio Shack. Any kind of happiness you can imagine is beamed into our greenery, where we might be sheltering our own poignant quandary about life.

The Fabulous Unknown versus The Fundamentalism of Shopping. That's the showdown.

(Matter-of-fact, even tough, speed up.)

After 9/11, when we stood in circles in Union Square and passed the talking stick, we started by not having answers. We were surrounded by the big smiling eyes of the missing loved ones posters of the 9/11 dead, the "Amy call home we miss you" scrawled in Sharpie ink. We passed the stick. The world hadn't solved the riddle of hate—and why? We're caught between Bush and bin Laden. And then we passed the stick to a new person. Each of us tried so hard to ask a new question, to get closer to "Why don't we have Peace?" And we passed the stick to another stranger.

We ended each day with a sea of questions and an action, say, a march thirty blocks to Times Square, toward the army recruiting center, The *New York Times* building, and the international media green zone.

(Sotto voce.)

How can we stop the bombs from falling? Have faith in that question and don't stop asking. Now, all these years since 9/11, the wars have made the question a wordless sigh. We don't ask it anymore. It isn't printable or audible in the air. In some way that we don't understand the war bombed the questions into the wrong answer. Amen?

(Back, for a series of declared statements.)

But always—our faith is in the First Amendment. It guards our questions and our questions have a way of creating a scenario, another life after Consumerism and Militarism.

The First Amendment is a protective law that can take the shape of a beautiful park. It leaves the wild-park-center for people to be with other people in a state of questioning, and that is not the state of governments or corporations.

A bold question is the radical seed of change.

This is the forgotten self-correction that was once imagined for our Democracy. It was supposed to be designed in by the balance of powers and the Bill of Rights. Now it is like a famous secret, whispered only by the strongest of the activist dead.

(No-nonsense tempo.)

Let's review today's message a moment. What ground have we covered? Where are we going in our journey?

You remember my dedication at the top? "And there never was a place like Union Square Park for bringing together all the issues at once. If we go stand there, between the Lincoln and Gandhi statues, within a few seconds everything progressive that can possibly happen and the conservative reaction to it, will bristle up your skin."

Union Square is a place for Radical Americans.

The arguments, songs, seductions, and pronouncements that marched out of America's wild commons. The defining moments in our history always originated in the wild grassy gathering places deep in the center of town—something very powerful there—and Union Square is one of those sacred places. The Continental Army's first stop when the British left New York. The May Day parades and open-air free university during the Depression and the vote-for-women marches and reproductive rights and anti-sweatshop and forty-hour work week rallies. You can feel the shouts of radical Americans put to entrenched power.

Change-a-lujah!

(Band strikes up, clear the air with Amens, change the lights, take a breath and begin again.)

Alright. It's June first today. And we have a park. A park is the natural world—it lives in the grasses, flowers, birds and bees, and trees. Amen? It is life, and life is the most concentrated form of mystery. Life is never really explained. It doesn't come to us in the form of an answer. Amen? And so we meet it with our admiring questions. Are you with me so far?

And there is in our park, in our wild commons, sex. It is sex that we hear and smell and walk through, sensual life that we share in the common air, especially here in the burning green of spring. Amen? Oh, and we have it in us, don't we? The natural world beneath our clothing—all the signals in our high-heeled shoes, perfume, the way we lean into our legs to step across the mysterious Earth. And when all this extra-curricular behavior comes to the parks we gaze, flirt, talk with strangers, hold hands, and we kiss.

Now we're getting somewhere! Kiss-a-lujah! Now hold on . . .

I've seen three couples side-by-side on a park bench going at it, lunch-hour necking. The non-kissing citizens love it, tolerate it, smile inwardly or outwardly from the memories it arouses. It is the life of the park. I believe the police like it too, but officially they must not let their smile lead them to temptation. Their uniforms and posture are like the fundamentalist walls against sexual contact or the free-thinking radical in the commons of America.

I walk the park a few times a week. I look toward its center and let the park's complex life come up in me. And I peer out of the trees at the international chain stores and gentrified eateries, and above them penthouses and fancy lofts. A few thousand wealthy people circle the park and want to privatize it. Someone anonymous gave $7 million to reconstruct the pavilion as a restaurant—and we don't know who the donor is. So there is just this ambient feel of money, a high-end mall with a park in the middle. It squeezes our five freedoms in the center, is always closing in, the logos press against the trees.

Let's break down this squeeze on the Unknown. The business improvement district is always remodeling the park. The BID wants to change the park to stylistically match the surrounding storefronts. The pavilion is supposed to frame a haute sip of a chardonnay, a crossing of one's elegant legs, the pause in the shopping that refreshes the power to continue shopping.

As in so much of Consumerism, there is a hidden Puritanism in the plan. Getting back to our sensual burning green park—these conspicuous consumers only tolerate public affection if we're dressed well enough, if we have the innocent flair of a Doisneau photo. Call it the Fundamentalism of Gentrification. Private police, uniformed with badges but with uncertain authority, nevertheless are on the alert for bad behavior, of the sexual or of the political variety, or just someone doing something original. The corporate cops can even write a ticket for "inappropriate shouting" in Union Square.

The "attack on the peaceable gathering" would be the ACLU's phrase for all of this. Gender rights activists might call it "the Death of Fun." It's that damn consumerizing fundamentalism, children. Terrified of the questions, they have the single and ever so simple fascist answer: "You come to Union Square to shop, and we shouldn't do anything to disturb the customer."

And we say, "Yes, absolutely! Disturb the customer! You just might be loving your neighbor!"

Corporate marketing and police—both want to guide how we meet each other in the public space, First Amendment be damned. Our flirtation is mediated by corporate gadgets. We're cell-phoning and Blackberrying, using the corporate minutes as foreplay. Our unsupervised check-me-outs and arrangements might lead to a kiss or something worse, a crowd of ruffians who question society uproariously. What are we up to, under the trees?

Wait a minute, children. Do you . . . do you think that they can mall-ize our park? Let's take it into our bodies. Take it into our bodies. Feel the First Amendment! The park's right over there through that wall! Feel it? Bill of Rights-a-lujah!

(Go from protest back to the kiss.)

We can neck with each other just a bit and all the corporations and police are left out in the cold. We can pray to the Fabulous Unknown and they won't be able to guess what that is. What can they do? Tap us on the shoulder and sell us prayer books? Sell us condoms? Sell us perfume? The weak link in the park-privatization campaign is that they have to retain control of the mysterious—human and otherwise—on the ground. They have to reach across cold space and control the burning green spring.

But in Union Square—we're not shopping. We have our own love. We have our kiss. We have our . . . CHANGE-A-LUJAH!

Extend a kiss back out to protest. Think about it. The amorousness of speaking and singing in public places. The poet Kenneth Patchen had a phrase, the "amorous orator in the village commons."

I have a dream today. Make love not war. Silence Equals Death.

Even Sí Se Puede and A Change You Can Believe In. These phrases were nourished in public space, often in historic commons where passionate sweaty, shouting, laughing, and singing Americans gathered without permits. Oh, yes, nervous corporations and police know enough history to know that governments change, oligarchies are broken up, the powerful retreat into helplessness—when we gather in public space in great numbers.

When Paul Robeson sang "America the Beautiful" from the steps of the pavilion, when Emma Goldman rose to address a thousand young women about reproductive rights, when Dorothy Day prayed for peace—suddenly that thing happened that resembles two kids kissing on the park bench. Ordinary living, just the earthy life in us creating its desire for a new future, leaves us to touch each other.

Remember the old Ray Charles song? "Do the mess around! Everybody's doin' the mess around!" Our communication then passes beyond the control of the powerful. We stand together holding hands under George Washington's statue. And Mahatma Gandhi is right there on the corner with his walking stick. Abraham Lincoln is back over there across the lawn.

Everyone! Kiss the person next to you! It is the beginning of power. Go ahead! it is the way to honor this historic place of change. Our activist ancestors are smiling! Amen!

Emma-a-lujah!

(Glory-time. Choir whooping it up now, the band rolling.)

Woody Guthrie said in one of his songs: "I'll meet any living person in a public debate at high noon on the green grass of Union Square."

The corporations have landed on our shores, have imprisoned our Emmas and Malcolms. The super-mall is now the dream of four-year-olds. Real wars are normalized in video games. Cancer-worshipping corporations are attacking life as we know it, the Earth itself. Does anyone here doubt that it is time to flex our First Amendment? We've got a freedom battle here.

And so what do we have to fight with in our grassy commons? Our dead heroes, and our First Amendment, our kiss . . .

We look out from our burning green spring into summer and what do we see? We see products. That's what the Devil has for bullets today: Walls hanging with and shelves piled with and windows brimming with products. Mob rule by buying. The barbarism of marketing every-thing.

They see the whites of our eyes. Now the products are flying through the air, hurled from the sides of buildings by seventy-foot-tall super models. The cell-phones and video games and lattes and plat-inum cards and roasted chickens and dollhouses and Stephen King books. Catapulted into our senses, into our park, crashing into the gravity of the First Amendment. It's a siege of our American protest his-tory.

The products drive us back to one little circle, with one talking stick, and we light it and make it a candle, and we pass it around and each of us testifies about freedom. How is the old notion of American freedom fighting still alive? We ask Lucy Parsons and Norman Thomas and An-gela Davis and A. J. Muste and Paul Robeson and Florynce Kennedy and Elizabeth Gurley Flynn and W. E. B. DuBois and Cesar Chavez and yes, Woody Guthrie—we feel the freedom you gave us . . .

(Big preaching, soar.)

Let us pray.
We ask the Fabulous Unknown!
We stand in the center of our wild commons on the cusp of
    summer!
We stand in the place of furious questions and first moments of
    sex!
Give us the power to pass the talking stick.
The power of burning green unlogo-able questions.
Our park is where our public life waits for effective love.
So that six months from now, on the far side of this circle in the
    sky,
We can stop the evil super-mall of Christmas, the conversion of
    giving to buying.
By not converting life-honoring questions to consumerized
    answers.
We will stop the invasion of this historic radical park by the mall
    that surrounds us,
The logos they lob into our forest clearing will be repelled by our
    conscience.

Give us the power to have the intensity of a questioning public
   life.
So that we're ready to face the products!
Take us there now! Open the door
Let's march to Union Square!

9. Iceland: Holding Back the Dam

Action Camp

SAVITRI D

Midnight here is murky, a jar someone washed their brush off in. You can see, but distance is a trick: Everything is much farther away than you think and there are apparently no shadows, or everything is a shadow. I can't tell.

Only a few roads run between places, and rural communities appear suddenly, each one a surprise, ringed by steaming vents and tiny churches with graves in their green yards. In places, the volcanic rock is blanketed by thick sod and delicate flowers; elsewhere the porous stone is completely barren. It is a spirited land and there are birds everywhere.

In the city, along the water, what at first glance appears to be sand is actually deeply colored sea glass, weathered and whittled down to gem-like nothings. Boats bob all along there, too, and small European cars, but very few people. Reykjavik is not a crowded place.

Windows have thick curtains in Iceland, for making night dark in summer, but the shine slips around the folds and under the cracks and somehow there is always just enough light to read. We are mystified by time. Every once in a while Billy asks if we should get up. "Is it morning?" he asks. "Is it time to get up?"

We are staying with O, a poet, who jokingly welcomes us to his ancestral home. It's crowded with books and oil portraits of men with beards. The mantle has bones on it, and rocks. An enormous stuffed raven perches above O's desk.

O has hair that sticks up and an old-fashioned face, and someone told me he has a whole other life in London, but it is hard to imagine him anywhere but in this house in this pale Icelandic summer of 2007, surrounded by maps and flyers and scattered photos.

Also at the house are activists from all over the world, all of them members or guests of the group called Saving Iceland. We are all here to keep big dams out of the last pristine wilderness in Europe. As many as thirty new hydroelectric dams are planned on Icelandic rivers by 2020. Thousands and thousands of hectares will be flooded. Unspeakably beautiful places will disappear forever. The dams are being built by a handful of corporations virtually unknown to the citizens of Iceland. They advertise in pamphlets at the G8 and the World Economic Forum. They make deals with governments, not people. They all have histories of environmental and labor abuses.

Accompanying the dams and their so-called "cheap" power is the promise of polluting aluminum smelters across the land. If flooding and destroying a wilderness is the price of power, can you still call it cheap? The foreign aluminum and energy companies, Alcoa, Rio Tinto, and Alcan, and the Icelandic energy company, Landsvirkjun, are thoroughly enmeshed in government policy. Symbols of Iceland's new international standing, they promise jobs and prosperity: a future. They have apparently inexhaustible resources and are highly motivated. The activists are looking up at a crowd of Goliaths.

There are 320,000 people in Iceland and about fifty of them are willing to get arrested for civil disobedience on behalf of a cause like "the wilderness." Of those, maybe half are willing to get arrested repeatedly and of those, maybe a dozen are willing to lock their necks and vulnerable parts to heavy equipment in the middle of nowhere. These few may be the ones who save Iceland.

Iceland's democracy is one of the oldest in the world. Its people have survived serious famines and difficult conditions for more than a thousand years. They live longer than any other population and have more local newspapers per capita than any other country. Public space is plentiful, but quieted by a reluctance to be rude or offensive, so a kind of insistent silence suffuses the squares and sidewalks.

In Iceland, as in the UK and much of Europe, consumerism pervades the culture. Shopping is a form of entertainment and retail and service jobs already make up a sizable sector of the economy. However, unlike the UK and much of Europe, Iceland was never industrialized, so the people never had to organize against the voracious appetite of heavy industry. Iceland did not determine its course to independence through restive social movements, but through expert language and courtly enterprise, maneuvering itself out from under almost one hundred years of Danish rule through a legal loophole while the Nazis held power in Copenhagen. At the point when we are there, a little more than a year before the banking collapse, there has been virtually no history of radical social movements in Iceland; only a few people remember the riots that erupted when Iceland joined NATO in 1949 and invited American military bases onto their soil, effectively militarizing the country and bringing it into the Cold War.

Iceland remains a member state of NATO and, though it is also a member of the European Economic Trading Zone, it has never joined the European Union. Its citizens enjoy more personal liberties than those in almost any country in the world and have elected female majorities in both houses of government. In many ways, Iceland resembles progressive northern European countries like Denmark and Norway and most people would guess it has a similarly serious, forward-thinking ecological policy. It does not. The Icelandic economy has very little in common with its allies and former rulers on the European continent. Fish and cheap power are its only easily commodified resources, and the Icelandic government has made no secret of its eagerness to exploit the potential of both. Thus Iceland is far more vulnerable than its neighbors to the whims and demands of globalized markets, as it has no manufacturing base and lacks a substantial financial sector of its own.

Iceland also lacks racial and ethnic minorities; even religion is monolithic with more than eighty percent of the population claiming membership in the national church. Its inward-looking conformity results from a fairly homogenous population and conditions harsh enough to inspire cooperativeness and collectivism. Well into the twentieth century, long winters and chronic food shortages forced people to work together. The urge to wait and see what the rest of the group thinks and decides is very basic to Icelandic culture. One question facing activists now is: Who, exactly, constitutes the group and does it include corporations?

In Iceland, as in so many places, corporate capitalism is completely

integrated into everyday life. The presence of multinational corporations just seems perfectly natural, so natural that envisioning a future
without them is almost impossible. We aren't just loyal to them, we are
them. And so the people of Iceland call non-Icelandic activists intrud-
ers, but would never think of a company like Alcoa as an intruder,
much less the cruel raider it is.

It's a culture of mixed but logical signals—freedom married to uni-
formity, direct democracy in the shadow of serious conformity. We are
greeted by various forms of hostility at every turn. Xenophobia, name-
calling, the empty claim that the problem can't be addressed by anyone
except experts, seem strained and defensive—efforts to keep the heart-
break at bay and avoid the hard work of change. Saving Iceland's best
hope may be to get the place talking, and then stall the projects long
enough for the group to sway their compatriots toward protecting their
most precious resource, the land itself.

O has been following our work for years and invited us to come. I don't
think he has illusions about what it would mean to the people of Iceland to be shouted at by an American preacher dressed like Elvis. I
don't think he expects they would actually listen, or that we would
change their minds, but O has an instinct for the long-term course of
the struggle in Iceland. He tells us we could, at least, "rattle the per-
versely good mannered lot of them a bit."

A large group of us caravans to the southeast of Reykjavik for a four-
day summit on the land of a sympathetic farmer, where there is a small
building with toilets and running water and a conference room for
meetings. As we arrive the kitchen crew is hoisting an enormous mess
tent in the rocky field alongside the modest building, while giant pots
steam on the camp stoves. Billy and I are staying in a wooden hut down
the road, heated and powered by geothermal energy, with a hot pool
on the porch, a lovely little kitchen and a cave-like sleeping room.

The farmer's place lies on a long sloping meadow, beneath a series
of weathered, grass-covered buttes. As everywhere in Iceland, mysterious piles of rocks appear out of nowhere, thrown down from the heav-
ens by a careless god. The scenery is less dramatic than in other parts of
the island, but easy access from the city ensured that more kinds of
people could come to the conference, which would precede the less inclusive Action Camp. And come they do: families and couples and lon-

ers and bands of students, in bursts and streams, for talks and meetings, lectures, screenings. It is a four-day immersive course in heavy industry, and we hear amazing stories of anti-aluminum and anti-dam activism from around the world.

Attilah Springer speaks about the morning she realized she would have to do something about the smelter coming to her Caribbean community in Tobago. She and the women in her neighborhood started marching against the smelter, getting in the way, and she started writing more and more about the situation, surprising herself with her own obsessiveness, managing finally to grab the attention of non-local press outlets and then quickly building enough momentum against Alcoa to stop the smelter in a few years.

Cirineu da Rocha, from the Dam-Affected People's Movement in Brazil, talks us through less heartening situations along the tributaries of the Amazon, the increasingly precarious situation indigenous tribes face there. Da Rocha is a fierce Communist, of a kind we almost never encounter in the US, and his ideological language somewhat overshadows the details of his stories, but he finishes with a rousing call for an international workers movement against industry—still a good idea!

Helen B, a leader (she wouldn't want to be called that) of the roadless movement in the UK, describes protecting a much-loved hill from being turned under, paved and made into a highway. She describes the slow epiphany she and her fellow activists experienced defending the hill, not a dramatic wild treasure, not an unsurpassed and beautiful rarity —just a little hill with soft grass and a few trees and occasional flowers on its slopes. It can all be important, she says. We have to learn, she says, to make it all important.

Lerato Maregele of EarthLife South Africa tells us about actions in the heart of an industrial development zone (IDZ, aka export processing area, zona maquiladora, zona libre). IDZs are the black sites of globalized trade. Sometimes these miniature free trade zones are homes to distribution centers, sometimes factories, sometimes heavy industry. They make use of local labor and resources, but are exempt from VAT and other taxes, and exist in regulatory limbo, unbound by local laws. The zones are hyper-dystopian and openly militarized. The pitched contests between corporations and communities along their edges are crystalline visions of the impact of global capital on local communities—the killing fields of Juarez, the poisoned wells of Nairobi, the

chronic food shortages in Haiti. Lerato describes how the unfair alloca-
tion of public power to a smelter resulted in severe power shortages in
the surrounding country, affecting everything from hospitals to
schools to meal preparation in homes. She and a handful of people
started a long-term blockade at the gates of the IDZ, protesting the
quasi-privatization of public utilities as well as the damaging environmental impact of the smelter. She ends her presentation with a song,
"My mother was a washerwoman. My father was a gardener. That's why
I'm a socialist."

These human responses, acts of resistance led by relatively small
groups against powerful corporations almost always in league with governments and international development agencies like the International Monetary Fund (IMF) and the World Trade Organization (WTO),
are apparently simple, almost humble, but they are the natural response of a complex organizing system: community. As an organizing
principle, it is one of the most basic building blocks, the evolutionary
result of hundreds of thousands of years of cooperative ingenuity. Listening to the stories, I have the profound sensation that we almost always already know what to do. We get mired in strategy, but most of
the time we do know what to do. The trick is getting enough people to
do it.

That night Billy and I walk away from our house into the fields.
About an hour into our walk the wind picks up and suddenly it is so
windy that I am leaning into the wind horizontally, like some crippled
sailboat just inching along at a terrible off-course angle. We laugh for
the first few minutes, but the situation begins to feel almost threatening. We lie down flat just to get a break; the volcanic rock covered over
by about a foot of loamy grass makes a perfect mattress, and were it not
for hunger and descending temperature we could have stayed the night
there.

We slog on in the wind, heading toward what is closest, which is
sadly not our home, but a gas station/convenience store perhaps three
miles away. An hour later it seems maybe a little bit closer, but not
much. We continue tacking, lacking an alternative, and finally on the
road a few hundred yards away we see a jeep slow and then stop. A man
stands on his sideboard and yells something in Icelandic. We start running (not very fast) toward him, and finally collapse on his car. He tells
us he and his wife were going to the store for a movie DVD; do we want

a ride? We slide into the backseat, speechless. These people are wonderful! We collect ourselves in the three minutes it takes to get to the store. The couple is going straight back on the same road so we can ride back with them too. A miracle!

The store is foodless, more like an emporium of vice and decay—just cigarettes, booze, movies, magazines, and an outrageous amount of candy. I buy some salty licorice, a Norwegian favorite, and stand in the window watching the wind. A small herd of dreamy Icelandic horses lingers just on the other side of the highway. They have an unnerving direct stare and seem never to move. We get in the jeep and head back toward our house. Then the man, who clearly knows we are visitors, but must have mistaken us for tourists, misled by Billy's Italian sports jacket, begins to warn us about the dirty hippies, the commies, staying on his neighbor's farm, how there are even "colored" people there. I can feel my heart starting to race and see Billy's eyes jumping around. Finally, Billy shouts over the wind moaning around the car, "That's us! Thank you for noticing us and our friends and thank you for saving us from the wind. We're gonna stop the big dams—we're gonna try!" We ride on. Another Iceland pony stares at us from the dark field, her mane streaming.

That night I am actually sore and feel as if I had been in a fight. For the first time since we had been in Iceland we sleep through the night. The next morning we walk the two miles over to the camp. We ruminate on the previous night's mix of generosity and fear in the jeep. When we'd gotten out, I'd offered, "Isn't Iceland a magical place?" The wind is gone. And we get dive-bombed by birds on the road. At the camp, Billy gives a sermon about Crazy Horse. I keep thinking how much the sloping field outside the window reminds me of the Little Big Horn, Lakota Country, the greasy grass.

After lunch we are invited to sit in on an all-Icelandic meeting in which a wide range of locals/natives talk about "next steps." There's tension in the room, and certainly ideological and tactical distance between the groups, some obvious—say, the differences between anarchist youth and an elder journalist—and some more subtle—the professional artists, for instance, versus the ruralists. The discussion revolves around whether to build, or try to build, a unified Icelandic movement against heavy industry, or to work separately. At times it seems the conversation will collapse and I think of how many times I have witnessed the gut-wrenching decay of meetings—sometimes the result of insurmountable racial and class barriers or gender differences, but more often the result of a perceived possibility that a racial or class or gender-preference "problem" might arise. In New York City much of the work of activism is just getting a representative group of people in a room together. Are we labor enough? Are we black enough? Are we gay enough? Are we New York enough?

It is sort of wonderful to see the exact same conversation about representation taking place among a group of apparently genetically identical people from a fairly narrow social class, and it reminds me that clarifying difference is at the very core of becoming a decision-making body (so obvious when you see it, but so easily forgotten when caught up in the urgency of a cause). We navigate the scope of difference to arrive at consensus, or at least tolerant agreement. Doing so requires that we temporarily expand and overemphasize our differences, perceived or real. Sometimes in the expansion, the distance seems too great to bridge. We talk about how different we are for so long we suddenly *are* different, too different, and can't think of anything else to say. Fortunately, after about ninety minutes, the Icelanders agree to move forward, toward action, strategies, and goals.

At this point they ask "the outsiders" to share our perceptions and reflections of the conversation and I tell them how much they have in common. I say the distance they have to travel, just to agree on anything, seemed almost imperceptible to me, though I know to them it was absolutely vivid. I ask them if their urge to find common ground and similarities might leave them more diffuse, diluted, or if they might perhaps be made stronger by amplifying and accepting their differences. In some instances, it can be our differences that protect us, that make us more complex than our institutional adversaries. This approach would play out in both directions—our responses to their moves and their responses to ours. Aren't our motives less obvious, less discernible, even less rational, because we have so many reasons to defend land, reasons far more varied than the single, obvious motive of extraction/profit that industry has? We defend land because we love it or because we are ideologically opposed to capitalism or because we own it or we don't think anyone should own it. We are bothered by the impact of development on animals or the impact on humans; some of us are xenophobic, some spiritually motivated, some of us think industry is ugly, and some just hate change. If we manage to get enough people in the room so that we do have this accumulation of the strange, wild, and unreasonable—we're dangerous.

Later we have a discussion—mostly in the form of questions, most of which go unanswered—about what we want to achieve in this work that would take place over the summer, including the direct action and the friendly outreach to media and the people. Do we want to reach the Icelandic people? The media? The government? Can we start a broad social movement in Iceland? Do people understand the facts? Can this battle be won outside Iceland? Who is not here who should be here? How many Icelandic people will it take to sway the whole country? Can we speak for Iceland? Which people are most open to our message? Will people listen to anyone who isn't speaking Icelandic?

Things move quickly, and by the end of the meeting we have a written statement and a plan for the next days of action.

We are going to the mall, since there are more people in one place there than anywhere else, and since as far as anyone can remember, no one has ever done anything remotely disruptive in a mall in Iceland, not even PETA, so the general consensus is that it will be unsettling, hard to ignore, and as we say in the Church of Stop Shopping, "RUPTUROUS!"

Twenty-five of us go to Kringlan Mall with banners and noisemakers and flyers. The mall is like all the other malls in the world. This one has a traveling exhibit that I happened to see at the United Nations a year ago. Photographs of people doing extraordinary things: athletes and scientists and artists and soldiers and explorers from all over the world, their enormous courageous faces, the very shape of human triumph. There is not an activist among them.

Billy is bellowing in the food court on the third floor. People seem bothered by the noise, and mistaking Billy for a "real" Christian, they ask us "please" not to "preach." I am handing out flyers about the dams and smelters, but people seem afraid of the information and refuse to take them. Billy keeps booming. I can hear the rest of the crew making their entrance on the lower level and we move to join them for a triumphant moment on all three levels of escalators. Just as we begin our descent, three security guards appear and spirit Billy away behind the Burger King. It's almost a record: three minutes to arrest. I move down the escalator and signal the contingency plan. Snorri, a young man of twenty, wears Billy's other suit and collar. He has a beautiful earthen voice and a rail-thin frame. He stands loose inside the suit and wails in Icelandic. Every once in a while he sings "Amen." We all respond, "Amen!" kneeling at his feet while others dangle an enormous "STOP THE DAMS" banner from the balcony. We are really loud. I feel the Icelandic politeness slipping away. Some shoppers are noticeably disgruntled, but others seem curious. Snorri starts a singing parade. We move through the mall handing out flyers. We are too many for the security detail, and so far the regular police haven't appeared. I look for the girl who is supposedly doing legal support, can't find her, and I leave the parade and run to the door in the food court where I last saw Billy. It's a claustrophobic maze of white concrete stairs and hallways. I start to run, looking for an open door, a sign, anything. I start shouting, "Billy! Billy!" as loud as I can. Amazingly, I hear his voice: "Savitri? Savitri?" I stop running . . . Billy? Savitri? Billy?

I think he is above me. I make for the stairs and turn down a hallway. Billy? He is farther away now. "Hold still!" I say. "No, you hold still," he says and I stop moving. We carry on this way, echo-locating, until he emerges from a door on a landing above me. We run down the stairs and out a door into a parking lot. We are sweating, gasping for breath. We take a moment to assess.

We make it to the side entrance just as the parade, still led by Young Reverend Snorri, approaches from within. The parade has grown. They are pushing an impressive armada of empty shopping carts of all sizes. They are loud, excited, and now there are real cops just behind Billy and me, pushing us through the door, back into the mall, as if to get us out of sight, as if we might be less threatening inside the mall. This occurs just as the security guards inside push the parade out the door. We meet in a glassed-in foyer, which happens to be full of news cameras rushing to the breaking story: Handsome Icelandic reporters trapped in a sunny cage with cops on both sides and activists bursting through toward them. We are singing. Billy starts a shaking exorcism in the charged moat, a prayer to the river gods: "You hidden beings in the waterfalls! You are in our dreams! Burst the dams in our imaginations!" It is fun now, strange and fun.

Back in New York the next week, we anxiously read the reports, watch the jerky videos, and send our encouragement. Attilah and Lerato have gone on a weeklong tour of small, remote communities and have been telling their stories to the people whose lives would be most directly affected by the dams and smelters. Meanwhile blockades and lockdowns were occurring almost daily back at the Action Camp. The activists were scaling heavy equipment, dropping banners, stopping traffic, invading corporate offices, and all the while getting brutalized by overzealous, undertrained police forces. Some Icelandic media seem to concede the issue, agreeing that the plans would be harmful, but the media uniformly decry the oppositional tactics, and activists are predictably vilified, called dirty, violent, dangerous, worse. Still they keep on through the end of the camp and then on into the winter months.

A year later, in the summer of 2008, they once again hold an Action Camp, and successfully disrupt and stop construction and work at several smelters and future dam sites. Many arrests take place, along with massive campaigning on the streets, and parallel actions at consulates and corporate offices in Europe as well. It seems there is more and more public support, though the activists are still demonized and treated badly by both the police and the media. "That's okay," I am told. "We don't care if they like us as long as they are listening." The cause draws a wave of international attention that seems to ignore the work of the activists entirely, but is nonetheless a direct result of their work, and I certainly feel they are making progress. Björk, the most famous Icelandic person in the world, and Sigur Ros, a famous Icelandic band, are getting behind the cause. There are glimmers of hope.

Then, in October 2008, as world financial markets start their slide, Iceland experiences a near total economic collapse. At the time, Icelandic debts exceed the nation's gross domestic product of 14 billion euros by six times. Staving off total disaster, Iceland nationalizes its three major banks, separates the domestic accounts from foreign accounts, and defaults on foreign debts. Inflation jumps to eighteen percent overnight and the banks lock their doors. Iceland immediately starts negotiating with the IMF for bridge loans. The Althing (parliament) goes into emergency session and the Icelandic people take to the streets en masse, surrounding the parliament in Reykjavik for weeks on end, demanding an immediate resignation of the government.

The Icelandic government finally resigns in January of 2009, and a left-wing coalition is formed within a week.

Iceland was just the front wave of the global collapse. Within months of their crisis the entire international financial system had plummeted into apparently inexorable and permanent chaos. It seemed like an opportunity, a game changer. Headlines read as if they had been lifted verbatim from Billy's sermons: "Retail Economy Unsustainable," "Development Hinged on Unsound Financing and Corruption," "Shoppers Stop Shopping, Start Saving." We were looking at pictures of empty ships lined up in ports throughout Asia. Big auto companies were renting thousands of acres of parking lots to house their unsold cars. In Dubai, foreign workers were abandoning their cars in airport parking lots and taking the first flight home, leaving mortgages and credit card debt. It was the Shopocalypse!

We knew that the proposed solution to the crisis would resemble the cause of the crisis and that the world, at least the human world, was not ready for, and had no provisions for, a real course change. Bailouts, duct tape, and hastily printed money would save the day, avert a great depression, get things back on track.

As the global economy collapsed, aluminum prices fell drastically, mostly a result of the slowdown in the manufacturing of airplanes, automobiles, and all the various things that use aluminum (except, of course, the weapons trade, which continues its incredible expansion). So there was also cause for optimism, with aluminum so cheap and abundant that the profit motive for creating smelters for companies like Alcan, Alcoa, and Rio Tinto disappeared. This is where the wicked nature of the IMF really shines through, because the IMF has power vast enough to offer conditional grants and loans to nations like Iceland, and the resources to subsidize the aluminum industry in Iceland. This is exactly why we always remind people that the free market isn't really free.

Reports from 2009's Saving Iceland Camp made it clear they have absolutely no confidence that the collapse saved them from environmental disaster. Development is slowed, but still on course, though the players have shifted a bit. In late May 2009, Iceland elected a right-wing government, which seemed a bitter turn to many, but may have liberated the environmental movement a little. Claimed and unattributed actions show a rather more fearless and far less polite tone. An enormous banner was dropped from the highest point of the largest church in Iceland saying, "FUCK YOU ICELAND. Signed, Aluminum."

And someone has taken to gluing shut the doors at the homes of CEOs from the energy companies, making it just a little more difficult for them to go to work destroying the earth.

I think it is safe to say the activists of Iceland are no longer waiting to see what the group will do. People tell us there is at least the habit of action now, after the economic protests, when so many people were in the streets. The general move of so many people into public space shook up the status quo and even if it settled to the right, it still made for new space, new roles. Maybe just being exposed to activism makes room on the edges. "They can't quite call us freaks anymore, since we were all standing together in the street just a few months ago," a Saving Iceland activist explains.

Letter to Saving Iceland

REVEREND BILLY

A year ago we were with you in Iceland, the land of fire and ice and spirits. This year we get your news and images on the computers. Congratulations on the Century Aluminum Smelter blockade. You slowed down the output from that day, July 21, 2008. You're saving lives! Every hour that an F-16 is not yet in the air . . .

Wandering your website, I remember my sermon last year, in which I tried to conjure the memory of Crazy Horse and bring his spirit to your struggle for Iceland. Savitri remembers the recurring phrase, "The land is innocent and powerful." I don't remember much of the specifics of my talk that afternoon. I was overwhelmed by the beauty of the river valley from our windows and simultaneously by my boyhood love of the stories of Crazy Horse, from when my family lived in the Dakotas.

Putting your bodies on the line against the big extraction industries as you do—your work has so much dangerous hope in it. You teach us that the quixotic Crazy Horse strategy is also the practical one.

Your volcanic wilderness with its geysers and glaciers and cascading rivers—to Savi and me it feels like the American West. It is as if Yellowstone and the Alaskan fjords and the Black Hills were concentrated on this island just below the Arctic Circle.

Savitri and I went west last year. We returned to South Dakota, to the Black Hills and Mount Rushmore, which towers over the flat part of the state to the east, the four burdened-looking presidents' heads gazing from the mountain. It's like having giant rolls of paper bills, with Washington, Jefferson, Teddy, and Abe glowering down on the little prairie towns.

But behind the presidents stands another mountain and another leader emerging: the Crazy Horse Memorial. The great brave is rising year by year from the mountain, and as he rises on his pony he is pointing east at—what?—the United States advancing toward him. The Crazy Horse Memorial was the idea of the sculptor Korczak Ziolkowski and the Lakota Chief Henry Standing Bear. Ziolkowski's family helped build Mount Rushmore and got to know the native people, then began to convert the mountain into Crazy Horse in 1948. The work has been continued by the family and the tribe these last sixty years.

Crazy Horse. He studies us from the horizon-line. He will always sit on horseback in the sky, just beyond our American border that comes toward him in the form of a spray of bullets.

After the Civil War, the victorious United States Army turned its attention west toward the Indian territories. In the 1870s, the Iron Horse rode the rail all the way to the Black Hills on the edge of the Dakotas and Wyoming. The extractive industries were coming in as the larger wildlife—wolves, eagles, and buffalo—were killed off and any natives who might lay claim to the land were forced into new treaties and escorted to reservations. However, a large group of Sioux and Cheyenne migrated farther west in the 1870s, out of the reservation system. Tatanka Yotanka, known to us as Sitting Bull, a Hunkpapa Sioux, was the trusted leader and seer.

In 1876, the Seventh Cavalry of the United States Army marched into eastern Montana looking for this moving village. Major General George Armstrong Custer took the lead. Custer was a tall, handsome Civil War hero, a German American from Ohio, a kind of proto movie star. Custer was known for fearlessness in combat at Gettysburg and Bull Run. He led the division that trapped Robert E. Lee on the final day of the war at Appomattox. The natives called him Yellow Hair.

On June 25, 1876, eleven years after his heroism at the end of the Civil War, Custer's men discovered Sitting Bull's encampment and attacked it. They found, though, that no one was there to suffer their attack; all the fighters had slipped away. Within forty-eight hours, those fighters—a combined force of Sioux, Northern Cheyenne, and Arapaho warriors, led by the young Lakota Sioux war chief Tashunca-uitco (known to us Crazy Horse)—out-flanked, trapped, and overwhelmed the Seventh Cavalry. Custer and his 268 men died there. The Sioux called this The Battle of the Greasy Grass. Americans of European descent have called it The Battle of Little Big Horn, or Custer's Last Stand.

Crazy Horse, an Oglala Lakota Sioux warrior, was born on Rapid Creek near the present-day Rapid City, South Dakota. His birth name translates as "In the wilderness." His adult name—as we know it, "Crazy Horse"—doesn't have the humor of the more accurate translation: "His horse is crazy!" But despite this lighthearted name, the man was known for his self-possession and quiet. He rarely spoke. His life was forever marked by an attack on his childhood village by the US Cavalry. From that point, the young Crazy Horse began to experience the trance visions he would have for the rest of his life.

In preparation for battle, Crazy Horse was known to cover his horse with dirt, and then cover himself, too, and then ride into enemy lines right through the astonished enemy warriors, whose arrows and bullets would slow down, as if they were falling through clear honey. He whooped, in his trance—acting Crazy!—moving in and out of all that mean-spirited cutting metal. Crazy Horse whirled and leaped and charged all the way up to the enemy war chief and clapped him on the shoulder and let out his signature raging laugh. Then he'd suddenly appear someplace else.

Crazy Horse sliced his way back through entire battles. It was believed that he did not scalp his opponents; he demoralized them. He knew the rhythms and depth of focus of his enemy. He made them see things. He created a parallel world.

Crazy Horse always returns us to the relationship between the fantastic and the practical. He is famous for his call to his warriors, "Hoka Hey! Today is a good day to die!" He knew death well and how its closeness could create his untouchability. It seemed that Crazy Horse could re-play the slaughter of his childhood village when he entered a battle. He used his nightmare to vanish.

And he is uncatchable to this day. No one can square his personal facts. He is unverifiable. He was never photographed (and yet we are sculpting a mountain of him). Like the hapless men of the Seventh, historians strike out at this blurring brave, but can't make contact. Throughout his life he was seen here and there across the Great Plains, sometimes showing up in two or three places at once. No one knows where he is buried.

But for activists, Crazy Horse is very clear. He has a gift for us.

From the high, grassy ridges of the Little Big Horn, Crazy Horse studied the trajectory of Yellow Hair. First there was the speed of the cavalry, from Fort Lincoln to the east on a two-day marathon deep into Indian Territory. Less than a week before, Custer spurned offers of reinforcements, or faster-firing, heavier guns—all for speed. The "westward ho!" jerked Custer's focus farther west, into a harsh dream that stabbed at the horizon. Crazy Horse let him fly by, like a Tai Chi practitioner using the opponent's momentum.

On that day in 1876 as Yellow Hair squinted at the western horizon, he could see only his idea of progress. He was taking the measurements of national borders, of ranches and mines and railroads. Custer's neurotic hurry, riding the dying horse of his own myth, warped his military science. He wanted what all corporations want: Expansion and expansion. He ran his men west to claim square miles of natives, of buffalo, of gold . . .

Crazy Horse waited in his silence as the American raced toward the phantom village that would pull him in. Crazy Horse knew that he and his men could slow down as the cavalry sped up, and become invisible, lost in the grass, float up as a cloud, suddenly fall from the sky like the killing point of an arrow.

He covered himself with earth. Let's take that literally. The natural world has a lot to teach us activists. Take a few square feet of prairie grasses and the information is there for the asking. Follow a bird or animal for a few hours—it's all there. You've got your retreats, flight, circlings-around, counter attack. There are the endless disguises, like the killdeer bird who lures a predator away from her chicks by pretending to have a broken wing. There's the ever-present strategical music and camouflage. It's all there: Magic acts abound, swallowings, floats, upside-down bark-clingings, every kind of hiding and surprise tactic, murder mysteries of jealous poisons and quick flights into weightlessness.

I'm serious. Before battle get away from people and ask for directions.

Crazy Horse's instructor was the Great Plains. He returned always to his people and his land, his beloved Black Hills. He spoke repeatedly of his ancestors buried there, all around him, their power rising in a noiseless stream in the grass and trees. He knew the wind, the direction of it around storms. He knew what sounds would travel how far. He was a hunter. The scent in the wind fed him and his family. Custer and his men were running blind into a very sophisticated information system.

It seems to me that remembering your native knowledge of the land of fire and ice and spirits is a key to taking on the aluminum companies. The superior shape-shifting that you need from your fellow Icelanders, so that the corporations cannot manage your opinions and values, will take a very old power, from before corporations, even from before modern history.

Native Iceland is the perfect opposite of Consumerism, the opposite of this rushing Custer-like glitz—which is the final erasure of any nativity. And you call yourselves Saving Iceland! And that is the right name. It also means remembering Iceland. And what would Crazy Horse say? He would say that the earth guides, teaches, saves us. He would say that the land saves us.

When you joined Savitri and me in the action, taking the church service into the Kringlan super mall in Reykjavik, we were representing the wild rivers of Iceland in our human form. You met us at the airport and took us directly to the land of Iceland. You took us to the rivers, to the land beyond the edge of Reykjavik. We became haunted by something as you took us deeper into Iceland.

The representatives of Alcoa and Rio Tinto and Alcan would want to call us mall-invaders "romantic" and "eccentric" and "dangerous." That is how the mall spokesperson portrayed us to the press. Anything to delegitimize us before polite Icelandic society, but preaching about the rivers flows in a media all its own. People would speak of our church as if we were a crashing river full of potential electricity raging through the aisles in the land of simulated satisfaction. We were shouting to save the rivers, and we got our power from the rivers.

We defined the battle with Iceland as our language. The retailers lost control of the messaging of the mall. Their regime of appropriate consumer behavior was interrupted easily, by our ritual play-acting—a preacher and a make-believe church that became a native preacher shouting in Icelandic—we became more real as the shock wore off. If we succeeded as I think we did, then big retail was shown to be a fake religion itself, with the display booths, mannequins, and shilling celebrities in giant six-color prints.

Sensing the ease of our interruption, shouting about rivers, singing that we need to Save Iceland—we were left to wonder about the power of Iceland inside these big boxes. What revolutions in personal perspective would disrupt these passive consumers in this mall if an Earth-inspired community poured through the electronic doors?

Let's just go to the radical statement. We are made of the Earth. We are the Earth. We will save ourselves by saving Iceland. We are a river of charged blood and shouting air and we came from out there somewhere, and now we are an unstoppable flood . . .

The burden of all activists worldwide is to find where the corporations can be out-flanked. Their retail outlets, where they take cash from hypnotized consumers, the "Point of Purchase"—that is a weak point in their defenses, we believe. We have worked hard at aggressive ritual-making at the cash registers of the big-box sweatshop companies. With one hand on the register and one hand in the air, we watch a jolt go through the bodies of our American shoppers. There is an equivalent in Iceland. As Crazy Horse discovered with his penetrating study from the high ridge, there is a way to defeat an enemy who pretends to be speeding from the future.

Saving Iceland: Iceland will save itself partnering with you. Iceland knows the point of purchase, the vulnerable chink in the armor, of the aluminum companies. There is a way to out-flank them and overwhelm them. Let's go down deeper into the notion that Iceland holds in its life its own best defense.

You have extreme animism here. Your famous lovelings, flying sprites with spells coming out of their wands. You have the Huldufólk, the "hidden people," the elves and faeries. They are so thoroughly sensed by Icelanders—it's hardwired into your culture, like the belief in angels in the United States. You have told me that highways actually curve around suspected towns full of the hidden citizens. The Kringlan super mall was itself forced to re-design its foundation because of the belief that spirits would be upset by the original plan.

You see you have your Unknown. Your ancestors have left you a map for vanishing and re-appearing, as has Crazy Horse. And Big Hydro can try to dam you, but you fly, you dig, you transubstantiate, and there you are again. You have your own greasy grass.

Iceland is still becoming. It seems to be arriving from the deep, struggling with steam shooting and glaciers descending and volcanic fire and weirdly blue pools in the crevices. The consciousness from all of time presses against everyday life. It's tragic, but it makes sense that the war companies would find so much electricity by placing their turbines in these rivers. Our sense of hope comes from the inevitable feeling that all this energy is formed by beings, consciousness, the hidden people doing their job. Your island is haunted in the most practical way.

The Icelandic people are famous for being reserved, polite. The mountains, on the other hand, shout with their fire and ice. And it is a given that Iceland has very few people. There are sweeping vistas that have no houses. That land, though, is saturated with flamboyant nether-people engaged in stories that everyone knows, involving every sort of plot twist. You have an important clue here. Alcoa has already been forced to make concessions and give assurances that the Huldufólk and elves would not be displaced before the construction of one of its smelters. The Icelandic people had to be satisfied that attention was paid.

Your hidden people require their own kind of Environmental Impact Statement (EIS), then. The environment is defined to include the invisible personalities. The corporations have managed to keep the EIS of this kind separate from its impact reports on reindeer, harbor seals, pink-footed geese, and rare invertebrate species. I'm speaking of the Karahnjukar dams. Your strategy could combine the two, and let the spirits of nature imbue all the opposition to the dams, so that the specter of the entire earth stands before the corporate strategists. The endangerment of life in this last great wilderness of Europe cannot be separated into powerless parts, with the Huldufólk consigned to cultural superstition, and the bird species to the concern of ornithologists, and so on. Make their earthy opposition all one power. Spook 'em! The

Sioux painted their faces and screamed bloodcurdlingly, as they represented the whole rage of the violated Earth.

Your Icelandic elders, who have lived for all those seasons of midnight suns, tell stories that come from those mountains. When the old
ones talk—that's when we can really feel the power that cannot possibly be dynamited into the shape of the new, corporate rivers. Like Puck,
Oberon, and Titania in *A Midsummer Night's Dream,* the hidden people
are caught up in mischievous adventures. They are not bad or good, so
much as interested in change and even chaos. The native Iceland stories come to the light like angry life, like the fire and ice, and don't you
think they will call out to you before the river dies?

It is easy for a latter-day westerner to be suspicious of such talk to
the point of laughing out loud at the idea of a post-ironic effort to communicate with the Earth. We can dispense with a hipster's derision of
warmed-over indigenous rituals of the New Age variety. We don't have
time to be self-conscious. Just go for it. Fake it till you make it in the direction of the hidden people of your island. Eventually partner spirits
will come.

Progressive activism has long ignored the ancient bridge to the in-
effable, while favoring strategies that are often redoubts of intellectual-
ism that only academics can understand. Perhaps we identify the old
ways as weak, as we watch the indigenous people fall before the on-
slaught of the globalized economy. Nevertheless, in our work in the
Church of Life After Shopping, we have found that all people retain old
working souls whose relationship with the spirits of the natural world
is still going strong. It is an act of remembering something that we
can't Google. In our work, we have seen many different kinds of people
energized by a memory that precedes and then prevails over the coer-
cive faith of corporations.

You do have allies, the living things that Icelanders have accepted
from the land. The land is innocent and must be defended, but the
land is powerful also and gives you the opening for your response. The
Huldufólk are whispering to you. The defenders on your national seal
are the eagle, the great fish, the giant, and the bull. Let the other world
throw its voice through your mouths. Now that's a rebel shout! And
this will be a more straightforward, compelling kind of talk to the Icelandic people than the pallid stories of corporate marketing. All the

myths of this island are full of revolution. Every Icelander will recognize what you are doing, not via the news only, but from the Earth.

Well, Saving Icelanders, all of you brave souls! You know that we believe that prayer works. We believe, in fact, that human speech came from a million-year-long duet with the language of animal and plant and Earth life around us. We believe that there is power to re-cycle back through us. Activists who allow the life of the Earth—both the life forms of species and the folk forms of spirits—to come into their protests have a far greater force. In the case of magical Iceland, how would your hidden people rise up? We can't wait to see!

And so good night to you, and thank you for your invitation to come to Iceland and learn so much from you and your land.

Crazy Horse saw Yellow Hair in the distance, galloping from the east. He listened and watched and prayed. And then he covered himself and his horse with Earth.

10. Berlin: Tear Down This Wall

The Third Generation of Feeling Fine

REVEREND BILLY

Savitri and I traveled to Berlin for a festival in January 2004, with our choirmaster, James Solomon Benn, but we couldn't bring our Stop Shopping singers. The festival producers had enough money to fly only the three of us. The plan was to hire a Berlin choir for the performances, and so we emailed out to Europe our "Stop Shopping" and "Remove Starbucks and Disney" anthems as audio files. Our German hosts said they had found a wonderful local gospel choir.

The festival, called Maulhalden, presented comics, storytellers, singer-songwriters. It loosely translates as a cross between "Verbal Heroes" and "Funny Big Mouths," according to the festival staff. We took the producers' word for it that we fit the bill. The festival's site, the Tempodrome, was a Barnum and Bailey–sized yellow and red circus tent, but with central heating and a whole interior village built for show-biz. The Tempodrome amazed us, as European venues so often do, with multiple, moveable stages and miles of lights and sound equipment hanging everywhere. The big theater where we would perform seated three thousand. The Germans treated us graciously and we were excited to be in Berlin. Our hotel was embarrassingly classy, across from the old SS headquarters (now a small wilderness of a vacant lot) in downtown Berlin.

The second day there we met our German gospel choir. We stared at these super shiksas beaming with every beat, but I mean loving *each* beat. That is, the god they sang to was on Quaaludes. There were men in the bass section. One of them considered himself the lead singer. He wore Harley-Davidson leathers and did slow motion *Saturday Night Fever* moves with a shit-eating grin on his face. All that afternoon we re-hearsed, clapping hard, shouting Amens, and sort of dancing at them, trying to ignite some gospel bounce.

We had gone on local TV, received impressive newspaper coverage, and the three thousand tickets sold out. And so once again our popu-larity in Germany—we've performed there annually for seven years—challenged our idea of how we are perceived. Germany is post-religious. Many Germans don't know what a televangelist is, unlike people in Spain, England, or Russia, where the raging pentecostalists roam. The Germans tell us that Reverend Billy is simply very "American" to them, a sort of Elvisy cultural mishmash, with the priest's collar and the big hair, a mixed metaphor that resembles a picture of an American city—nothing matches but everything screams.

What we always wonder when our performance is transplanted to another culture is: What happens when things occur onstage that are beyond cultural symbols? Our American idioms can be deciphered by most Europeans even if I don't slow down my delivery or widen my gestures till I'm playing charades. But what about the thing that orga-nized religion gives a thousand names to? I pray before every perfor-mance that thing will fill the room. We call it the Fabulous Unknown.

Back home in New York, we've known this for years: If the Un-known doesn't sweep through the audience like a wind from deep space, then the show doesn't make sense in some basic way. The inef-fable, the universe, the Buddha, whatever it is—it must make its ap-pearance here in the middle of a comic take on a preacher. If it doesn't show up, then the audience will have an empty feeling and not know why. It's not just American and not just German. It lives in all of us—but will the spirit rise for this upcoming hour-long partnership in the Tempodrome? We could only pray.

We met our German gospel choir a second day and kept preparing for the show. But we were not sure what kind of entertainment—or pol-itics or spirituality—would rise from this singing. Would this be glori-ous? They thought so. The singers were non-stop happy. They smiled when they sang, when they tied their shoes, and even when they sneezed. Then we would listen to another song and wonder if the choir's schlogging beat was the embodiment of the troubled oxymoron in the phrase "German gospel choir." Their persistent nostalgic distance from gospel was subjecting us to the same instability that our performances inflict on doctrinaire critics. What will this be? Comedy? High church? Here were these stately women and slo-mo men who laughed and laughed as we sped up their gospel. Little did we know, the choir was not the problem.

Then—the way these things happen—suddenly, we were waiting to go onstage. A local comedian was out in the spotlight spewing his German and the crowd was roaring with laughter virtually every time he stopped to inhale. This relaxed us. I remember we were calmly whispering to each other in a backstage area that was a floor below the stage. We talked near the bottom rungs of a ladder that angled up to the back edge, feeling confident about the show and even forgetting that we had any reason to be afraid, as the tall Fräuleins kept laughing with a powerful abandon, their manes of golden hair on their shoulders like a dream of fire. The women looked radiant, their pleated robes shining from the light bleeding around the curtains. Meanwhile, the waves of audience laughter continued to rise and fall in the Teutonic world beyond the curtains.

We got the YOU'RE ON signal. We started singing our way up that ladder and a festival helper took us through the long black curtains that hung down from the dark swoop of the tent. The curtains parted, the lights burst on us, and the three thousand faces focused their frowning eyes. We were singing as we entered the stage, a stepping procession with the phrase "Stop—STOP SHOPping, Stop—STOP SHOPPing" and we could hear our voices echoing through the vast tent. James and I ran out to the front edge of the stage like rock-n-rollers, our choir trailing behind with their happy harmony. I felt my job was to PUMP IT UP. That was my first response to the immediate reality we faced, which was that the audience had stopped laughing. Why? Three thousand Germans sat erect and stared at the shouting people onstage without blinking. I needed to commit to this. PUMP IT UP! I was gonna be the raging spirit-touched preacher. Here I go!

At some point in the second number, the dozenth of my "change-a-lujahs" echoed out of the powerful speakers into a world of stunned silence. I looked out across the thousands of people and suddenly they appeared to be just a few feet from me. It was as if there was a wall abruptly rising from the edge of the stage, and the wall was made of stern faces and stolid folded arms, made of a generation of Germans who were the children of their war, forgetting it and finding something that could make them feel good, to laugh, to eat and consume and travel, to have a life with no past, only a future forcing its way into the present. And a gospel choir of their daughters led by a big black man and a big-haired shouter in a KFC suit—this was not the orderly arrival of the past-destroying future.

The aisle up the middle of the audience offered a way for me to prove that this wasn't just a wall. I made a running start and I leapt off the edge, directly into the Germans, and yes, the wall fell away. Now I was running alone about half-a-football-field deep into the motionless mass. At least I was daring them to turn their heads as I passed. If they turned their heads, maybe that would begin to break the ice. But no, they seemed to continue to look straight ahead. Behind me I could hear the gospel wail, "STOP SHOPPING!" That's what I was saying, too.

Choir director James Solomon Benn pulls out the stops onstage with Reverend Billy and the Life After Shopping Gospel Choir at the Black Forest Theater in Dallas, Texas, 2005. (Photo by Fred Askew.)

Maybe none of this made sense? My responses had a giddy quality now. Was my behavior in danger of becoming permanently inappropriate? Was I stranded out here with my wireless microphone? I put my hand on a man's shoulder and he slapped it. "Lighten up! That was my I-cure-you-of-the-Evil schtick!"

I turned and walked back up the aisle toward the stage. There, the blond gospel choir was standing, slack-faced. James looked out at me across the still heads. He carefully whispered the words, "Help me! Help me! I'm in Comedy Hell!" James! Oh, they came to laugh but they can't? Damn! I turned and shouted, "LET US PRAY!" This is an old standby that always works: Audience participation. Get the blood flowing a bit. "Berliners! Let's put our arms in the air like our hands are receiving signals from God and you are a flesh television. Amen?" I tossed off that flesh TV reference, you see that? Soon I'll have zinger after zinger. I'm a comedian now, see.

"Everybody! Get the arms up! Hands out! I know we're in a circus tent but here we go! People, now look. What if God showed up speaking German and sang a nice gospel song about your Consumerism? Now get those arms up, cup your hands like little satellite dishes. I'm teaching you the classic gospel gesture! All right. LET US PRAY!"

Suddenly Savitri was hissing from the orchestra pit. "Billy!" Her eyes were burning. She was speaking in broad emphatic tones: "They think you're Hitler!" Honey, wh-what?

I looked out at my German audience. They were trying to get their hands up but their arms were encountering a glass ceiling at about the height of their frowning foreheads. They couldn't raise their arms. Savi then shouted at James, "Oh Happy Day! Do it! Oh Happy Day! Quick! Get them clapping!" Oh, all right. I walked back to the left edge of the stage. Savi must have thought something was very wrong. Harley Man dropped his robe. He was all zippers and leather now!—and he was hitting his Travolta poses. Oh, God. Will he turn out to be the hit of our show? James was trying to get the choir to rock their hips, but they smiled as he waggled his ass back and forth, then pointed to their lower bodies and shouted, "Do it!" Language problem.

Savitri pulled my ear down to her mouth. "They think you are Hitler. Hitler was a fake preacher too! That's what the producer told me. Your gospel pose, the arms up—it's like Heil Hitler." Oh. I did a double-take at the audience. My . . . GOD! Oh my GOD! NO! Some were still frowning and waving their arms like they were broken. The rest went back to the concrete-block-in-the-wall position.

Now, in my thirty years in the theater, I have looked into the eyes of audiences who were visibly upset by how bad I was. I've seen that look of distaste. It's actually more like frightened anger. But in my life in the theater this has taken place in ninety-nine-seat theaters, smaller performance art venues, or community spaces. This German circus comedy experience—this was a different nightmare. It was their Zen-like stillness: that's what worried me.

Then I had a moment of active resignation from my collar and Elvis hair and white suit—I became estranged from all that stuff on the outside. I would leave that with the German public as a gift. They could have the Billy surface; I would wear it only outwardly for awhile. And so my survival tactic was: emotional disengagement from my own identity. It might seem like an extreme measure, but the idea was living to preach another day. This withdrawal would give me time to go into my dark interior—a visualizing technique, where I place myself in Coney Island, on the beach, on my old towel with the little space-ships . . .

Then Savitri reached from the edge of the curtain, yanked me back and the garish footlights blinded me. She had noticed my detachment and said coldly, "Billy, do something *energetic* in this circus tent for about half-an-hour. If you don't we won't get paid."

OK! A new frisson of terror! So we sang and preached in this unearthly world for the half-hour just stipulated. We heaved our barrage after barrage of "Change-a-lujahs!" at the wall of frozen Germans in the circus tent. We worked and worked with the happy gospel blonds, the sentimental gospel based in the handsome daughters' effusive happiness. We rode those fearless, unknowing smiles to the end of the night. Our choir could, in fact, sing "Oh Happy Day" into the Lake of Hellfire and come out the other side all smiles.

We always leave our Fabulous Worships the same way: high-stepping in grand style up the center aisle—although usually it's through cheering throngs, not statuary. This day we were sashaying in a vacuum, through busts of the burghers, concretized as all the laughter inside them died. We were marching into the vanishing point at the end of the highway. Hoping for deliverance from this stillness, freedom from their eyes, which did not even watch us leave. They were looking straight ahead at the now empty stage, their orgone accumulator that would bring them a more entertaining future.

Then: a body in the back rows moved. We sensed him before we saw him. Someone was singing along, clapping and whooping. And the old Germans around him were casting sidelong glances. The young man loomed larger and larger. We kept stepping forward, feeling the relief of fewer and fewer glazed faces . . . and there he was again. Yes, this was really happening. There was actually one very thin guy who seemed to be applauding.

In fact, he was standing and screaming: "Oh, YES! Oh, YES! I will STOP my SHOPPING! Oh, YES! CHANGE-A-LUJAH!" I couldn't help but smile at him, and smile back at Savitri and James and then back at him. Oh! Our audience of one! "You're our audience of one!" I chimed at him, as we drew near. He stood up. He was like a beardless Abe Lincoln at nineteen. And then he said a strange thing! "Follow me." He added in his thick accent, "Yes, I know I am sounding like Jesus, but I do now repeat to you—follow me!" As the German audience burst into the relief of laughter—a three-thousand-person laughter responding to the comic dressed in lederhosen who was now onstage, pushed there by festival producers hurriedly trying to save the show—we turned to this tall kid: "Take us from here! You—friend!—lead the way."

Soon, Savitri and I were alone with him. His name was Clement— and he asked us in a phrase that he lent a good broad American inflection: "Have you ever heard of the Third Generation of Feeling Fine? Ah! Well, the Third Generation of Feeling Fine is the slogan that was adopted by the designers of the 'Arkaden'—I am taking you there. It is—you will see!—like the Mall of America! That size of a super mall here in Berlin! But it isn't just the mall that is the Third Generation of Feeling Fine. It is the people, too! The German consumers! That is this comedy audience that will never laugh or pray with you, back here at the Tempodrome. It is the state of this country now, and the US too, yes?"

We walked and walked. Suddenly we wondered: What happened to James and the choir? Maybe they were just happy that the show was over. But we didn't look back much; we couldn't. We were drawn forward powerfully by our new leader, deeper and deeper into this strange Berlin night. Something was in the air. As Clement talked we kept hearing the sounds of crowds shouting, an occasional siren. He told us that we were near Checkpoint Charlie, and so the Cold War had great symbolic meaning in this part of Berlin. The super mall he was taking us to, the Arkaden, was built as a triumphalist consumer paradise here in Potsdamer Platz, near the former Wall.

Arkaden was a shrine to freedom. Buy anything you want! Park your car and stay all day! The mall went on and on—escalators rising into the clouds. The Third Generation of Feeling Fine was a German promise that in three generations the war would be forgotten, and the glossy products accelerate the necessary forgetting. Consuming would replace soldiering, and we would all feel fine! But in this agitated night, the consumers were gone—or they were back in the circus tent, still sitting there, getting their giggles going again.

The first floor of the mall felt like a rock show. Clement pulled us to a gleaming silver escalator, while explaining to Savi that all three public universities in Berlin were on strike, and that many strikers were expecting Reverend Billy to preach. I remember the last thing he said before we got to the mall balcony at the top of the silver stairs: "The Berlin city government got caught in bed with the big banks, and meanwhile they are cutting back on the humanities, because the leftist professors seem to come from the humanities or because it's not a part of the school that is a profit-center—put it that way. IT IS CORRUPTION! It is the Sin of the Devil!" Oh, a German televangelist!

This was happening fast. I turned and this heavenly garden of the Berlin middle class was packed with sexy young radicals as far as the eye could see. Waves of Allelujah! Allelujah!—"They know us," Savitri was coaxing me, because I had the performance bends. Rising from the audience made of high-stress concrete to this flight of the rock stars, I was gasping for psychic breath. A supersonic Dante journey, up from the circus tent of Hell and up and up to the opposite problem. The identity destroyed moments ago was now crowned and glorified on what basis? We had a crowd of biblical proportions here. And what pillar of fire were they following across what desert? They were laughing, fist in the air, shouting "Allelujah!" Savitri said, "Shout with them for awhile. Just be Billy." Fortunately for the expectations of my congregation, I can crank up an Allelujah for large churches. (When the New York police kept taking my bullhorns, I studied with an opera singer to create that prayer that shatters glass.) AL LAY LOO YUH!

Over the next hours, all I remember is sermon after sermon, calling out from various promontories, up on railings, up on counters next to cash registers. We hunted every store known for its sweatshops and got up on their shelves. My arms were in the air, and words echoed through the utopian super mall cleansed by the Cold War. Whatever was going on here, Savitri translated what she could, and I would plug in new details on the spot. The sensation felt palpable that a good shouting preacher was a momentary answer to a silencing that the young Berliners had suffered. As the hour of shouting in the Third Generation of Feeling Fine wore on, we recognized that we were hearing the same stories of silencing we experienced in the United States. Gradually the message became the global nature of the corruption, censorship, and militarized response by police. That became the universal evil, and we folded it into the apocalyptic rhetoric of the American televangelist.

Consumerism has taken all the language of freedom from history, and emptied those words of meaning by using them to sell products, from breath mints to war. So we need outside languages, and we offer from our work a mocking back at hyperbolic right-wing apocalyptic Christianity, through which we do battle with their use of "Democracy" and "Freedom" and "The Third Generation of Feeling Fine" as their banners. We can steal words, too, and re-up them, reversing the transubstantiation of advertising to happiness, of militarism and big money to a consumed violence and debt. In the Arkaden, the students swept us up into the delight of a cultural flip; we were momentarily weightless, a fundamentalist religion turned on its head by shouts of adulation to the god of no shopping.

It was so exhilarating it was hard to stop. And Clement and his student leaders, constantly conferring with Savitri, didn't have an endgame in their design. I was told to indicate a soccer field as a destination, but there was no theory or strategy for me to fulminate over. They kept me moving and Billying into the night. The creation of excitement, a relief from a standoff with official Berlin, was the point. I preached from the mouth of the subway, from the edge of a six-story parking lot, on every false balcony. We thought we saw the remnants of our former Maulhalden audience slowly retire to the brat houses along the leftover Berlin Wall. Then something so familiar to us—like an old enemy so familiar it has become a kind of friend—loomed before us. Oh yes —of course!—the Arkaden Starbucks.

It was surrounded by khaki-clad soldiers with their arms folded (like the unwilling audience at the comedy show—now seeming so long ago). Erect, chins up, and feet apart, the police stance of the ages. I didn't see weapons; it was just that they were seven feet tall and blond, these soldiers. I didn't know that there still was a German army. I knew that they refused to go to Iraq, so I thought they were, peaceful? How they arranged their vehicles and uniformed bodies for the maybe-mock-church from New York made us laugh. This was priceless. The exact mise-en-scène of our play. The café itself was closed, the baristas waving from in back of the stalwart bodies. And so—time for one more sermon with the soldiers staring from behind me, glowering at the mysterious believers. "Allelujah! Children! Here we have an American company. Starbucks. First, it is not a Fair Trade company. Will somebody here give me a Change-a-lujah!"

Gute Nacht, Berlin

SAVITRI D

As we left the mall in a wave, I noticed a group of jackbooted police over my left shoulder, shadowing our movement. The students protected us, keeping solid body mass between us and their legion. As we swung around a corner, crowd force whipped us out to the edge. The police, agile predators, moved in and locked us both in grim custody in under a minute. They were rough and we were cooperative.

The police, these anti-riot giants, were the biggest men I had ever seen outside a sports arena. As they maneuvered us to a row of trailers behind a line of barricades, it dawned on me how hard the rest of the night would be if we were both in custody. We had no legal support. We didn't even have phone numbers and I wasn't sure I could remember the name of our hotel. The lead cop was talking on a phone. The others were clustered around Billy, demanding passports, handcuffing, milling around. Taking a chance, I ducked out from under the arms of two officers and walked as fast as I could back to the crowd, my heart racing. They followed, but not far. By then the media were swarming and I knew Billy was basically safe. I had no illusions about rescuing him. He would sit in that caravan until the protest was over. They would never let him go until the crowd broke up.

Clement saw me coming, grabbed my elbow, and whisked me toward the other side of the crowd. "We are going to the stage," he said. "You'll have to speak."

For a short time in the early '90s, my close friend Anne was a tour guide at the famous No Man's Land near Checkpoint Charlie. She walked small groups out onto the grass, careful to point out that the exact same movement would have gotten them all shot just a few years earlier. Hundreds of people were shot, she said, hundreds. The groups stood in the center of No Man's Land and looked at the city. Anne would point out various landmarks, which ones were visible from where, and what role they played in the endless propaganda campaigns of the Cold War. Then, inevitably, everyone would stop talking and the sound of the city would recede to what felt like utter silence. Such was the illusion of the field's size and the intensity of its emptiness. I suppose we were also impressed by the change, she said, how fast it was all happening.

Even then, she said, you could feel the flood. City planners were hard at work and construction cranes blossomed against the sky. Anne was in architecture school at the time. She spent afternoons and evenings exploring, wandering along the seam where the Wall had been, and then talking her way into the buildings. She walked the rooflines and stairways; she sat in public spaces. She loved the neighborhoods in the east, but said they felt only different, not better, already aware of the hazard of sentimentality that would later be called Ostalgia, a longing for the old days, for East Berlin, for strong feelings, she explained.

When they built the Arkaden mall at Potsdamer Platz, she was not surprised. But when No Man's Land got landscaped and civilized, she was deeply disappointed. The logic of the place, she said, was undone.

Potsdamer Platz (PP) began as a crossroads. Around 1700 it was designated as a marketplace outside the city walls, a trading zone for refugees, Huguenots, Jews. For one hundred and fifty years the market thrived and the fast-growing city of Berlin eventually encompassed it. PP became a primary market and cultural center. By the 1920s and '30s it was home to legendary cabarets, grand department stores, and Europe's biggest restaurants.

The Third Reich installed itself there, ensuring regular attacks from allied bombers, but the district recovered from the leveling with astonishing speed, and when the war ended, the markets were already flourishing.

Potsdamer Platz was carved up by the allies at the end of World War II, and like most border regions, it supported a fertile black market, especially as working conditions and quality of life deteriorated in the east. After a brutal Soviet crackdown on a worker uprising in 1953, travel to the east was severely limited. Families and workers were denied access and the border hardened until 1961, when the East German government put up the Berlin Wall.

In those years Berlin was, for most of the world, a static symbol of a power struggle that was playing out dynamically elsewhere—in Afghanistan, Central America, Asia. Berlin was the local frontier in a covert world war and West Berlin a beacon of light in the grey prison of the Soviet Empire. The Berlin Wall made PP less practical and more emblematic, less crucial as a center of exchange and more important as the site of an escalating and increasingly pompous display of cultural might. We are the greatest! No, we are the greatest! No, we are the greatest!

In 1989 when the Wall came down, the government handed the area over to Daimler-Benz and Sony and the conglomerate that built the Arkaden and penned its motto, "The Third Generation of Feeling Fine—a pure experience." These transnational corporations invested mightily and for several years Potsdamer Platz was the biggest construction site in Europe. In 2004, its development was handed over to J. P. Morgan and the Swedish banking subsidiary SEB.

PP was always a place where one thing ended and another began, the edge of two districts, the meeting of five roads. It was naturally rich, a thriving ecosystem, like a shoal off the coast or the fringe area between a forest and a field. These are the teeming places. Power is drawn to them, springs from them.

Clement and I were walking across what had been No Man's Land. Now it is the roof of an underground parking garage; behind it is the Arkaden Mall and the largest casino in Europe.

I am watching a crowd of ten thousand assemble. I watch their wide faces as they talk and shout, cheer and laugh, and bounce up and down to recordings piped over the sound system of North African drum and bass. The city has receded. Its history feels old and impossible. Brandenburg Gate is just there, and the Reichstag. I can see the government buildings, the Arkaden, and the needle tower in the east. Amazingly, the sky it still ringed with cranes. A flock of blackbirds is flying below the clouds and Berlin feels like a city that will change before my eyes.

With Billy absent, Clement is pushing me onstage. I have to give an impromptu sermon. I address the crowd:

Berlin! I am honored to be here tonight.

They just locked us out of the mall. What are they protecting? Who are they protecting? There are riot cops at McDonald's! Finally our government is protecting us from these corporations. Finally we can sleep soundly.

Berlin!

Fifteen years ago we stood around televisions and radios all over the world watching you pour over that wall, so weightless. I was in a bar in the mountains and we drank and danced on tables all night. We thought we could do anything. Berlin! The "Antifachisticscher Schutzwall" came down! The iron curtain came down!

Berlin!

I regret to inform you that it did not take long to put up another wall, and in the true story of our lives, this new wall is just as dangerous. This new wall is the real American sector. It is the surface of imaginable space, of digitized space, of television, of advertising. It's the unobtainable misinformation of celebrity life, of revised history, of your unknown desires. Berlin, Berlin! There is already another wall. The commodity wall is here and they built it before the old one even came down. It is all over our skin and in the reflective surface of those clouds. It is on your matches and the bottoms of your shoes. It's in your eyeballs, on my tongue.

Berlin!

What's on the other side of the commodity wall? It's not East Berlin. It's the rest of the world: It's the sweatshop and the gold mine, it's the clear-cut and the oil field, it's an urban slum and the monsoon, a tranny in a refugee camp, an orphan at a sewing machine. What's on the other side of the commodity wall? All the trash and all of the wilderness. All of the hope and none of the opportunity.

Berlin!

Corporate capital has a perfect disguise and it's only a matter of time before we are ALL on the other side of the commodity wall. Your universities, your professors, your education are at the top of the list. Berlin is a colony and you are its natives.

Berlin! Berlin ! Berlin!

The commodity wall is ours to tear down, ours to rupture, ours to offend—it is ours to tear down. Be vigilant, be crazy, be wrong. Show up late. Unearth, dislodge, surprise! Upset their expectations, stop shopping! Turn your back on the advertising, talk to each other, move each other, don't let it get between you. Tear down the commodity wall. Tear it down.

Gute nacht, Berlin! Vielen dank!

11. Resurrection

Kings and Thieves

REVEREND BILLY

In April of 2007, the season finale of *American Idol* really went over the top. The show pixilated visions of quick fame, record deals, critics in love, and even a kind of democracy. But that's not why nearly thirty-one million Americans simultaneously gasped. That's not why thirty-one million of us blubbered and cussed, why our shoulders jumped and buttocks clenched, why we dropped our beers and massaged the wrong person. What did *American Idol* do that night?

In airports and living rooms, on computers and in bars across the country, America went still. The host, Ryan Seacrest, halted the big song-slam. He told the audience that there would be a break in the show, that two special guests would sing, that it would be a duet by Celine Dion and "the world's greatest idol of all time."

Dion walked out from an upstage shadowy area, and with her strode a mysterious duet partner. They entered a brilliant house of light on the edge of the stage, raised the microphones to their lips and began to sing. And America saw that. It was Elvis Presley. What? It's *him*. The standing ovation *before* the song prolonged into breathless screaming. The two stars sang "If I Can Dream," a blend of power ballad and gospel song, the lyrics about wanting your dream to come true. Elvis and Celine harmonized perfectly, together building the passionate intensity of the song. At one point, with Elvis's face so close to the camera it was out of focus, we saw Celine Dion gazing out at the crowd as if seeing across the decades.

This is a good YouTube of the three-minute miracle: http://www
.youtube.com/watch?v=hOg9-OpG0G0

The *Idol* audience that night shook off death for a few moments. Its
hyperventilating fit was the consumer version of religious ecstasy. We
lost all self-awareness. Out in America, we sacrificed ourselves to the
glowing box on the wall. We offered up our personal identity to the
stage, to the miraculous King, to resurrection-as-product.

Product? Elvis more than anything made the sale. He did it by
demonstrating the power of a newfangled fundamentalist church, part
Christian and part Computer. The perfect storm of stolen faiths, the
monster religion Consumerism, was sealed in the three minutes of
blinding euphoria. Among the thirty-one million, there wasn't much
mental dissent. Nobody quibbled, "How can this be? Elvis died thirty
years ago!" We long ago learned to suspend disbelief (or destroy it) for
the duration of an ad, a song, or any of the thousands of quick seductions in the American consumer's average day.

But this—this was the Second Coming. Like electrocuted seals, clapping and screeching "We buy it!" we were also ready to consume and
worship the secrets of the miracle. How did they *do* that? Go ahead,
pull back the wizard's curtain and we'll buy that too. Sure enough, a
YouTube was posted in the next days, entitled "How They Did It!" and
it became a runaway hitfest. The Resurrection Reality Show rolled on
and on.

It turned out that *American Idol* had hired the special effects engineers who beamed up Scotty in the *Star Trek* movies. These are experts
at altering worlds and film stars, and creating explosions the size of the
sun. Working for months, the team managed to lift the videotaped
Elvis—three minutes and thirty-nine seconds of him—out of his *1968
NBC Comeback Special* and "re-composite" his glittering remains on the
American Idol stage forty years later. Because the background of the original 1968 "Dream" was infinite black, the engineers could cut out the
singing body of the King and place it into the large video game on the
American Idol stage. Somehow they constructed a hologram up there,
the size of a house, and Elvis walked into it, singing in three dimen-
sions.

The unforgettable image of the *1968 NBC Comeback Special* is Elvis
in the black leather bodysuit gyrating in a boxing ring surrounded by
screaming housewives. But the song that concluded the hour-long spe-

cial, "If I Can Dream," was impressive in a new way for Elvis fans. Elvis shed his motorcycle outfit and got dressed up from chin to toes in his bright white Sunday best. His performance was an energized prayer, without a flicker of the impish smile or the leering what-have-you-got gaze. Elvis's song seemed to rise and rise.

> *There must be lights burning brighter somewhere*
> *Got to be birds flying higher in a sky more blue*
> *If I can dream of a better land*
> *Where all my brothers walk hand in hand*
> *Tell me why, oh why—*
> *Why can't my dream come true?*

I watched Elvis and Celine sing "If I Can Dream" a hundred times, slowly working through the ultimate sensuality of resurrection and its omni-faith punch. I showed the tape to Savitri and the singers in the Life After Shopping Gospel Choir. We all sensed that there was some kind of seed down deep, a generative power in this remarkable product. The words of the song, unnoticed—never mentioned in the "How They Did It!" tape—had a separate and stand-alone life outside the trashy miracle. Something was inside Elvis, something beyond this alchemy of selling traditions, something that the consumer was not supposed to see.

Play it again.

I hit play again, and the doll-size *American Idol*ized Elvis emoted from the computer screen.

Elvis was in his gospel whites, with his hair politely combed for church. Midway through the duet with Dion, a multi-racial gospel choir, dressed in matching white, walked upstage to accompany the preacher—Elvis took the preacher persona here. After all his dalliances with stock American characters in his films—cowboys, race-car drivers, boxers, surfers—his gospel self rose more and more into public view, dramatically revealed in that *1968 NBC Comeback Special*. With the addition of the gospel singers in the 2007 show, his new *Idol* producers were accentuating the reverence in the gospel-singing Elvis, and tacking against the rocker-looking Dion, who was wearing a tight jumpsuit with a zipper running conspicuously down her posterior.

That night on *Idol*, they manipulated our American love of expansion; our western horizon got a new door, a soul flew up, and there was a new vista for all of us to see. Preachers are powerful here on this western horizon if they can persuade us that they are arbiters of the unknown, just beyond our view. Elvis stood at this sexual and musical line across the mountains, but now, wheeling his arms and bracing his legs as if in a tunnel of heavenly wind, he was singing a prayer of grand frustration. The American idea of horizon was recoiling back on him, surprising him, and demanding conditions, and among them is violence.

Elvis returned from thirty years in the netherworld, rising before us, glowing. And what was his message for us? What were we doing while he was gone? Elvis on that *American Idol* stage seemed to be working his way free of the luminescent impersonation that the computer engineers erected. Elvis was come back to life and with every word seemed ready to actually escape *American Idol*. He was about to run from the stage. This was not the later self-mocking Elvis. There was something deadly serious here. Were we hearing him? Did we get it? We noticed Celine kept trying to catch his eye, but that Elvis ignored her, dedicated to the delivery of the song on his own. He so urgently hoped to reach us with the news that something had gone terribly wrong, something had stopped this Dream.

With all the troubled duets of real life and special effects, of Christ and Elvis, of gospel and rock, and the Comeback in '68 and the Resurrection in '07, Presley insisted on singing this song. All the dazzling cultural clues were obvious to see, but he kept singing. Or, is it more accurate to say, despite his supercharged delivery, that it was the song that kept singing? Looking back on it, was Elvis really on *American Idol?* No, *he* wasn't. The song was, and is. He gave it to us. It belongs to us. Back to the words.

What Are the Words He Keeps Singing?

I played the YouTube again and heard these words in a quiet moment near the beginning of the song:

> *There must be peace and understanding sometime*
> *Strong winds of promise*

that will blow away all the doubt and fear
If I can dream of a warmer sun
Where hope keeps shining on everyone
Tell me why, oh why—
Why won't that sun appear?

Through the screen of the TV, through all the hysteria, we can hear that phrase "peace and understanding sometime." It's the quietest line in the song—just a bit of common sense, really. We need peace and understanding, don't we? The song quickly builds to its glorious sailing heights, but its foundation is this modest, everyday logic. "There must be peace and understanding sometime." Elvis was trying to turn the frenzy in another direction.

So this is a Peace Song.

The Original Song, the Original Story

We thought we should follow that peace-and-understanding to its source. We looked up the surprising history of this Dream.

By 1968, Elvis was culturally beside the point. He was hidden for the most part inside his mansion, called Graceland, in Memphis. Colonel Parker, his Svengali-like advisor, had narrowed the Elvis product-line to a series of terrible movies, which made a great deal of money and took only six weeks to make. Elvis was aware of the tumult of change that had risen from the Civil Rights and Peace movements. He didn't like his increasing feelings of irrelevance, and against the wishes of Parker he made plans to tape a national television special. It would be his comeback and showcase his more playful and spiritual side. It was slated for the summer of '68. And then, in quick succession, Dr. Martin Luther King, Jr., and Senator Robert Kennedy were shot.

The high, racing wave of the sixties, which left Elvis Presley so out of cultural time down in Memphis, suddenly halted in midair. Elvis watched history stop. The cities burned inside a painful, planet-sized silence. How much had the two dreamers, King and Kennedy, guided this cultural revolution? That spring of '68, in the sound of gunfire and flames, we wondered—was peace possible now? The stage was emptying. Malcolm was gone. Che was gone. The Vietnam War, which by this time already had claimed a million lives, raged on.

Isolated as Elvis was, he had friends who stepped into and out of the heat of the radical dream that grew from the mid-fifties to that moment. His awareness of Dr. King and civil rights came from the direct experience of the south, and from the assassination only a couple miles from his home. Critics have fired accusations of racism at the Presley legend from afar, but it is more instructive to read James Brown's biography—how the two grown-up-poor southerners snuck into gospel concerts together. We can't know for sure how it happened, but Elvis suddenly wanted a new song for the finale of his television show, and this would be "If I Can Dream." Elvis turned to one of his composers, W. Earl Brown, and commissioned him to write a song that could serve as high prayer for that hurt time.

Brown seems to have done a bold thing. It seems he re-read the work of Dr. King. In a matter of days he created a song with phrases echoing Martin Luther King's speeches and sermons, fashioned to the rhythms and rhymes that Brown needed for his song. The "trembling question" and "beckoning candle" are clearly the writing style of Dr. King, influenced as he was by the Psalms in the King James Bible.

> *Deep in my heart there's a trembling question*
> *Still I am sure that the answer is gonna come somehow*
> *Out there in the dark, there's a beckoning candle . . .*
> *While I can think, while I can talk*
> *While I can stand, while I can walk*
> *While I can dream, let my dream, come true, right now . . .*

In 2007, Elvis's dedication to the dream of justice blew right by poor Celine, who kept pretending to be sharing the conspiratorial sexual glance of two celebrities caught in the same spotlight. In death, Elvis has so much power that when he sings, "While I can stand, while I can walk . . ." we believe him. Elvis feels the dream "deep in my heart," and he senses the dream "out there." He has faith that the change is "gonna come," but he demands of an unnamed god that his dream come true "right now." This is a big embrace: It includes all of us, and it's Dr. King's design. And we believe Reverend Martin Luther King.

And the heartbreaking title of the song? "If I Can Dream, Then Why Can't My Dream Come True?" This is what we get when a bullet hits the phrase "I have a dream today!" Earl Brown took it upon himself to re-cast the courage of Martin Luther King, to inhabit the bewilderment of a thwarted—an assassinated—activist. It's an amazing switch. On paper, the re-worked quote, "Why can't my dream come true?" almost sounds like the unreasonable question of a child, or a rock-n-roller, or a utopian American preacher. With Elvis it is, even on *Idol,* the implacable demand for a moral life.

Here is—sans Celine Dion—what the television audience witnessed in 1968, at the end of Elvis's special: http://www.youtube.com/watch?v=9CMlYVu9J4g

What dream is that?

The dream of peace and social justice in 1968 was re-manufactured by *American Idol* into a dream of instant fame. Of course, that is the show's bill in trade: rags to riches, an audition to a big career. Not much in the way of politics there. Would they ever permit Elvis and his "If I Can Dream" to remain as fiercely activist as it was at the time of the *NBC Comeback Special?* Of course not. The Fox network would never risk that Dr. King's meaning would be updated to demand peace in Iraq and Afghanistan. This would never happen now. Not in this carefully de-politicized commons of *American Idol.* But it would be inaccurate to claim that censorship was not around in those earlier days. The original "Dream" almost died in 1968.

As the television show approached, Colonel Parker wanted the finale of the program to be a cover of Bing Crosby's "I'll Be Home For Christmas." When Earl Brown brought in the new composition, and Elvis started singing it and realized what he had, everyone making the show rooted for this special creation over the Crosby song. Colonel Parker found there are times when even a Svengali can lose—at least this one time—to this fiery preaching of a song.

There are three takes of the song in the public domain. They are edited together in a posting on YouTube. If you watched the YouTube above, you'll recognize in this next tape, the take on the right as the one that director Steve Binder and Presley chose for the *1968 NBC Comeback Special,* and the one time-machined to Consumerism's coliseum in 2007: http://www.youtube.com/watch?v=mfvsepvgCCc

The song succeeded in America's summer of sorrow in much the way that Elvis hoped. It became a public song of mourning, anguish, and renewal. It had all the more impact because it came from this surprise pop source, Elvis Presley.

The song is also clearly a rededication of those two assassinated dreamers' lives, sung in defiance of the murders and the encroaching conservatism that the collaboration of King-Brown-Presley-Binder seemed to anticipate. We know what happened. You can follow the arc of the swing to the right in the fortunes of "If I Can Dream." With its soulful debut forty years ago it was a hit single. But now, in part because of the *American Idol* technical trick, it has secured a place in the Easy Listening rotation. A lot of political songs are there with it, stranded in saccharine: old Dylan anthems and Marvin Gaye's "What's Going On?" and John-and-Yoko peace songs, and Bob Marley too. No wonder they were confident that we would never hear (much less remember) Dr. King's words.

Right now, in this time of forgotten dreams, permanent war and the crisis of the earth itself, Dr. King's words could not be more important for us. With "If I Can Dream," though, we were out-maneuvered. In 2007, the shadowy international entity that owns *American Idol*—the corporation CKX, Inc.—also owned the rights to the Presley songs. But CKX's fortunes fell when the value of its Las Vegas real estate holdings crashed in the recession. As of this writing, the *Idol*-Elvis industry was in play; circling hedge funds and entertainment entities were in a bidding war to seize the empire. Elvis's brave performance will dim and come alive again and again as the money rises and falls.

American Idol reveals the nature of censorship in the consumerized culture of the United States. We don't have the clumsy crackdown of an Iran or a China. Our media elite buy the means of broadcast, and then dazzle us away from the truth of the matter. In the case of "If I Can Dream," time wore down its moral clarity and the special effects took the pop glow of the messenger and resurrected him with his passion, but without his meaning.

In the end, the *Idol* people created their idolatrous profit center, a gushing income stream for their quarterly report. The season finale of *American Idol* would sustain its highest advertising charge, $650,000 for thirty-second ads selling Apple iTunes, AT&T, and Coca-Cola. The host called Elvis the "the greatest idol," and the short radical sermon of a song was ripped from its pulpit in the Civil Rights Movement and beamed over to the other side, the preaching of war, celebrity, shopping. Elvis was re-branded. Did you notice the *American Idol* logo circling and circling Elvis's famous face like a drunken shark?

The "I" in "If I Can Dream" was assumed to be all of us when Elvis sang it live in 1968—and he was right. He was our "amorous orator in the village green." *American Idol* accomplished its theft by making Elvis into liquid capital, re-locating the identity of our "I"—the crowd of thirty-one million concentrated in front of our TV sets forty years later. Resurrected, he walked toward us not on our stage, but in a hellish bubble-wrap of timelessness and placelessness that leaves us frenetic yet unresponsive. That is, we consume him with our standing ovation, but are unresponsive to where we are, surrounded by the language of peace made unhearable. We cheer the Peace song while we continue to be officially in at least two wars without knowing why.

Corporations own the song, the show. Can they buy the dream? As corporate ownership of more and more of life becomes the political question of our time, we must, as Kurt Vonnegut said, "counter-punch with society." The words of "If I Can Dream" still have their own life. They are not a product and cannot be privatized.

We need to help one another hear the song of this afterlife duet of Martin and Elvis. If one of us notices the lyrics, feels that power, then we need to repeat those words.

If I Can Dream

SAVITRI D

Billy was muttering in front of his computer when I got home. I stood behind him, staring over his shoulder, but I couldn't quite make sense of what I was seeing: a gigantic audience, people with their mouths open, clapping, some jumping up and down. Swirling lights, a smiling man with a microphone and then the enormous *American Idol* logo swooping into view. Billy held his head in his hands.

I had never seen *American Idol*, though I had read about it plenty in the paper. Ratings winner! Savior of the recording industry! Somehow I knew all about it in that ambient way we know about celebrities and popular cultural products. So many people were watching it that paying it some attention was in order. The serious study of Consumerism requires research.

Billy started the video over. I thought I saw Elvis walking toward me out of a bright light onstage. It was definitely Elvis. Elvis! And there was Celine Dion, the most perfect pop instrument on the planet. They emerged from a white light. Wow. They were really glowing. "Oh it isn't real," I told Billy, as if he didn't know, "That's not really Elvis. They put a face on someone. What a great song."

Billy was shaking his head. He had been doing some research of his own. He sat me down and showed me the original version of "If I Can Dream," at the end of Elvis's *1968 NBC Comeback Special.* Do you know who wrote that song?" he asked. "Do the words sound familiar?" I shrugged. "Lincoln?" He told me his discovery and made me listen.

"You mean to tell me that Dr. King wrote a song for Elvis?" Billy explained the theory: "Earl Brown may have patched the song together from old sermons, I don't know . . ."

We watched both versions again. That digital trick really was amazing. We quickly became obsessed with the whole thing, aware of a riddle caught in its surface: behind the opacity of the television phenomenon was something that would help us understand our own work. Billy started developing a sermon trying to unlock the meaning of the broadcast. We bounced around inside it for a several days. We listened to some of Dr. King's sermons. We talked about Elvis, washed up in Hollywood in 1968, trying to become significant again, struggling against his own commodification. We talked about Celine Dion, shiny heroine of the monoculture, straight off a half-billion-dollar Vegas residency.

What a bloodless decision to pair her with Elvis, or maybe she is the only one with the chops to carry a duet with him? Is he that good a singer? Is she that good a singer? Is she herself a digital creation? Why is this the most popular show on television? And why now? Is it just the spectacle of their pairing that is so jarring? His resurrection? Or maybe we are astonished that *American Idol* ignored the basic elements of the song—America's most famous gospel singer singing a song made out of the words of our most famous gospel minister—sad that inside that particular temple the meaning of their union is rendered inert, made into a plea for celebrity and wealth, not peace and justice. Billy's sermon was coming together.

Because we are in a made-up "faith" that has no text or liturgy, Billy has to establish the basic values of the "faith" every time he preaches, then explain them and apply them to the subject of the sermon. There is no shorthand in The Church of Life After Shopping. We can't just say, "I refer you to John 3:16." I'm sure one reason working on the Elvis sermon was so interesting to us is that there were such supercharged building blocks to work with: Elvis! Dr. King! *American Idol!* Television! These are such broadly recognizable and interpretable elements, part of a cultural alphabet familiar enough to our audience to give the sermon plenty of traction. And that familiarity freed Billy to expound, or, as our choirmaster Brother James would say, to "speechify."

Some sermons really work right away. This one failed a few times, though it was always entertaining. At first, Billy couldn't quite find a way into its ending. He hadn't figured out how to close the loop and turn it back on the congregation. The sermon started out comedic and very physical. He began by imitating Elvis's entrance on *American Idol*, and the fans clapping with their jaws on the floor, caught in what Billy called a "pure Consumer moment." Billy reasserted the political value of the song and the remarkable effort Elvis was making at a healing gesture, bringing solace to a nation that had lost its moral leaders in quick succession. Essentially Billy re-narrated the *American Idol* episode from a moral position, enforcing a moral lineage: Elvis as carrier of a message, Elvis redeemed. It had good bones, but somehow it wasn't all there. Billy and I went for long walks after each attempt, talking about the sermon, why it kept missing.

I was keeping a close watch on *American Idol*, a little desperately; I knew there was something more there for us. One day I got a call from our diva, Laura Newman. I could barely hear her. "There are ten thousand people here," she said. I had no idea where she was. "I'm in New Jersey! At the stadium! I'm auditioning." "What for?" I asked. "When are you up?" "*American Idol*," she said. "I got a golden ticket." The prospect of losing Laura to *American Idol* was horrifying, but maybe she could be an inside agent, perform a little subterfuge. I started to explain but she interrupted me: "Gotta go. I'm almost up!"

During the 2008 election cycle Billy's sister Julie went off to Pennsylvania to register voters and we went to her empty loft in New York (because we don't own a television) to watch our first live *American Idol* episode, a special election edition. The contestants started with a series of supposedly inspirational songs. Half an hour in, we were almost dead from advertising. I alternated between complete boredom and dangerous over-stimulation. The candidates were nowhere to be seen. Ryan Seacrest said, "Hey everyone! Let's get voting in an election that matters: Who's going to be the next Idol?" Then Bono appeared on a gigantic JumboTron and said:

> Save a life, tomorrow change the world. That's what we are about in one.org. Just get online, one.org. Okay and if you're going shopping, these are red glasses, Shop Red! And you know this is a year of big election, it's, you know, everyone is talking about this election in America, all three candidates are talking about this new America, and they are all trying to imagine a new America. The new Americans are the people that are picking up the phone, and writing checks, and sending in their pocket money to *American Idol* right now, and that's the America that I want the world to see. As a fan of America, that's the America that I want the world to see.

This was not just a special election edition, it was the "Idol Gives Back Special." Every vote generated money for Bono's multinational ONE Campaign. They told us to check online for special messages from the candidates. I turned to Billy: "What the hell? *American Idol* hosts the presidential candidates, but they get relegated to the Internet so Bono can tell us that our citizenship is best expressed through consumerism?"

I found the presidential candidates' statements online, and immediately understood why the producers cut them. They were boring. I guess when you have the highest rated show on TV you can make moves like that. But why would the candidates agree to letting Bono beat them out of prime time? Were they seduced by *American Idol's* "participatory democracy"? How can we explain that just because something *feels* democratic doesn't mean it *is* democratic? And really, does a democratic sensation ever lead to a democratic process? It seems obvious enough that consumerized democratic participation just reinforces consumerism; it does nothing to teach consumers to participate in democracy. Thirty-five percent of *American Idol* voters think their vote on a season finale is as or more important than their vote in a presidential election. But maybe that says more about our government than it does about *American Idol*.

More votes (580,000,000) were cast in the last season alone than in the last five presidential elections combined, so there is obviously real power there, enviable energy. But to what end? "Idol Gives Back" has raised $185 million for the ONE Campaign. Isn't it audacious for a show worth more than $6 billion to ask its viewers to give back? Aren't we giving back by watching the show? There are more than four thousand product placement "events" per season. Shouldn't *American Idol* be giving back? A thirty-second advertising spot on an *American Idol* finale goes for $1.3 million; the show's advertising revenue tops $800 million annually. Head judge Simon Cowell was reported to have been offered $144 million for his last season on the show. And the presidential candidates were telling *us* to give to *Idol* too, for Africa—for Africa!—when their own legislation has done so much to keep Africa in a state of war and poverty? But none of the candidates even mentioned policy. All they could do was ask the audience to give money to *American Idol,* to Bono, to the ONE Campaign and then to vote for them in a totally trivialized presidential race. It's an unholy alliance: consumerized democracy at a low point, money the medium through which all else flows.

This is simulated resurrection, a thrill that locks the prison door instead of freeing us. The audience is not resurrected, along with the old Elvis or the new Bono—we don't transcend the walls of commercial programming. "Idol Gives Back" is taxation by spectacle; the taking and spending of the money is mystified. You don't get to know what happens to the cash you send in and there is no accounting. *American Idol* and Bono's ONE Campaign operate on the theory that there can be no life after shopping. In their world, our hopes to change the globalized economy cannot be structural; we can only try to shop our way out of poverty. Their projects evoke the sensation of democracy, even the sensation of radicalism for that matter, leaving no space to wonder why we aren't doing the right and admirable thing when we send a check. But can we shop enough for Africa?

Billy and I started mapping out the Elvis sermon again, fueled by anger, determined to crack it. I called Laura to hear about the audition, see if there was some grist there. She said she sang really well, but the judge sneezed just as she started her song and then spent the next minute with her back to Laura "looking for a tissue, I guess, and then blowing her nose, and then my time was up, so she kind of missed it." Laura said, "I mean, I sang my ass off, and it was an interesting experience, but—I don't know." She was good-humored about the whole thing, but her account reinforced my sense of *American Idol* as a mechanized moneymaking machine, playing on all of our deepest vulnerabilities, contestants and audience members alike.

What is so disturbing about *American Idol* is not just how they could literally project Elvis into another realm and then demand that the TV nation turn with all the weight of our nostalgia and worship him as nothing more than an Idol. After all, we have been doing that to Elvis for decades. The crime is that *American Idol* took that song, the moment in Elvis's life when he made his single most meaningful political gesture, and used it to shill their show, their gigantic floating logo, their advertising slots, things you can buy. All the most charged moments of our history will soon disappear into advertising, drained of their power. One by one the great promises of the past will be hollowed out, their surfaces slicked up and sent out into the future in the form of shopping imperatives and retail assignments, bypassing the present moment entirely. That's Consumerism.

We know Elvis didn't entirely escape the trap of Consumerism when he staged his *Comeback Special.* He himself was by then a living product. But did he break through the commodity wall at all? He defied his handlers and producers and brought the song into the show, which, covered in advertising, product placement, and shopping opportunities was certainly the *American Idol* of its day, or at least a spectacle of equal proportion. So he was certainly trying, straining toward immediacy, agency, the present moment, "And if I have the strength to dream, I can redeem myself . . . Right now! Right now!" And perhaps he redeemed himself, at least for a time. But that doesn't help us with the sermon. Personal redemption is not enough.

We watched the original video yet again, and the duet too. And it was suddenly so obvious. All along we were praising the messenger, trying to unlock the meaning in the wrong place. It's the message itself that matters. It's Dr. King. Dr. King breaks through the commodity wall, tears through it, in '68 and again forty years later. It's Dr. King, not Elvis. Because his words are full, made of action, and so powerful that all those layers of production, of Consumerism, of commodification cannot intervene. Forty years on we can feel his feet on pavement—radical, outrageous, in motion, still in the present tense.

We went to our dress rehearsal with some hope and forty-five copies of the words to "If I Can Dream." We started an extended improvisation, drenching ourselves in a memory of Dr. King's words to the point that we were able to riff on them, play on the rhythms of key phrases: "Deep in my heart there's a trembling question," "Strong winds of promise," "Hope keeps shining on everyone."

At the pitched finale when we could feel the thrill of change coming through us, Billy was shouting "Right now! Right now!" and some of the choir harmonized on key phrases like "as long as I have the strength to dream" and the sermon became a field of sound, with stabs and shouts punctuating the voice tones. Then we started over and I asked Billy to sing the song and we created a duet between him and the choir, call-and-response, feeling the strength of Selma and Birmingham—all of us grateful to live within the legacy of that dream, and filling the room with powerful emotions. Still, we left rehearsal somehow unappeased, without having solved the riddle. We still felt hemmed in, left circling the same sentimentality, recalling the courageous moments of change, but not yet transcendent. We wanted to find our way off the end of the song, where the song points but doesn't go. The history-making that the song demands but can't do by itself.

We got it right at the Highline Ballroom a couple of weeks later. The room was packed, and there were fifty of us onstage. Billy, excited by the choir, got way underneath the details of the *American Idol* episode and sang his way deep into the sermon. He started to make demands. We were nodding along, and some of us stood spontaneously, shouting "Amen" and "Yes!" with our hands in the air ready to move, ready to go "right now."

And it was suddenly very clear what we had to do. As long as we remained on the stage, within the confines of our own version of entertainment, we remained simulations ourselves, Billy another Elvis impersonator. So I was electrified by the arrival of our solution. We simply had to walk from that "right now" and carry that purpose back into public space, into present-tense activism. And it was happening on its own. The choir vamped, an exalted crescendo of voices on a big major chord. "If I can dream, if I can dream, if I can dream, if I can dream," up and up and up and hundreds of bodies were standing in the Highline, parents and children, hipsters, radicals, tourists, and artists were shouting, moving. Billy and the choir were halfway off the stage and the crowd was halfway on the stage, and the band played on.

Billy shouted, "And IF you dream, then why can't your dream come true? Well IF you dream it then it WILL come true!" He continued: "I'm going to be radical, right now. I'm going to stop shopping, right now. I'm going to do something for peace, right now. I'm going to work for the earth, right now. I'm going to be a citizen, right now. Right now. I'm going to dream! I'm going to dream! Right now! Right now!"

I edged up next to Billy as we moved toward the door of the Highline. "Where are we taking these people?" I asked. "Outside," he said to me, then to the crowd, "Right now!" Right now!" I handed him the bullhorn. "Lets go to the pier," he said. "West to the river! South to the pier."

The Christopher Street pier, recently refurbished, had become a gathering place for teenagers, especially queer youth, many of them thrown out of their homes. Lately the police had been harassing them, writing them tickets or arresting them and throwing them in with the general jail population, forcing them to call their parents. Into the teeth of this fear and shame was a citywide call for support and solidarity. The choir was excited. "To the pier!"

When we got there we found a dance party under way. It was not a totally comfortable fit—at first they thought we were a preacher and a choir there to save them. But eventually we all relaxed into it and it became clear we'd come to save ourselves. On a Sunday in the late afternoon, with the sun soon going down, there was life after shopping. Billy shouted, "If I can dream!" And the crowd, filtering across the pier, sang back: "Right now! Right now!"

12. Theater, Justice, and Holy Spirit:
A Conversation with Bill Talen and Savitri D
ALISA SOLOMON

ALISA SOLOMON: Let's begin with Reverend Billy's beginning: How you got the idea and built the character and how you studied, physically and vocally, to develop it. I'd also like to talk about the nature of belief and the authority of a clergy figure. I wonder if granting that authority, believing in it, runs parallel to theatrical belief, the countenancing of the dramatic as-if. What do you think it means for people to have faith in your church? Simultaneously to engage the irony and the sincerity? That's my agenda for this discussion. And then to widen it out to questions of activism—and to wherever the conversation leads.

Billy, you spent significant time in the South as a young man and you have said that the preaching you heard there made a big impact. Do you remember the first preaching you saw in the South that really excited you?

BILL TALEN: It was in New Orleans churches. And also, the child preachers in the Latin Quarter are really something. The parents would put their little kid up on a soapbox—he might be eleven years old—and he'd just be preaching. I loved that. It was so strange, mesmerizing. But I was completely afraid of it too, because of the content. It had the same threats that the Dutch Reform people I'd grown up with had: hell and damnation. I was afraid of that.

But also excited because I was raised by Lutherans and Dutch Calvinists from the Dutch Reform Church, where there really isn't

Reverend Billy and Savitri D tussle with State Police outside New York's Javitz Center, 2008. (Photo by John Quilty.)

preaching going on. It's a Protestant reaction against the Papacy and there is no inflection in the voice, very little decoration of any kind up on the altar. I remember Dutch Reform Churches I was in where there was a man in a little narrow Goldwater tie in a black suit with a table and an old Bible on the table and that was it. And he never lifted his voice once. So preaching was a revelation to me.

AS: When did you start to preach? Which is another way of asking: How was Reverend Billy born?

BT: I was performing in my own two-, three-, four-character plays while I was co-artistic director of Life on the Water Theater in San Francisco. I produced myself once a year. My plays were falls-from-grace stories. I would play characters I was supposed to have been in life—architects, bankers, news anchors. A neighbor of my theater started coming to my plays—Sidney Lanier. He took me out to lunch after one of these plays and he said, "I don't know, you have some talent there, but there's a prophetic note in your voice."

SAVITRI D: He said there's prophetic energy in you. That's what he sensed. That Billy was wild and on fire in that very old-fashioned, John Brown way—forceful personalities with a lot of energy. They aren't common, those kinds of personalities. I think that Sidney first of all wanted Billy to use that energy—and I mean energy in a very literal way. I don't mean it in a woo-woo New Age way. I mean his actual physical energy. And to use it together with his love of language in a sort of spiritual pursuit. Sidney gave up on the church, but he never gave up on spirituality.

BT: So Sidney, a lapsed but not defrocked Episcopal priest, became my teacher, mentor, business partner. I moved to New York City under his guidance in the mid-'90s. He got me a job as the house manager at his old church, St. Clement's Episcopal on 46th Street and Ninth Avenue where he and Wynn Handman had started the American Place Theater back in 1962. He took me to scores of church services. In the beginning, I resisted significantly. I didn't want to have anything to do with Christians. They beat me up psychically when I was a kid. Let *Saturday Night Live* make fun of them, I didn't want to do that.

But he kept taking me to services and I fell in love with preaching because after all, I had been producing David Cale, Holly Hughes, Reno, Karen Finley, Spalding Gray in the Bay Area and I was in love with monologuing.

Sidney said that to listen to preaching I had to learn to turn off the text. He explained to me the strategy of using Bible narratives, religious characters. I think I had such a tough collision with Christianity as a child that I didn't want to know about a lot of that, but Sidney explained that Lenny Bruce was a Jesus character, that Lenny played every religious character that he could possibly play in that period from '58 through '63, up to his death. The character he played in the last couple of years of his life was just a lawyer, but he had played a nun, a priest, a rabbi, and a televangelist.

Sidney had been Lenny's friend, and he made me sit down and listen to Lenny Bruce monologues, which I had already listened to. But he was mixing Lenny in with these Pentecostal and Baptist preachers in the Bay Area that he took me to listen to.

AS: When he said you have to ignore the text, did he mean that you have to watch these guys at a level of their performance and never mind the content of what they're preaching?

BT: Exactly. They're warmongering, racist homophobes, many of them. But he said there's a wonderful instrument there. He explained, it's an American vocal tradition, like the blues, like auctioneering, like the announcers on the trains. It's one of the American traditions. It's one of the biggest ones, one of the strongest ones.

AS: So you studied the technique itself, the vocal and physical technique of the delivery and the metaphor-spinning and storytelling of the sermons.

BT: Yes.

SD: I've seen clips of some of that. Even with Sidney coaching you for a while, being with you and teaching you so much, you didn't really become a preacher until you cared about what you were saying, until suddenly the text wasn't fictional. And I've always thought that was so interesting, that you can't fake preach, you actually have to mean something. So finally, when you were mad enough about Times Square, mad enough at Disney, mad enough at [New York mayor Rudolph] Giuliani, suddenly all that information and all that teaching came out, came through you, and it registered in your instrument. It's like you had something to play finally.

BT: I did believe fiercely in what I was saying. I had been feeling overwhelmed by Consumerism, lonely, and I went down to the vortex of logos in Times Square and began to shout. When you have belief in what you're saying, the rhythm and the colors of the words—suddenly it's Rachmaninoff's Piano Concerto Number Two. It's really a vast landscape, and people start lifting themselves up into it. You see it in the congregation's eyes: they forget about their faces, their eyes go up. Some of them are in a memory place.

AS: How is that different from acting?

BT: There's definitely an overlap. It can be the same thing, but I don't think that my acting was ever that good!

SD: I think a great actor can perform the role of a preacher. But that's really different from preaching. With preaching, I always think of delivery. I use the word "delivery" literally. You're not reading lines, you're not performing a text. You are actually rooted in meaning and you have something important to say. And I think that's the primary difference. I mean, actors often have important things to say, and a play can be very important, but that's not the primary thing you're doing, or working from technically when you're acting, necessarily. I think as a preacher, and also because it's improvisational, largely, you're pursuing meaning and delivery all the time. The text isn't behind you, it's in front of you; you're going after it, and you're not remolding, reshaping, and finding an honest and authentic way to live and breathe a text. You're actually in pursuit of a text, you're trying to get to the meaning, at the same time that you hand it to someone. So it's very strange as a performance form. And the mastery of it is very mysterious. It's much more like singing, probably, like what happens with a great song. It's really falling off a cliff, I think, when preaching is powerful and strong, it is really like . . .

BT: It's flying into the air off a cliff.

SD: It's jumping off a cliff. You really don't know what's going to happen. And that's why the meaning and the belief are so important: because you can always return to that. That's why so many preachers work their sermons around a specific passage, some kind of text, and they always return to that. It's like an anchor; over and over and over again, they go back to that text and then they start that journey again. Out, out, out, away from the text, off the cliff and then they lose their way and they go back and they start again. It's really different from acting, though as I said, I think a great actor can perform that role.

AS: I have heard you use the word "appropriation" to talk about Reverend Billy's role. Can you explain? What are you appropriating from the traditional preacher? Form alone?

SD: In this country preaching has mostly been a Christian form. It came up through churches and certainly it came up in parallel to the blues, gospel music . . .

BT: Slavery.

SD: . . . work songs. It definitely came out of a lot of things that weren't natively Christian. I think part of Billy's fear of preaching was the Christian part. Do you have to be Christian to preach? Does it rely on its Christianity, and then how much of that do you have to appropriate? How much of the Christianness is Christian? How much of what we see as Christianness is actually Christian?

Well, as it turns out, not very much, amazingly. The rhythms of preaching have nothing to do with Christianity. Nor the physical life it has, the way it expresses itself in a body.

I've been to a lot of Baptist services, in Virginia, primarily. Deep Southern Baptist preachers are really among the greatest performers I've ever watched. I cannot believe the way they can talk. The way words and language just roll out of their mouths, the liquid poetry coming out of those, mostly, men—it's astonishing. Unfortunately, yes, a lot of times what they're saying is disturbing. There's a lot of damnation and talk about hell, and there's not a lot to look forward to necessarily. (Laughter) And then suddenly there is. And it's transformative, and suddenly it's all forgiven. I remember going in particular to a church service for a young preacher who had died of AIDS, that must have been in 1991, '92 . . .

AS: Before you were involved with Reverend Billy.

SD: Yeah. My mom and I went, because of a wonderful preacher we knew. When my sister died, we buried her on our land, but the law in Virginia says that at a burial, you have to have a religious figure of some kind, who's registered with the state, or something. So we just opened the phone book and called the first name, Doctor Reverend Johnson, and he came out there and he helped bury my sister. We had a pond there with some fish in it, so he said, "Oh, do you mind if I come fish in your pond? I love to fish." We said of course, and so he started inviting us to his services, and we would go and I couldn't even believe what

I was seeing. He has two churches, Pilgrim Baptist Church and Zion Baptist Church, one in the middle of town, and one really a country church that's been there since the Civil War. It's one of the oldest churches around there. Anyway, it was his son who died of AIDS, and he was a preacher, too, and when he was buried, it was a four-hour service and there were only a few songs. Four hours of preaching by preachers and pastors from all over the South. And you would think in a setting like this—it was just all forgiveness. They were very open and honest talking about his AIDS; they were very open and honest talking about his being gay and his love for Jesus. I was amazed by that. That totally broke me open to the whole thing. Because up until then I shared Billy's "Oh my god, no, it's homophobic, it's damnation, hell, damnation." Because my mother and I used to go visit churches when I was a kid. Every Sunday we'd go to a different church, kind of hoping that we'd find a church that made sense that we could go to, and none of them did. We'd actually by then been to probably a hundred church services together, even though we're not Christian. So I've seen a lot of preachers, and priests, and religious people, standing up talking about the Bible, and the thing that makes it ever forgivable is when people mean it, and then you know you can at least fight back or give back or be in an engaged conversation with them, when they mean it.

BT: It's not marketing.

SD: Even if you disagree with them at least you know it's direct. That's another thing that really distinguishes the preaching form from acting. The more direct it is . . . well I guess that doesn't distinguish it so much. The more you talk about the difference between the two, the more you see that they're almost the same!

My early directors always said, "Go to the text, go to the meaning, when in doubt, go to the meaning, say the line, drink the tea." So when I say that a preacher has to be direct, it's a lot like a note you'd give an actor: Be direct. And if it's a great text, you really don't have to do much. You just have to say the words.

BT: Right. And a good preacher may be a bad actor. A great preacher might even be the opposite of charismatic, yet have an empathic note in his voice, a hard-to-pin-down sincerity that makes it possible to speak movingly about life and death, love and work. And bad preaching is indirect, just like bad acting.

SD: Exactly. So maybe the thing that ruins them is the same, but the thing that makes them great is very different.

AS: "Indirect" is such an interesting word in this context because with preaching, the best sermon texts are metaphorical. They often spin out on long, winding metaphorical journeys that you could call indirect.

SD: Well, it's like when you see a picture of the space shuttle or something, and you know that there's that astronaut who's dangling from the rope out in space. He is still directly connected to that machine; he's getting his oxygen through that dangling thing. A great preacher is like that rope. He is taking you way out until you're really not sure where you are.

But you're still there, you're with someone, you're not alone, you're with the preacher and then normally, usually, you're with God too. The preacher is touched. But then he can bring you right back. You're safe.

BT: Partly because you're in that amazing thing: you're in that community of believers.

And they're breathing and sighing and laughing and shouting all around you. You feel their body heat.

AS: A theater audience, presumably, is like that, too: also breathing and sighing and laughing, and you feel them as an actor on a stage as well. There's a kind of belief—the suspension of disbelief—that makes them, in a way, a community of believers. When I've seen you perform, particularly in the indoor settings of theaters, the suspension of disbelief is a theatrical one, right? At least that's how I experience it: I'm playing at being in church. I'm not really going to church.

SD: The language is so funny: Suspension of disbelief. Or is it, suspension of belief? Because some people go to our church service and they're Christians, so they're actually putting their belief on hold, right? Not their disbelief. That's fascinating, too. There's also this going through the motions—the fake-it-till-you-make-it scene that happens in the show. That if you start saying "amen" enough, suddenly you mean it, or you're playing along, you're muscularly, you're physically involved, you're emotionally involved, you're laughing. And then there's a moment you're in agreement. You have been broken open enough to agreements. You know the old trope about comedy: make 'em laugh and then—how does it go? Punch 'em in the nose? Grab 'em by the heartstring? There's a little bit of that going on. It really depends a lot on the position of the person coming into the show. Whether that person is truly secular—and those people exist—or whether you're a deeply spiritual person who's never had a religious home or a format for your spiritual life, or whether you're a straight-up radical and this is your politics and you would be going, "Yes!" or "Hell, yes!" or you would be shouting along in a call-and-response on the street or in the audience.

BT: Preach it now, preach it!

SD: You just mean it. You share the meaning. And then other people are discovering it. We've had amazing experiences with audiences when we felt they were completely not participating, not going along with it. And then at the end they just go crazy for it.

AS: I expect you need to have a certain familiarity and comfort with some religious tropes to create and appreciate that process. To, well, have faith in it.

BT: Savitri and I share something in that we had severe fundamentalism in our parentage, and then we also were both confronted with communities where there was a New Age proliferation of religiosity mixed in promiscuously with indigenous beliefs. Savitri was in New Mexico and I was in Marin County. But then we both had—Savitri, in your case I think of your mother, in my case, Sidney Lanier—we had wonderful teachers. The leap from fundamentalism to that big smorgasbord of warmed-over religions that is the New Age is a dangerous weightlessness, but we both had lucky relationships, we found good teachers.

SD: And our privilege. I was always given an imaginative outlet. I was given a place to have ecstatic release that didn't rely on anything except my own mind and that's the privilege of our specific kind of education, seeing that in art as opposed to religion.

AS: Savitri, you mentioned searching for churches with your mother. What is your religious background and how did it prepare you for the Church of Stop Shopping? You were born on a commune, right?

SD: Yes, a non-denominational spiritual commune, in New Mexico. At the time, my parents were NYC artists who left here and bought a big piece of land in the early sixties. They were sort of ahead of the sixties wave. We lived on a mountain in the wilderness and they had a rigorous spiritual life. Then my father went to Jerusalem just as I was born and converted to Islam. But my mother continued on this other trajectory, which was essentially a community-building one and in some way the legacy of my parents in my life more than anything has been this community-building, which I feel I've taken into another generation.

When I was about eight, my mom and sisters and I moved to Virginia, because she and some friends had determined that that's where the best public schools were. We went back and forth to New Mexico sometimes. And sometimes I would go live with my dad in the Middle East. I lived for a year with my dad in Mecca, right in the heart of the Muslim world. Everyone is a Muslim in Mecca. I'll never experience that again, being in a place where every single person shares a faith. It's really an amazing feeling, and when it's prayer time, all over the world people are praying to where you are.

AS: While we're doing biography, tell me how you became an artist.

SD: I finished high school when I was fifteen and I went out west and was an apprentice to a painter and a jeweler, and somehow I ended up in college in Montana and I took a dance class. I had always been a dancer. My mother couldn't afford dance lessons, so I didn't have dance schooling, but I always loved it and it came easily to me, so when I finally took a dance class, it was so great. That's how I came into my theatrical life, and I expanded from there. When I finished school, I moved back to Virginia and started a company with four other dancers, the Zen Monkey Project. We were in rehearsal all the time. We did a choreographic cycle where we each made a piece a year and we committed to doing that with each other. The piece in the end was not the point; it was this incredible rehearsal process.

AS: And coming to New York?

SD: By the time I moved here in the mid-'90s, some part of being a theater artist, being in a rehearsal room all the time, had kind of played out. I was looking out at the world and a part of me was waking up. I realize now it was my radicalism, trying to figure out how to make art political, which I had been struggling with all that time: How do you bring what's happening in the world into these settings, into these rehearsals, onto this stage? I thought I was able to do it as a writer, but I couldn't do it in dance. It just seemed impossible. You'd make a dance piece and people would think it was about aliens, and then in theater, there is just so little control over content, and as an actor, politically, it's just such a disempowering position to be in, especially as a woman. I had made five or six movies and I had a lot of work as an actor. I was touring sometimes. And I suddenly realized that every decision that got made—whether I had a part, whether I had a job, where I was going to stand onstage, what line I was going to read—were all being made by men, not me, and I thought this can't be my life, I can't devote my life to this. That all coincided with my moving to New York. So it was funny that just when I got here, I lost interest in being a performer.

BT: That was a kind of turning point time in 1996. It was the last great political Broadway season, with *Bring in 'Da Noise, Bring in 'Da Funk; Twilight: Los Angeles, 1992;* and *Angels in America.* They were all on Broadway simultaneously.

AS: Which meant there was more—or less—of that kind of energy downtown? Was it a great bubbling up or the end of an era? Or . . . ?

SD: When I came here, I couldn't feel the heat, I couldn't feel the energy. I looked around and where I saw the energy was on the street. That's where I found the magic in New York, the most dramatic situations, the most interesting language. I didn't give up theater—I didn't stop going to theater or stop knowing theater people—but I felt my passion for it shifting. Of course when that's happening you don't necessarily recognize what's happening to you, you just notice that suddenly you're not compelled to do the thing that for ten previous years you had done all day. So I started writing a lot and making a lot of visual art . . .

BT: And you became a theater manager.

SD: And I got a day job in a theater. My interest in theater, as an artist, had changed fundamentally and I didn't know how to make the change, I didn't know what it would look like. My radical education was so limited. I couldn't look back at a body of knowledge and understand what was happening to me.

AS: But by having lived outside of Consumerism—which is such a rare experience—maybe you had an unusual sense of possibility, or an absence of a kind of brainwashing.

SD: Absolutely. I trusted that I didn't have to have a certain kind of career or that my validity would not have to come from certain kinds of success. I always knew that. I had great role models that way and very little brainwashing on that front. In that period, I spent a lot of time in the street. I spent every spare moment when I wasn't working, wandering the streets of New York and just absorbing, looking hearing feeling, just trying to make sense of how you translate it if you can.

When I was in my teens I was very political. I organized lots of things at my school—hunger protests and peace concerts, and I was very active. It was when I became an artist that I stopped being politically active. They were very distinct pieces of my life; I didn't know that I could put them together, though that seems so obvious now.

Then a lot of things coincided—meeting Billy and September 11th— and over about a year's time, I had the sudden understanding that I really had to dedicate myself to justice in a different and new way, that would be the life I wanted, that was meaningful to me. Yeah, I could continue being a dancer and performer and making plays, but there were a lot of people doing that and a lot of people doing it really well and that world wasn't necessarily going to miss me. But I had a sense that I had a set of skills and experiences that could feed a different kind of movement in a much more powerful way, and that was all sort of fermenting when I met Billy, who I think was having a similar set of experiences, although he is older than I am and was a little further along in that evolution.

AS: It's amazing that when the two of you met and got together, even though you were the manager in the theater where Billy was performing, you hadn't ever seen his work.

SD: True. I was managing The Culture Project and he lived upstairs and performed downstairs. He happened to perform on Sundays and I never worked on Sundays, so I never saw those shows. It wasn't until about five months after we met and started going out, when I produced Billy's show at the band shell in Central Park—that was the first time I'd seen it.

AS: What did you think of it?

SD: It was a disaster!

BT: Alisa, you were at a lot of those shows. Were they that bad?

(Laughter)

SD: There was a lot that wasn't bad. There was something in it that was totally wild, something I had never seen before and I didn't know what it was. There was a power that was overwhelming to me. Its theatrical shape was disastrous, but at its core was something not disastrous at all. I kept asking myself, "What is this?" And that was the striking part for me, the "What is this?"

AS: What were your reservations, Savitri?

SD: Initially I was concerned about whether you should make fun of religion like that. Having grown up with so much religion and so much ecumenical spirituality . . .

BT: Respecting each other's symbols . . .

SD: . . . I was one of those people watching, thinking, "Are you allowed to do that?" But it didn't take long for me to realize how intrigued I was by it. I still am. I still have that same feeling: there is something in it that is out of control. Part of it's Billy, but part of it is being in this country and taking that form and trying to undermine what this country was built on, so there is something really tense and exciting about it. I still have lots of doubts about it as a form, I still have a lot of doubts about its effectiveness, but ultimately I still don't know what it is, so I'm still interested in it. One thing that struck me right away was that lots of different kinds of people came to it. I hadn't seen that in New York. At other shows, I always knew who was in the room and that was very disappointing to me, terribly disappointing, that this form that I had invested my whole adult life in could be so predictable in that way.

And the choir was always fascinating to me. I thought, here is this funny body of people and some of them are really good at what they do and some of them are not. As a sculptural possibility it was always great—they always looked odd and strange. They don't look like actors or performers. They were highly imperfect; it was wonderful.

BT: The choir has the community in it, people who live real lives, and are going to rehearse only once a week . . .

SD: And that's in part about breaking through the slickness, the trend toward incredible slickness. It was everywhere in the late nineties. You'd go see a show, even if it was some off-off-off-Broadway house, and you'd have to poke through all these layers of production just to get to the thing.

AS: And yet there is a lot of rigor in the Reverend Billy performance. Going back to the beginning, let's get technical. So, Billy, you had a lot of energy, some of it trained through acting and solo performing you'd done already. But what specifically did you have to learn vocally, physically, and about writing to create the character or the persona —I am not even sure how you relate—maybe to *become* Reverend Billy?

BT: We had lots of failed attempts. We had a preacher in a play. We tried that. That was only a bridge from my old work. We tried re-creating

New Testament stories from a sort of secular-humanist-comic perspective. That had to do with Sidney introducing me to [the religious scholar and expert on the historical Jesus] John Dominic Crossan and giving me the Gnostic gospels to read and the whole historical Jesus movement, which he linked up, of course, to Lenny Bruce and to certain characters in Tennessee Williams's plays. (Tennessee was Sidney's cousin.) But the first step was finding the right setting for the character and the right setting turned out to be the sidewalk in front of the Disney Store at 42nd Street and Seventh Avenue.

And then I had sidewalk preachers on both sides of me and I developed my shout, my whoop.

AS: Your "whoop"?

BT: It's a shout that has your own colorations, your own vibrato, and it's really a collection of shouts. You have many different kinds of shouts. "Mickey Mouse is the Anti-Christ" [he demonstrates, melodiously] "Please! Don't let your chillll-dren come into this den of iniquity!"

AS: Did you develop it by imitation?

BT: I did partly.

AS: Whom did you imitate?

BT: I imitated the sidewalk preachers who were on either side of me. I would just go and listen to them.

SD: Technically, it's right on the edge of singing. It's as if you are about to sing and instead of singing, you shout. But it's the same impulse as singing in a way because it has rhythm in it and it has melody in it and you risk losing control. You're lifting up into the voice. And muscularly—you use a different set of muscles. Technically it's lower in the belly, it's more driven by air. It's much more like shouting than it is like talking. You make the effort to sing, and then shout. And it's a little scary-feeling. It's not a natural thing to do with your voice—wouldn't you agree? It's work.

BT: (Chuckles) It's natural for me now.

SD: But it's always work.

BT: There were a few months there in front of the Disney Store, where boy, it really was work. I lost my voice several times. I had the loud environment of Times Square to deal with and I didn't always have amplification because the police would come and take my bullhorns from me. You have to learn to do the shout in your body and you have to learn to accept that for long periods of time people will walk by only showing you the side of their face.

I had to decide whether I would be funny. It turned out there was a mixture of being mesmerizing and being funny. "There's only one sin!" [Song-like preacher's voice.] "And that is the sin of toooourism!" So I would say that in Times Square in 1997, '98.

SD: It's so different—that preaching—from the preaching Billy does today.

BT: It's come a long way.

SD: Because your theology, so-called, is so much more developed. And the joke is on the surface and then you almost don't have to express the joke.

AS: What's the joke?

SD: The Elvis joke the—

BT: Elvis-impersonating televangelist

SD: —impossible silly hair and white suit. Oh, it's obviously not a real preacher—the joke of reality! The reality joke.

BT: That's a bond with the community at the beginning of the preaching.

SD: Or something to overcome with the community because they're resistant because it's fake.

BT: We were in Tompkins Square last night. They're converted. That's the congregation.

SD: There's no one to apologize to there. They're relieved that it's fake. They're like—phew! Or in Europe, "What a relief! He's not a real preacher. Thank God!"

BT: Some of the people want to call me religious. Some want to call me political. Some want to call me theatrical.

AS: Does what they call you matter to you?

BT: In the first few minutes of a good Fabulous Worship, the people will be relieved of the label, of religion, the arts, or politics. That's where the resistance to Consumerism is in the form. In a good service, that's working, I won't be a product in the sense that I won't be a label.

SD: Within the confines of a theater space, there's an understanding and a knowledge of Reverend Billy. At this point it's very rare that there are people there who don't know in advance what to expect. I think it's much more dangerous and in a way much more interesting on the street where most people really don't know. Even in New York City if we go outside to, say, a park right now with the choir and Billy, a lot of people there are going to be unnerved by it. They don't have the safety of a performance to protect them. It is dangerous and startling.

AS: Dangerous how?

SD: It's dangerous for us because they might hate us, there might be incredible hostility. They might actually attack us—that's happened before. Or it might be dangerous in the other direction: That we really offend them, that we startle and unnerve them or overwhelm them. I think those labels—I don't even know how to apply those labels when we are in public space. What do they even mean? What is art? Who cares? You really are a preacher with a choir when you are in public space. There's no confusion there. On the street in public space— that's where the magic of these mashed up forms really works and does what it is supposed to do: which is make consumers feel confused, which is the opposite of how consumers are trained to feel by Consumerism.

AS: Namely, comfortable? Knowing what they are looking at and want?

SD: Yeah. Passively sated. "I have what I need." Or "I know how to get what I need."

AS: But just unsatisfied enough, right, to keep wanting just a little more, or the next new thing.

SD: You want more, your desire is activated. But you understand it. It's not alarming.

BT: So the preaching is different in different places, different altars, different sidewalks. Generally the preaching has developed over the years,

Reverend Billy and the choir baptize a four-month-old baby at the Christopher Street pier in New York, 2009. (Photo by Brennan Cavanaugh.)

from my attempting virtuosity to my attempting to know what is happening at this time among this group of people and what is happening to me. Starting from that place and then going toward flight.

AS: Will you talk about the evolution of the theology? Or the politics? Perhaps they are the same.

BT: It began with identifying the place to preach in front of the devil—the Disney store. Trying to save the souls of the tourist-consumers. That was millennial time. A lot of the language was millennial. When the preaching started hitting its stride for the first time it was arranged around compelling evil—the sweatshop basis for the economy of Disney; the twenty thousand sweatshop factories around the world; the marketing juggernaut that especially attacks childhood imagination; the pushing aside with eminent domain and Rudy Giuliani's police and so forth, of local eccentric people of any kind, just people who didn't seem to have credit cards; the pushing out of small independent shops, local culture; the privatizing of the sidewalks and streets; trying to turn Times Square into a mall. There was a ten-foot-tall statue of Mickey Mouse just in back of me at the entrance of the Disney Store and there were hundreds of Mickey Mouse logos everywhere. So the doorknobs were silhouetted silver Mickey heads. Mickey carpeting. It was a Mickey environment. The logo—which is so intense at Times Square, with all the mega-corporations wanting to have their logos there, and many of them sweatshop companies—the logo was a big part of my definition of evil. So I had a very dramatic and well-developed devil in this theology.

At that time my saving of the souls—because I didn't want to be a Christian, I didn't want to be a Jesus guy—was something called God-sightings. God-sightings were difficult to do outdoors. I would have my God-sightings in St. Clements. That is where I started what later became what Savitri directs: the Fabulous Worship, cobbled together from any worship service I'd ever been to and full of inventions of my own. And one of the inventions of my own was this thing called the God-sighting. This is where secular humanist ironist hipsters could come forward and say, "I saw God." And they would sit with me, like in a talk show, up in front, and they would describe, when they were eight years old and they saw a drop of water on the tile in their bathroom with the sun coming through the window, and suddenly there was a rainbow in the drop of water. And that was their God-sighting.

SD: Wasn't that Samuel Delany's God-sighting? That was his!

BT: When I first came downtown and I was no longer the house manager at St. Clements, Tony Torn was my director. We presented Millennium's Neighborhood at Judson Church. And the first places I was invited into were Charas-El Bohio Community Center in the Lower East Side and community gardens, which were under attack at that time. So I was a part of that whole effort to save the gardens that were about to be bulldozed by Rudy Giuliani. When I started preaching in the community gardens, it was the beginning of pastoring. The pastoring came into my preaching in a quieter voice. I was in gardens instead of out on the sidewalk on the corner of 42nd Street and Seventh Avenue. And people were coming up with their babies and asking for blessings.

AS: Did that surprise or disturb you? Did it freak you out?

BT: It just felt so good. I remember being in the Esperanza garden [a vibrant, more than twenty-year-old community garden at East 7th Street and Avenue C in Manhattan, destroyed to make way for an apartment building despite community protests]. I was preaching to about twenty-five people and every one of them was dressed like a vegetable. Tomatoes, zucchinis, broccoli, and a croaky frog. Twenty-four hours a day there were people there with fires, people living there. And mother Alicia Torres [the founder of the garden] next-door. So that was another kind of preaching, with a softer voice, and pastoring.

AS: That's a point when the performance aspect—to whatever extent there is self-conscious irony in the performance of Reverend Billy, whether on street corners or in theaters—disappears. In that setting, people were sincerely asking you for blessings.

SD: What's fascinating, though, is that it does both. The irony does and doesn't disappear. Because there are different people in that setting. That is not a monolithic group of people. And that's a perfect example.

In Esperanza, you had Puerto Rican grandmothers and you had straight-up anarchists.

BT: And some of those Puerto Rican grandmothers were the daughters of Puerto Rican nationalists . . .

SD: . . . but they had raised kids, they probably went to church a lot of them. So you had people there—just take someone like Brad Will, sadly not with us any longer [he was shot and killed in Oaxaca, Mexico, in 2006, during demonstrations by striking teachers that he was documenting], a kid in his twenties, educated, middle-class kid, anarchist, squatter, fearless, willing to fight with everything he had for this garden that he probably just encountered for the first time a few years before. Standing with him, a woman in her seventies who nurtured that garden and cleared it of needles twenty years earlier. What Brad needs from Billy is totally different from what the grandmother is expecting from Billy. So for Brad, the irony, the performance is the way in for him.

AS: That's an important point. Say more about the audience member or the encounter with the person for whom the irony is not part of it and whether there's any anxiety or squeamishness on your side of, "Oh my God! They're taking me completely seriously. Am I lying to them? They are asking me for a blessing! Can I honestly give one?"

BT: Absolutely. But I was scared. I was on the phone every day to Sidney. Tony Torn and Savitri were telling me, "We don't need this parody in your voice anymore." They were telling me consciously, "Get real. We need a preacher here in the Village. We need a preacher." At that time, right after Millennium's Neighborhood, which was November 1999, I was trying to get the self-referential tone out of my voice and come straight from an emotion that was in the room and in me. Then I had a choir for the first time. The pastoring, the choir, and direction to reduce the parody and find the compassionate preaching all happened together.

SD: It's the choir that lets Billy do that. The choir is the authority in a funny way. Because when Billy is insecure or it doesn't seem possible that this hetero white male with blue eyes and white hair can be in that position, with him at his side and really actively engaged in the meaning, movement, and the values, is a representative group.

BT: Diverse in gender, race, age . . .

SD: It's not just outward legitimacy, though. It's inner legitimacy, Billy knowing: These people agree with me. I'm not bestowing the blessing of me as an individual. I'm bestowing the blessing of this group of people, this community.

AS: Have you ever said to somebody who authentically wants your blessing: "Well, I'm not a real preacher. Maybe you better go to your local parish if what you need is a real blessing"?

BT: In New York City and any of the places that we frequent, in European capitals and progressive communities with activists in small towns that are trying to save themselves from super malls, the combination of the collar with a big polyester suit—there is a cultural aesthetic fence to jump that lots of those people around have already jumped. But if you walk with a cobalt blue suit and white collar into a Episcopal or Anglican or Roman Catholic community, that's not the right costume for them so it's quite rare that that misunderstanding takes place . . .

SD: Or if it does take place it's more likely that people assume, based on the costume, that he is part of the invented Christian church, which is self-proclaimed to a large degree anyway, the Evangelical traditions, Pentecostal traditions. There is more latitude there. People don't necessarily think he has to go to seminary, but I don't think anyone has mistaken him for a Roman Catholic. When we have been in Europe, especially in smaller places, you do see women of a certain age kind of deferring to the collar. I find it awkward, a little unnerving. I want to say to them [whispering], "It's fake."

It's interesting, because there are two dilemmas there. There's the dilemma of you pretending to be in a faith that you don't take seriously and then there is offending someone else's faith. They are really quite distinct. I think the first one is really interesting, how a political person who is really deeply involved in social justice has to be really careful not to take that power, which after all, has been at the root of so much of that injustice you are fighting.

BT: And then of course there is the wonderful connection that we occasionally get to feel to the liberation theology of South and Central America. Father Julio Torres was smuggled out of El Salvador by Bishop Paul Moore and for years he was the vicar at St. Mark's Church and he invited us in there.

I did recently have the kind of experience you were talking about. I was walking in my neighborhood in Brooklyn, Windsor Terrace, and it was twilight and my bright blue suit got kind of darker in that light. It's a Catholic neighborhood of old Italian and Irish families and a lady called out to me from her doorstep, "Father," and she needed a priest to pray for someone ill in her family. She was in tough shape. I just said, "I wish you the very best. I'll pray for you, hope things are okay," and did not want to represent myself as being anything but Reverend Billy.

SD: But you didn't say, "Oh ma'am you've confused me for something I am not. I'm not a real reverend." You chose what was real in yourself, which was an honest compassion: I'll pray for you and think of you.

BT: I do try to represent myself honestly. I told her I'm not a part of the Roman Catholic faith. But I am pastor in a church—that part of this project has been growing over the years. Savitri and I together minister to people who are ill, who are giving birth, the life passage events, that is where the pastor has work to do and that continues to change and deepen.

SD: Just as we try to deepen the aspect where people take their relationship to the economy and to their immediate culture seriously enough to bring values to it, I think that we make ourselves available to that kind of pastoring because we are constantly talking about this other elemental relationship that people have with the world around them: What are you spending your money on? How are you living your life? Because we raise these moral and ethical questions all the time, we open the door for this other kind of pastoring. I always feel like I am trying to refocus people back toward the political, toward justice—because I feel like in a way we can be good friends to people, we can be compassionate human beings. Billy has really learned to be open in that setting, that pastoral role. It's a listening state more than anything, which is funny—the performer to evolve into the listener.

AS: You mentioned that this is a more recent development in the evolution of Reverend Billy and that a lot changed after September 11, 2001. Would you elaborate?

BT: A tremendous thing happened after 9/11, which was most of the theaters closed their doors. Our instinct was to open the doors immediately, and we were performing within weeks. We were at Union Square all that week, we were performing outdoors. I was Reverend Billy in Union Square right away, and soon we were performing indoors, too.

And there was something special going on that I couldn't put my finger on, but with some notable exceptions, basically the theaters were shut, and that was a point where we sensed we had a ritual responsibility. We had people who were hurting. There was a funny combination of celebrating and sorrowing going on—

SD: —which we can still barely talk about.

BT: People were meeting each other in the middle of the street, people who had been living next door to each other for years, introducing themselves; there were no cars below 14th Street; there were some really interesting things going on in Union Square.

AS: Until they swept it up and shut it down . . .

BT: Until they took all our flowers away, and candles. 9/11 was very clarifying for us. We opened the doors. That was our instinct and we knew we were doing the right thing. It was just the basic need was so clear and that was when we realized there is something decisively different between what we do and *Tony and Tina's Wedding.*

AS: What was the need that Reverend Billy was uniquely able to address?

SD: I think people wanted to be in rooms together. They wanted fellowship. But these are post-religious people, people who did not have a religious setting to go to, or a faith setting to go to, and there are so few spaces left in New York. What happened with us also illustrates that.

So you come here because you *can* come here. You can come here because these doors are open. We can be together. Maybe they were just coming for that, just to be in a room with other people and not be alone. I don't know.

BT: That's the thing about ritual—I mean ritual that doesn't come from two hundred years of religiosity. We didn't know why everyone was there, but we were trying to find out. Opening the doors and saying we're here was key. And folks knew we had a kind of immunity from fundamentalism and yet were praying and singing in big groups about all the big life questions. New Yorkers make spiritual lives for themselves with relationships, art, work, sex. But it's not easy to pull off a secular spiritual expression in a large group and not be vulnerable to the bureaucracies of an official priesthood or fundamentalism or deity. That's not a risk with us.

SD: I think it was early October that we opened, we did about six shows in October and November at the Culture Project.

AS: I remember the intensity of those shows and the eagerness to be in some kind of social space . . .

SD: . . . protected in a way, knowing you're not going to get in a fight. If you started talking about the attacks at the deli, you didn't know how people were going to react. I remember several dinner parties that fall that we completely busted up.

BT: We said we are against bombing Afghanistan and people started shouting at each other.

SD: So it wasn't necessarily a time when you wanted to be in a room with a lot of very different opinions in it. There are times when there is something to be gained from being in a room that filters out political opposition to some degree. It's helpful sometimes.

AS: You said you were singing and praying. And you told that woman in Windsor Terrace you'd pray for her. To whom? Who—or what—is the *theos* in your theology?

BT: I think that originally *theos* was the 713 stories that each of us is made of. I made that up. I declared a whole psychology system, where, from very early in our lives, we start accepting and rejecting certain narratives into our bodies. It's like we anthologize ourselves, we are the editors of our own DNA. And some of the stories are unforgettable because they're traumas, and some of them are glorious, some are minor and you don't know why you remember them, but we have memories, dreams, experiences that we gather. And then we build ourselves, and ultimately become unlike anyone else. That building is a duet with life that we perform and we end up with 713 stories. And I'm saying that the evil corporations want to delete certain stories that they consider powerful, the stories that bind the stories together.

SD: But why are you trying to find a God?

BT: To keep a deity out.

SD: That's it. There is no deity. The answer is, there isn't one. And if there is one, it's a game we're playing. If there's an answer to that question, it's the community. The answer to the question is: There's too many. The answer to the question is: It's New York City and that means we're all in the room and we're diverse and it means that there are Christians in the room, Mohamed's there talking, it means Jesus-God is there, there are Jews in the room. We're all here, so we don't have to choose one, we don't get to choose one. And that's different from an ecumenical gathering. We're not saying that they're all the same or that we honor them, each one. We're saying, that's not what this is about. I think, personally.

BT: Oh, is that what you believe? (Laughter) 'Cause you're preaching!

SD: If there's an answer, it's the Earth, it's the thing we take cues from. If the *theos* is there to give us cues and information and we're supposed to honor it and respect our relationship to it above all else, it would have to be the Earth, and the reflection of the Earth for us is the community of people, because we live in New York City. That's how the Earth presents itself here.

AS: Do you believe in God?

BT: You know, I—uh—I believe in the Creator. I don't want to assign God a sex. I don't make up a personality for it. Lately—since Katrina—we've being saying: The only authentic preacher is the Earth and the Earth is preaching to us in no uncertain terms right now, with tsunamis and the two-mile-wide freak tornadoes.

SD: It's really hard for us to take a position on that, to express that. For one, because we believe in social justice, in radical justice, which means that you can't say no. Because does that mean that five billion people are silly idiots if you say no? No. On the other hand—we continue to wonder.

BT: Life, life! We believe in life and wonder! We all have that voice in the back of our brains that is marveling at life every second of every day. Because it is amazing, isn't it? Even the most cynical people have this question going on. So engaging that voice, letting that question—what is life?—get aired out once in a while, will make you jump and shout and do the damndest things. That's what we do in our church. We don't want that deity with the answers. We want that life with the questions. Amen?

SD: We continue to wonder. Now, a fundamentalist will laugh at you when you say that. My father—to him that's not an answer. You have faith or you don't have faith.

BT: But we don't believe in the answer. We believe in the question. When I was saying a prayer in the gardens, I would always make up a god/goddess mystery gardener on the spot. I still do it. Making up a new god every day is the solution. I read that in the Gnostic gospels, according to Elaine Pagels, there was a sect that she discovered of early Christian mystics before they were slaughtered by the proto-Catholics. They would get up every morning and greet the day and part of their responsibility to that day was to have a new name for the Creator. And that happened every day. That's something I started doing down in the gardens. It's a natural outgrowth of God-sightings.

SD: We are still learning a lot about this specifically. About the belief part of it. What do you believe? Those direct questions: What do you believe? What do you believe in? What do you want? It's funny because those are the same questions you ask activists. They're much easier to answer as an activist than as a religious person: I want justice, I want real justice. I want less of a gap between rich and poor. I want other priorities besides private property to drive our legal system.

BT: We found that there's a spiritual heat in effective lefty politics, or there should be! It works better for us, makes us braver and calmer.

AS: What about the activism itself, then? We spoke about your religious backgrounds. What about your activist backgrounds?

SD: Both of us came to activism in fairly roundabout ways—not through an education or a body of knowledge, but through a set of experiences and disappointments and anger. I think there is a tendency in many groups toward a kind of paralysis in which people say, "I can't do anything until I know everything." But if you scratch the surface of any radical history, you will find people who do things and have no idea what they are doing. To some degree we fall into that category, which I have mixed feelings about, but I'm saying it as openly as I can because I hope it will embolden other people to trust their instincts about basic things that are going on around them. That's the source of our citizenship: looking out the window and seeing something going wrong out there, not because you read a book about that being wrong, but because you feel it. To some extent both of us came to our activist lives from that direction, with different inputs. Billy came up in the sixties, and I don't think you can come up through those years without absorbing some of that idea. It's in you; it's in the landscape.

AS: I agree there's a kind of professionalization of activism that has happened in some spheres over the last couple of decades, a sense that citizenship itself doesn't demand engagement from us, that we should leave it to the experts, so I appreciate your idea. I know, too, that you both have done a hell of a lot of reading—from the Marxist classics through theories of spectacle and corporatism and so on. And of course, Jane Jacobs. All that informs your work, even if it is not quoted on the surface. And more important, perhaps, is that you are not bound to a particular ideology.

SD: We have neglected to attach ourselves to an ideology purposefully. It's not a useful way to organize people anymore. When I see groups organized ideologically they tend to be brittle.

BT: We try to use humor and music and openly welcome all people— that's organic to our design and -isms often just don't go with that. We want to resist all labels, which are a kind of Consumerism.

SD: But I don't want to say it's pointless, either. Ideology can be a useful training mechanism. I studied a kind of modern dance to learn how to dance, not because I didn't want to do any other kind of dance, but because the narrowing of the skill set is helpful in learning. You do these nine things over and over, or you think inside of these precepts for a while, to train your body or mind to think. So as a philosophical and political tool there is great possibility there. But I just know from trying to get people into the street that ideology hasn't seemed to work for my generation. It's not an effective organizing tool.

BT: Our approach is built around stories—telling a story about an experience that a family has or that a small business has and then sharing the experience of that story . . .

SD: Well, I don't know if what we do works either. I'm not saying we have the thing that works. I'm not sure what we do gets people in the street. Like most of my generation, I resist certain kinds of compartmentalization, of identity collapsing, of reductionism, but I also think there is a lot to be gained from the rigor of ideology and the rigor of thinking things through.

AS: The 2009 mayoral campaign you ran for a year must have had an impact in this area.

SD: Yes. We didn't necessarily come up with an ideology in the campaign, but because we had to formulate a platform, we had to go through a series of steps, think things through we had never taken the time to do before.

BT: Yeah, we had to create a platform. It was good for us.

SD: It was extremely helpful, and it's hard! And you fail over and over again and it doesn't make sense and it's too open or it's too specific, and you understand how people end up in meetings all day figuring out their basic manifesto. I think it's important that there are people doing that work. I know our proclivity is not towards that, our skill set is not in that arena. We have different sets of skills. We design events in public space, that's what we do as activists. That is strange and unusual and helpful to the movement as a whole.

BT: There is still a fight that needs to take place with bigger companies and in support of unions and we have sung for every picket line, UFCW [the food workers union], teamsters, SEIU [the union of service workers in health care and other fields]. For the campaign we were up at Stella d'Oro [the cookie factory in the Bronx that was closed in October 2009 after workers struck against pay cuts]. They were saints in our last performance. That work has got to happen. That is closer to some of the classic labor and Marxist questions, which have to continue. From the other side, though, we have something that is happening that is coming right from the heart of our Jane Jacobs preoccupation, which is that neighborhoods themselves have a kind of energy . . .

SD: I'm inspired by this. I think it's a much more integrated way to make change, from the neighborhoods. One of the things we can do is present a community that is diverse and shares values. That's not impossible, it exists, though there are so many forces telling us it doesn't exist and always segregating us. We are so segregated in this country. In New York you don't see it as much because we are visually mixed up, but you know how often things precipitate out and you find yourself in a room full of people who are just like you. Changing that is at the core of our work.

BT: At the end of the mayoral campaign we came to the idea that the Bloombergs are in control. They are in control of the putative government, but there has to be a colorful shadow government informed by a cultural revolution of humor and music. Community-making is taking place under the nose of the redcoats. Consumerism puts distance between people. But that isolation is being defeated right now; it's crashing. We are still trying to find a name for what's emerging—the Colorful Shadow Government? The sub rosa. . . .

SD: A lot of people in the environmental movement talk about this: We can't wait for government and institutions to do this work. They aren't going to do it, so we have to start doing it, and I don't mean as perfect consumers and how we shop. We have to go out and build things, plant trees, do it ourselves . . .

BT: We have to weatherize things, we have to learn solar and wind.

SD: . . . plant things in windows. We have to relearn skills that we forgot.

BT: We have to start drying our clothes on lines. Did you know that it is illegal to have a clothesline in many suburbs and cities? Talk about the old tenement image, which was once as Americana as you can get. But that is actually illegal in many places and there is a movement right now to reverse that. The research on the difference in our carbon output if we stop with high-powered dryers is astounding.

AS: This worries me a little. I agree with what you're saying, but at the same time there is a right-wing or libertarian anti-government streak you can find in some DIY imperatives that lets government off the hook for regulation. A lot of the mess we are in stems from insisting on keeping the state out of it. A certain kind of call for off-the-grid, out-of-consumer-society self-sufficiency can be a kind of demand for privatizing. I know you don't mean that precisely . . .

SD: I don't mean that at all—

BT: You have to run both at the same time. It's not an either/or thing.

SD: Right. You have to constantly pressure and invent and create and push on governments to do their job, which is so important and can't be done, we know, by any other agency. It can't be done by corporations, can't be done by families, can't be done by religious organizations. That's why we arrived at a government in the first place, an elected government, and it's still the best idea. But we can't, particularly in matters environmental and ecological, wait around for their solutions. We have to get to work.

Reverend Billy leads a parade to the future site of the Destiny Mall in Saratoga Springs, New York, 2008. (Photo by John Quilty.)

13. Benediction

REVEREND BILLY

THE DAY THE EARTH STOPPED SHOPPING

I was shopping and the Earth shook me and tried to wake me up.
"It's time!"
I said, "Who are you?"
The Earth said, "It's closing time."
I said, "But it's the middle of the day."
The Earth said, "That's not what this is."
I said, "Alright, alright. But the others . . ."
The Earth said, "They will be stopping soon."
I said, "They don't look like they . . ."
The Earth said, "Hurry up, we are stopping now."
I said, "Where's my car?"
The Earth said, "We're walking."
I said, "Where are we walking to?"
I turned. I was alone.
The wind was picking up. It was getting dark.
I looked back, and sure enough, everyone was streaming out of the
    mall . . .
And that was the Day the Earth Stopped Shopping.